*IMAGE
AND
INFLUENCE*

IMAGE AND INFLUENCE

Studies in the Sociology of Film

ANDREW TUDOR
Lecturer in Sociology

London   George Allen & Unwin Ltd
Ruskin House   Museum Street

© George Allen & Unwin Ltd 1974

ISBN 0 04 384002 7

Printed in Great Britain
in 11 point Baskerville type
by Unwin Brothers Limited
The Gresham Press
Old Woking, Surrey

Preface

When I first decided to write this book I believed that the cinema had been criminally neglected by sociology. I was wrong. Criminal though its treatment may have been, it certainly had not been neglected. Though there is only one recent text on the subject (by I. C. Jarvie), there is an enormous and uneven amount of general literature. Over the past few years I have had both the opportunity and the inclination to read much of this work. I can report, in all honesty, that the game was not worth the candle. The few outstanding studies are all but submerged in a sea of mediocrity. But why? A few years ago I might have produced another glib observation: that we need an exhaustive synthesising perspective, a reputable body of theory. But I would be wrong in that too, or, at least, only partly right. While every empirical study does need some such perspective, the difficulties besetting the sociology of film run deeper. For this we must largely blame the baleful influence of classic media research. A formidable combination of unthinking empiricism and cultural prejudice has stultified our understanding. So much so that all the energies invested in research have shown frighteningly little return.

I wish that I could claim to transcend these difficulties. But I cannot. This book is also marked by the mass communications heritage; it is a constant struggle to even avoid the same old traps. Yet there is some cause for optimism. Recent years have seen many sociological sub-disciplines finally finding their feet; there are even rumours of dissidence in media studies! In what follows I have tried to add my small push away from the scientism and objectivism which has so often characterised media research. Though I know that I have not entirely succeeded, I would like to think that I have moved a little way along the road. If others are persuaded that the route is worth travelling, then so much the better. It will at least compensate for some of my own failings.

This book could have been a lot worse without help from

many people. From my first sociology teachers, who have not received my thanks, though they do deserve them: Alan Dawe, Herminio Martins, and, especially, Roland Robertson. I have continued to learn from them all. Other friends have contributed, knowingly and unknowingly, to the views I express in these pages. They all have my gratitude, though it is only right that I single out Jerry Booth, Alan Lovell, Frank West, and Geoff Winn for special thanks. So, too, with Laurie Taylor who was kind enough to read and comment upon several chapters in manuscript. I owe a special debt to Terry Lovell who has always been a rich source of ideas on the subject and who made many detailed comments on the manuscript – a manuscript which was made readable by Pauline Emerson's industrious typing. I must also thank my colleagues in the Sociology Department of the University of York who allowed me a term free of teaching responsibilities; without it I might still be writing.

Finally, I doubt that I could have completed this book without the encouragement, aid, and tolerance of my wife Min. For this reason the book is dedicated to her.

Andrew Tudor
November 1973

Contents

Figures

Tables

Chapter 1

Forthcoming Attractions!

In 1922 Lenin made his now famous statement to the effect that '. . . the cinema is the most important of all the arts'.[1] It might even have been an understatement. Certainly it was born of the recognition that here was one of the most socially significant innovations of the twentieth century. While much 'educated' comment saw the movies as of little real significance (except, perhaps, as a bad example to lower-class delinquents), the Soviet leader recognised the new medium's potential for creating change – and create change it did. Try to imagine a world without the movies or their inheritance. Though their days of universal popularity are gone, their influence still waxes. They have left us a characteristic imagery now thoroughly embedded in our cultures. The gangsters, the cowboys, the clean-limbed heroes, the vamps, and all the many characters, come to us in our childhood and remain with us for life. The genres, the techniques, the very conventions of the fiction film have undergone only minor changes in the modern shift to television. Until the forties the worlds which the cinema created reigned supreme in western popular cultures. They gave people a common reality however different the actual locations of their everyday lives. We have not shaken off that inheritance, nor are we likely to do so in the foreseeable future.

There is no immediate need to document the ways in which the cinema has entered our lives. A moment's reflection by any but a recluse is sufficient. With the coming of film, for the first time there was a widespread common articulation of the beliefs, aspirations, antagonisms, and doubts of the huge populations of modern societies. For the

first time men could share the same sentiments, simultaneously, and in every place that could run to a picture show.
Going to the movies rapidly became *the* leisure activity,
there to laugh helplessly at Charlie Chaplin eating his boots
in *The Gold Rush* or Buster Keaton shuffling soggy cards in
The Navigator; to weep with the mourning populace of
Odessa in *Battleship Potemkin*; to experience Mae Marsh's
hand-wringing anxiety in the modern story of *Intolerance*; or
to share some part of the pioneering spirit of *The Covered
Wagon* or *The Iron Horse*. It mattered little, then as now, that
the movies were 'unreal', that they were not obviously
'morally uplifting', that few recognised them as Art. They
thrived. They moved, literally and emotionally, and soon
they would also speak. It is to their credit that they survived
the stuffy demands for moral uplift and the snobbish cries
for Art. The cinema came just as near to tumbling lemming-
like over the precipices of aesthetic liberation as it did to
burial in the grave of commerical pap. The point is not
unimportant. Take as an example the films of John Ford, a
clear talent whose career spans almost the whole of film
history. He demonstrates the division. In the thirties and
forties he was praised for giving us 'moral uplift' and Art in
films which succeeded only in looking like maudlin tales
exquisitely dressed as Serious Things: *The Informer*, *The
Long Voyage Home*, and *The Fugitive* immediately come to
mind. Yet that last vulgarisation of Graham Greene's novel
came just one year after the delicate perceptions of *My
Darling Clementine*. It seems impossible to reconcile Ford's
great achievements – *She Wore a Yellow Ribbon*, *The Searchers*,
and *The Man Who Shot Liberty Valance* – with these almost
embarrassing essays in pictorialism.

In a way they are irreconcilable. There is something
about Ford's vision of the world, his whole aesthetic sensi-
bility, which causes him to excel in the fixed universe of the
western, and fall flat on his face elsewhere. This is a sad
failing of a major talent, and no doubt partly a result of the
artistic values which have gained currency in the cinema at
various times. But for us it should demonstrate that the art
of film lies in making movies which directly communicate

the dynamism of their world without being sidetracked into demonstrating their capacities as Art. It is this ability to reach people directly, without mediation by the over-intellectualising tendencies of much modern art, which so distinguished the cinema from its predecessors, but it had also an unfortunate influence on the ways in which students sought to understand the workings of film. Since the movies were rarely Art, then they could hardly be a 'good thing'. Or so it went. From such a simple prejudice flowed an endless sequence of misunderstandings. In one area, the 'language' of film, analysis declined into discussion of the methods of the more acceptably artistic movies. It is only in recent years that the 'everyday' cinema has begun to receive the serious attention that it deserves.[2] More important in this context, the sociological study of film retained a certain negative emphasis. The major empirical researches – the Payne Fund studies of 1929 through to 1933 – were motivated by the feeling that everday cinema was having dire moral effects on all and sundry.[3] They were forever recommending that children should be taught a 'serious and distanced' attitude to the movies, and their value as sociological analyses is limited by the imbalances in this brief.

So, allowing that the all too familiar negativism and condescension are misplaced, what would a sociological account of film look like? What does it mean to have sociological knowledge about the movies? Off and on various people have suggested provisional schematics for a sociology of film.[4] I have no such intention here, though this book as a whole might partly contribute to such a process. Ultimately, sociological knowledge of film would surely mean a body of 'true' statements about the role of the institution in society, its effects, the organisational context within which it operates, the nature, attitudes, and preferences of its audience, and the interrelations between these and endless other factors. In short, an exhaustive, intersubjectively verified, consistent, and generally applicable account of the many social worlds of the cinema. It goes without saying that such an account would be impossible as of now, next year, or next century. Sociology cannot scale such a peak in any area of discourse let alone on a topic which has been almost systematically neglected. We do not have even the first precondition of such an achievement: a rigorous accumulation of knowledge about film. What we do have is discrete and disorganised, filled with gaps, guesses, and dubious chunks of received wisdom.

No doubt this sounds like the familiar sociologist's complaint: 'we are only just beginning; please don't expect too much'. It is an understandable appeal in a subject which spends a good deal of its time in attempting disciplined formulation of things which many consider to be obvious, but it does have two justifications. One is that the things which people take to be the case quite often are not. For instance, the mass media clearly do not have the dramatic, immediate, and direct effects suggested by successive waves of 'media panic'. Sociology can thus try to demystify. The second justification is a claim of a different sort. Sociology is *necessarily* in the business of trying to construct disciplined formulations. If it sometimes seems a long way round, then that is because it is. The sociologist takes common knowledge, the random information that comes the way of any perceptive member of a society, deliberately gathered information, this, that, and the other, and tries to shape this unwieldy mess into some sort of order. He starts by constructing a simplified picture, something easily handled, as a provisional guide; this is his first stage in 'making sense' of a subject. Then he takes the picture back to the information, perhaps directing his attention to filling in the gaps. Revision follows. And so it goes on, as more is incorporated into the picture and less is left outside. When most of the gaps have been filled he might have something approaching an acceptable theory.

The sociology of film has no such beast. We have some bits and pieces of theories, certainly, and they help to make sense out of some bits and pieces of information. Such minor applications are scattered through this book. But basically we are still at the stage of early systematisation, of trying to make primitive sociological sense out of a mixed body of data. This task is not helped by the fact that sociology is so defensive of its specialisms, for it is above all at this stage that the sociologist needs all the help he can get. In dealing with the cinema (and other media) this introversion has had one fatal consequence. Where sociology could and should benefit from the insights and interests of film criticism, it has instead tried to present itself as distinct from, and even superior to, such 'subjective' endeavours. This has often manifested itself as an elaborate 'methodologism' whereby sociological methods, such as content analysis, are claimed to supersede the random perceptions of the inferior critic. This is rubbish, and pernicious rubbish at that. Although the insecurity that it reflects is intelligible it is not to be justified, and I trust that this book is imbued with my belief that a sociological study as primitive as this must take what it can get, where it can get it, and how it can get it. It is in his subsequent treatment of these materials that the sociologist begins to part ways with his critical colleagues; though not mutually exclusive, their interests are finally slightly different.

So to the book itself. There is a good deal here which derives from the practice of film criticism, especially in the later chapters where the links between meaning and socio-cultural context are discussed. To make these analyses slightly more methodical I have given their basis a separate consideration in Chapter 5; this discussion of film language is perhaps the most complex and abstract section of the book, but it is an essential prelude to the empirical discussions that follow it. In effect it divides the whole account in two, and in several senses. The first part (Chapters 2–4) is broadly microscopic in its focus, concerned primarily with the process of communication, and often takes off from criticism of established sociological studies. It is in this area that we find most research, and so these chapters are a mixture of critical commentary and further development. Chapter 2 offers a general organising outline – a 'conceptual scheme' – while Chapters 3 and 4 flesh this skeleton out with some empirical detail. These are the traditional areas of mass media research. Chapter 5, the dividing chapter, alters the emphasis. Though its discussion of 'film language' grows

B

out of my analysis of the communication process, its main implications lie elsewhere. It leads to three chapters concerned with cinema as a pattern of culture within society: one conceptual, two empirical. So, where the early chapters are microscopic the latter are macroscopic, and where the former looked at communication the latter look at culture. And since these macroscopic interests are historically neglected in media research there is less critical commentary and more exploratory discussion. The net result is a considerable stylistic and substantive difference between the two parts of the book. This seems an inevitable compromise in trying to write a general book on a subject so selectively and differentially studied. It also reflects one of my main beliefs: in studying the media we *must* turn increasingly to macroscopic issues of the relation between the media and society.

The materials I invoke are drawn from a wide variety of sources. Where it has seemed helpful I have considered particular cases at some length, sometimes for their value as examples of my more abstract analyses, sometimes as a part of a more speculative research process. Thus, I have illustrated my discussion of 'movie communicators' by analysing the Hollywood system in its heyday. By contrast, I have selected the western, the gangster movie, and the horror movie as case studies from which to develop a theory of the popular genres. Similarly with so-called 'German expressionism' in my discussion of film movements. My intention throughout has been to organise the materials as much as they will permit, whether one case or a range of examples. Obviously, then, this book is *not* a sociology of film. It is a partial account, an interpretation of the various social worlds in which the movies are to be found. It is necessarily incomplete, sometimes confused, and always provisional, and it is far from unified: do not expect a general theory of film here. It reflects my belief that the cinema is a vital art as well as being an omnipresent part of our cultural scene. It rests on my feeling that we must look to the methods of criticism if we are to understand the communication of meaning. But above all it shares Lenin's belief in the enormous social importance of this characteristic twentieth-century institution. If for no other reason than this we have no choice but to try to understand such a vital social process.

References

[1] This is the usual form in which the phrase is quoted, though the source appears to be: '. . . so you must well remember that, of all the arts, for us the cinema is most important', a comment made to Lunacharsky in February 1922. (J. Leyda, p. 161 – see Selected Bibliography for further details.) In a Soviet Union about to face the challenge of NEP Lenin well recognised the problems of bringing about cultural change to match the political revolution.

[2] Much of this renewed attention was stimulated by the work of *Cahiers du Cinéma* and, rather later, *Movie*. For a stimulating discussion in book form see V. F. Perkins (Selected Bibliography); Perkins was closely associated with *Movie*. For a discussion of the situation which gave rise to some of the emphases of film criticism see A. Tudor, *Theories of Film* (Selected Bibliography).

[3] The studies focused basically on the influence of the movies on young people, and used the methods of interview, survey, experiment and content analysis. They will figure in the discussion of later chapters, especially Chapter 4.

[4] See, for example: E. Morin, 'Preliminaires à une Sociologie du Cinéma'; W. Dadek (see Bibliography); G. Huaco, 'Toward a Sociology of Film Art' and his *The Sociology of Film Art*; T. Lovell, 'An Approach to the Sociology of Film', and her article 'Sociology and the Cinema'. (See Selected Bibliography.)

Chapter 2

Patterns of Communication

Hugh Dalziel Duncan's *Communication and Social Order* ends on a note of rhetorical appeal.

'We must return the study of man in society to a study of communication, for how we communicate determines how we relate as human beings.'[1]

While one can have every sympathy with the criticism implicit in this claim (that studies of man in society have tended to neglect the subjective element in interaction), it is surely significant that the statement makes as much sense turned on its head. We must return the study of communication to a study of man in society, for how we relate as human beings determines how we communicate. Which formulation you prefer depends very much on current perceptions of the state of the game. In a situation where the social sciences seem to betray a heavily objectivist bias then Duncan's version is indeed understandable. People communicate, interact, and exchange meanings; they are not merely the pawns of larger objective forces. Ten years ago his claim had the justice of a cry in the wilderness, but in the early seventies things are changing. The coming thing looks to be some form of subjectivism. Man, on this reading, is no longer a pawn of society. Instead his character as communicator becomes all, his society merely a residual sludge. From man as epiphenomenon we come full circle to society as epiphenomenon.

Yet anyone who can leave the front lines long enough to reflect on the good sense in both thesis and antithesis is able to recognise the synthesis.[2] In its formal outline communication is a process of interaction in a partly given social situation. To study the one is necessarily to study the other, and, contrary to the claims of the various polemic positions, that observation (it can hardly be given the honorific 'insight') has really been central to the mainstream of the sociological enterprise. Sociology has almost always recognised the dual importance of objective constraint and subjective action. Though the issue has provoked much tilting, it has been mostly at windmills created by exaggerating thesis or antithesis. One could hardly deny that communication is interaction, and that interaction is invariably embedded in a partially objectified social situation.

Communication, then, is social process, and social process is communication. The study of man in society implies the study of that which makes man so unique – the capacity for meaningful interaction. Whatever the peculiarities of behavioural psychology, general sociology has usually taken that proposition rather seriously. Which makes its comparative neglect in mass communications studies all the more peculiar, until we realise that studies of mass media have rarely been part of general sociology anyway. Of course the problem has been commented upon, noted, and bemoaned. All of us have been willing to demand that mass culture be looked at in terms of meaning; that communication be conceived as a social phenomenon. Janowitz and Street for example:

'To study the impact of the mass media from a sociological point of view, it is necessary to think of communications as a social process, involving a focus on interaction. Interaction encompasses the communicator, the content, the audience and the situation.'[3]

The important term here is *interaction*. It is not simply a question of identifying the elements which together make up the structure of the communication situation, although that is indeed important. There is also a need to identify the particular patterns of relations which come to characterise specific communication processes.

There is an obvious perspective implied here. All processes of communication are usefully treated as cases of the same fundamental interactive process. So, the process whereby Arthur Penn, Sam Spiegel, Lillian Hellmann, and Marlon Brando create a complex of meanings called *The Chase* which is then offered to a collective audience, this process is *formally* the same as that which I use when talking directly to an acquaintance. Which is not to say, as some have suggested, that mass communications are an inferior version of inter-personal communications; they might be just as complex, subtle, or effective. There is no question here of trying to build in a covert evaluation of mass culture except, perhaps, the view that we ought to take it seriously. The questions raised in this perspective are of a different sort. What is it that distinguishes different types of communication situation within the general class of such processes? In what ways do different media emphasise different aspects of communication? Does so-called *mass*-communication foreshorten the general communication process in determinate ways? Is there any predictable variation in the manner in which the different elements of communication are patterned into specific process?

This is not a simple case of arguing from analogy, with the limitations which that involves. Rather, we start from an analysis of communication in general and work down to the various special applications. Of course, our initial general account does not suddenly emerge from the blue. It derives from the various things which sociologists have already learned about communicative interaction. In effect, mass communication is a special case of communication process in general, which is itself an integral part of any picture of social interaction, and just such an image has been developed in the history of anthropology, psychology, social psychology, and sociology. Which is not to say that all those working within these disciplines are agreed on the minutae of inter-action; far from it. However, it is possible to build up some sort of picture which would not be hounded immediately from the page. Besides, whatever the perils of such generalisation, the task is imperative. To borrow some famous terminology, it is a precursor to intelligible discussion of the processes of mass communication that we should formulate a *unit act* of communication. It may start as little more than a checklist of elements derived from *ad hoc* findings and an ungainly mixture of theoretical perspectives. But even without such a simple framework we cannot begin to understand the workings of communication let alone its larger societal implications. How we relate as human beings determines how we communicate, and how we communicate determines how we relate. But how do we communicate?

HOW DO WE COMMUNICATE?

Many have suggested answers to this question, directly or by implication. Indeed, any analysis of social interaction is some sort of answer, in that interaction (where it is social) by definition involves the transmission of meanings. That emphasis can be found in Weber's concept of social action as meaningful action; in Parsons' 'voluntaristic' theory of action; and in Mead's category of symbolic interaction. Always the crucial element is the expression of meanings in terms of symbols, and the interpretation of those symbols. Interaction involves the complex interchange of these symbolic messages, intercutting each other, colliding, undergoing reformulation. Nor is this a process of transmission and receipt in a single pulse. The telegraph wire which carries its message only one way at one moment, and in a strictly governed language, is an extraordinarily simplified version. The elements are there – communicator, receiver, and medium – but their combinations are drastically limited. Interactive communication uses multiple media, crosscutting messages, partially clear languages, and almost permanent simultaneous transmission.[4] Any telegraph wire would rapidly become an electric fire faced with this sort of overload.

This then, is the complexity of communication *process*. To try to understand it we must first take it apart. Of course this is a hypothetical and abstract procedure. A process of communication is a process of communication; we cannot concretely pick up one of its elements and take it apart like a distributor from a motor. But it can be done by imagination; we can abstract. So to answer the question 'How do we communicate?' we have to start with the elements and work up. It is sometimes said that this destroys the totality of a process; that it somehow denies the richness and immediacy of the face-to-face situation. That it is not true to 'reality'. Often those who argue thus propose an alternative account of interaction which is literate or even literary, i.e. they claim that their 'impressionistic' rendition of social interaction is somehow truer to the real process. Surely not. If they seem 'truer' it is because of a particular property of these accounts themselves as communication processes. They are couched in conventions, in languages, more familiar to most of us—the sorts of languages in which people normally offer accounts of the 'real' world. For this reason such 'literary descriptions' seem more legitimate than more systematic and abstract analyses.

Such an approach to interaction is, however, as much an abstraction from 'reality' as one which breaks a process down into its elements. We are simply more used to it. It is not the actual abstraction (which is unavoidable) that is important. It is the degree to which analysis is methodical. By starting with the minimal elements and working outwards on the basis of our knowledge and our conjecture we can at least hope to trace mistakes, omissions, and redundancies.

As we have recognised in the case of communication the basic pieces are very simple: communicator, medium, and receiver. Of course, there may be more than one of each, and the receiver may simultaneously be a communicator. The medium itself may have all sorts of levels, overtones and undertones, hidden meanings and subliminal signals, but the lowest denominator is shown in fig. 2.1.

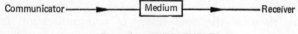

Figure 2.1   THE ELEMENTS

What should be added to this? First of all, the communicator's output does not come from a vacuum. He does not simply suddenly want to say something. All sorts of factors might reasonably be expected to impinge on what he says, when, and how. He has attitudes, for example. He might be concerned to make a moral comment; he might have certain feelings about the form in which such comments should be communicated; certain views as to the facts of the matter. No doubt he has a perception of the receiver to whom his message is directed, and this perception will no doubt colour the form and content of his message. He probably has all sorts of motivational and psychological attributes which have some effect on his communication. Perhaps he is in physical pain. And, of course, he does not exist in a social vacuum; he is an ongoing part of a social structure which he shares partly or wholly with the receiver.

Much the same considerations apply to the receiver. What he makes of the 'message' sent to him, how he interprets this process of symbolic interaction, will be influenced in some way by similar factors. So, to the basic elements we may now add some further factors (see fig. 2.2). This is

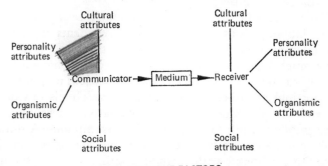

Figure 2.2   THE FACTORS

simply a general classification of the sorts of factors likely to be important in a process of communicative interaction. We all act in a complex of contexts and for a variety of reasons. It has become conventional in sociology and social psychology to classify the elements of this totality in some such terms as these.[5] It does not follow that all of them will be equally important in all situations; they will be weighted differently and interact differently from time to time and place to place. The fact that someone had trodden heavily on my toe thus causing my *organism* considerable pain may outweigh all other considerations in my subsequent communicative act. Or the fact that I live in a *culture* which incarnates the value that pain should be suffered without demur, that I exist in a *social* situation where my standing depends on living up to such an expectation, that my whole *personality* has been socialised into a 'stiff upper lip' belief, all these may outweigh the pain. Similarly what I make of something I am told, whether I believe it or not, how I interpret it, may depend entirely on the fact that I am somewhat paranoid. To me all communications are covert attempts at persecution. This might be hindered by the fact that I exist in a cultural context which stresses that people are generally truthful, helped by the fact that my social situation does not allow me any control over my life, and unaffected by the physical pleasure I derive from the fact that it is a nice sunny day. We know some of the answers to some of these questions for some people some of the time. The purpose of the classification is to tell us what sort of answers to expect.

There are still three things very much wrong with this formulation. It is atomised, its various elements unrelated; the medium is completely unspecified; the whole process is very much a one-way picture. To enlarge, we have a loose idea of the factors moulding a communications act, but they are focused at either end of the process. This is obviously unrealistic. Any process of communicative interaction, at least implicitly, has some set of *shared* assumptions. A simple two person unit act situation is itself an action system; its own little 'society' with a culture and a social structure specific to it. Looked at in total (and unreal) isolation its elements are: two personalities, two organisms, a culture, and a social structure. But any little 'society' of this sort is virtually certain to exist within a larger unshared context. The two members have 'outside' social and cultural experiences; they have specific personality and organic histories. Thus while the receiver may interpret one communicative act just as the communicator intended it, because he understands it in the light of the same cultural assumptions and the same social constraints, he may interpret another entirely differently because of 'outside' influences. The extreme case is the pair who have no shared language in the normal sense of that term, and who come from entirely different cultural and social backgrounds, Chinese and American for instance. Their situation looks something like fig. 2.2; the factors influencing their interaction process are completely independent of each other. Their only shared characteristic is the fact that they are there trying to communicate at all.

Clearly this extreme is unusual. What must be built into our 'reconstructed' communication situation is a simple distinction between shared and unshared elements. Between influences internal to the unit act and those technically external. There are several ways of doing this, and for the moment the detail can await diagrammatic presentation. Only one point needs to be drawn out here. If we are focusing on communication then the crucial point of conjunction of these various factors lies in the 'language' in which the communication is couched. Most languages are imperfect. They do not give rise to complete symmetry between intended and received meanings. There are two general sources of this imperfection. In the one case the language rules are entirely shared but ambiguous; the ambiguity itself is part of the shared culture. In the other the language is distorted by unshared characteristics, by the external predispositions which the actors bring to the situation. Either way the crucial focus lies in the *language* of the medium in question. It is here that we are best able to see the imbalances brought about by the different contexts in which communication is continued. It is through some concept of *language* that we can hope to specify our understanding of a medium.

The third problem, that of unilinearity, manifests itself in various ways. Generally, of course, the communicator and receiver roles are interchangeable; the whole thing can be reversed. More specifically, the interaction is not simply a product of all the various factors we have singled out. The process itself changes the nature of its shared elements. One has only to think of learning. This involves a continual series of situations in which what is learnt effects the socio-cultural context in which 'teacher' and 'pupil' exist. Now interaction is almost always a learning process, though perhaps less so as time goes by, and so the situation is perpetually undergoing reformulation at the hands of the interaction itself. Our 'snapshot' of structural elements must allow for this possibility, although by definition it cannot do more. That task must be faced in analysing process.

This revised communication situation can be given new diagrammatic form (see fig. 2.3). Some of the apparently

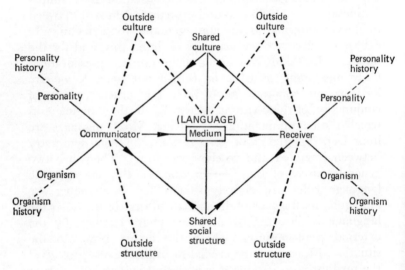

Figure 2.3 THE STRUCTURE OF COMMUNICATION[6]

independent factors might be related in particular cases. For example, a brother–sister communication situation would almost certainly be informed by a linkage at the level of 'personality history'. In the interests of stopping somewhere, however, personality and organism components have been left unlinked. This is a skeleton, not a body. Once given this picture of the components of the process, the next step is to explore their differing importance in specific communication situations. In particular, of course, in the so-called 'mass communication' process. For this reason I shall look at the apparent failings of traditional mass communication imagery in the light of this perspective.

PROCESSES OF MASS COMMUNICATION

Most classical studies of mass communications rested on an implicit and highly simplified model. If pressed their authors would no doubt admit to the richness and complexity of face-to-face interaction, but their image of the mass media was much simpler. Either by default, or because they felt that mass communication was somehow inferior, many of the factors obviously important in general communication were neglected here. Gone was the variability of particular personalities. Gone were the subtleties and inflections of expression long since recognised in spoken language. Gone was the interactive response of the receiver to the communicator. The audience in the darkened cinema, round the box in the corner, or peering from behind their newspapers were not seen as part of a situation of social interaction. Mass communication was not a social process; it was merely a process.

There were two main reasons for this development. One was seldom formulated explicitly. This was that it was so much easier to handle a complex process by minimising the complexities from the beginning. The much vaunted methodological obsession of media studies took off from here. The second reason was more plausible, if only sketchily developed. This suggested that *mass* communication was indeed a special case.[7] It was so in the sense that many of the elements so characteristic of communication in general were absent, or minimally important, in the mass media. Mass communication was a sort of *foreshortened* form lacking the sophistication of the more familiar face-to-face situation. The whole thing could be compressed into the simple image of the hypodermic.

There is a ring of truth to this position. Any potential for interactive response is seriously restricted in the 'mass' situation. The role–images of communicators cannot be formed and adapted in the immediate process of interactive communication; they must be mediated through things like box-office, critical response, popularity ratings, and public debate. 'Messages' are generally created once and for all; they cannot often be adapted to immediate responses from the receiver. Media languages are variously underdeveloped and unshared. There is an asymmetry of control and authority as between communicator and receiver: the one has all and the other virtually nothing. In effect, communicator and receiver do not 'know' each other. They are like strangers meeting for the first time.

It is possible to understand the force with which this view developed as a response to the awe-inspiring spread of the media in the post-war era.[8] The prospect of an ever increasing 'lonely crowd', of an anonymous mass society, had a frighteningly Orwellian ring to it. So, as a characterisation of a whole society we were given the mass society thesis. Its direct counterpart in the more microscopic domain of communications research was the now familiar 'hypodermic model'. The two were intertwined in such a way that the assumptions of the one were legitimated by the apparent empirical claims of the other. To argue against the mass society thesis was to invite the reply that the communications studies convincingly demonstrated the hypodermic power of the mass media. The fact that they did not was successfully ignored. Similarly, to attack the communications image was to learn that this was the inalienable nature of mass society. It was not but there we were. A frequent backdrop to this ideology was an élitist belief in the value of traditional intellectual and aesthetic culture. High culture versus low, and art versus pap.

All this made it fairly easy to avoid recognising that the hypodermic model and the mass society thesis were deeply misleading. Even so, the fact that variants of both positions have survived so long is rather curious. Whatever the rhetorical, ideological, and social pressures in their support there was at least one important influence weighing against them. Much of the development of social science (as opposed to communications research) led in a very different direction. Specifically it developed the view that people can be expected to be really quite active in their responses to meaningful stimuli. The mass/hypodermic images suggest that people are the passive recipients of whatever the communicators care to 'inject'. It is now clear that this was a considerable over-exaggeration. In contrast to some 'golden age' community of idealised face-to-face communicators this might have seemed so. In absolute terms, as we shall see, it was hardly accurate.

The easiest way to pin down the deficiencies of this hypodermic model is in terms of the conceptualisation in fig. 2.3. At the *communicator* end of the chain plenty of credit was given. Some versions of the general thesis even go as far as implying conspiracy; media men as manipulators of society.[9] Even in less extreme versions there is no necessary foreclosure in the hypodermic model as far as the communicator is concerned. What he does is seen as a function of a number of factors including almost all those suggested by my general model. The first three of Lasswell's famous questions – Who? Says What? In What Channel? – could be extensively answered.[10] It is at the *receiver* end that the model

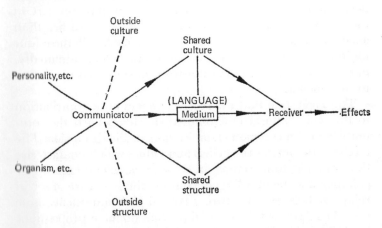

Figure 2.4   ASYMMETRIC COMMUNICATION (HYPODERMIC MODEL).

becomes compressed. This is shown in fig. 2.4. Everything is dictated from the communicator end (although he, in turn, may be dictated to by the outside socio-cultural context). But the socio-cultural world of the receiver is exhausted by that shared with the communicator. He may have other potential contexts (his family, for example) but they are thought to be of little importance. His conceptions are created through and by the media; there is no interactive element. A message passes through the medium, is understood by the receiver in terms dictated by the communicator, and he is effected accordingly. The needle reaches a vein, and the infection takes. The capacities of the language and the medium are also defined by the communicator – he knows what is good for the audience. Depending on your political preferences we have either benevolent dictatorship or totalitarianism. In fact we have neither because the picture is grossly inaccurate.

What precisely are the compressed elements? They are easily identified by comparing figs 2.3 and 2.4. First of all there is now no feedback from the receiver into the shared socio-cultural context. This derives entirely from the communicator. Second, the receiver is shorn of his 'outside' socio-cultural context. He reacts in a vacuum except for that provided by the communicator. Third, his individual personality and organismic characteristics play no part in the communication process. Lastly, he *re*acts rather than acts; he does not participate, he is effected. All these four limitations are rather wide of the mark, some, admittedly, more so than others. Let us illustrate each in turn in relation to the cinema.

The suggestion that the receiver makes little contribution to the socio-cultural environment he shares with the communicator is a common claim in mass media discussion. The media man dictates the beliefs and values which characterise the shared culture (either in self-conscious cynicism or by default), and he also largely controls the structure of social relations between the two. Like all such statements these must be relativised. Compared to what do these propositions hold? Nor are they necessarily linked. It *is* largely the case

First, the myth that beliefs and attitudes may be transmitted whole from medium to receiver. As in almost every other process of social interaction the characteristic attitudes of the receiver 'interfere' in the process of receiving. We make things meaningful for ourselves by fitting them into our preconceptions. They come to us raw, and we dress and cook them. The standard term for the process is *selective perception*. We see what we wish to see, and we twist messages around to suit ourselves. All this is demonstrated classically in the famous 'Mr Biggott' studies.[14] An audience was shown a series of anti-prejudice cartoons featuring the highly prejudiced Mr Biggott. They were then subjected to detailed interviews. The gross result was that about two thirds of the sample clearly misunderstood the anti-prejudice intention of the cartoons. There was what Cooper and Jahoda refer to as a 'derailment of understanding'. The major factors accounting for this selective perception, according to the researchers, were the predispositions of the audience. Those who were already prejudiced saw the cartoons as supporting their position. Even those who understood the cartoons found ways of evading the antiprejudice 'effect'. Only those with a predisposition toward the message interpreted the films in line with the intended meanings of the communicators. The television series *Till Death us do Part* may well have produced a similar 'derailment'.

Not all cases are as dramatic as this one. Another piece of research into an anti-prejudice film (*Don't be a Sucker*) demonstrated a similar 'boomerang' effect, though selective perception was not as strong as might have been expected.[15] The mere fact that the cultural predispositions of receivers can and do interfere with the hypodermic process is sufficient to give the lie to the pure compressed model. As in social interaction generally, the expectations, images, prejudices and beliefs of the receiver are a crucial part of the culture of the situation. How crucial a part is an empirical question which may have varying answers from case to case. It certainly cannot be given the universal and *a priori* answer offered by the traditional mass communications imagery.

Much the same reasoning applies to the clearly social environment of the receiver. Although there are many problems here it suffices to mention only one of the more grotesque claims. This is the implied view that the receiver is effectively a social isolate – the postulate of the isolated audience. His social environment independent of the media situation is of no importance in the communication process. The principal research to be held against this view is again among the more justly famous research in the field: the 'two-step flow' or 'multi-step flow' conception, a development which has been aptly described as the 'rediscovery of the primary group'.[16] The insight is simple although the repercussions are extensive. Katz, Lazarsfeld, and their various associates demonstrated that what individual effects communications had were mediated through an 'external' social network. Generally this derived from the social structure of the particular community. They developed the thesis using the idea of 'opinion leaders': individuals whose opinions on specified subjects were accepted by other members of the group. These figures acted as links between the media and the receivers. Instead of the direct flow postulated in the compressed model, one or more 'opinion leaders' might intervene. Thus the social structure of the immediate group in which the receiver lives becomes a constituent part of the communication process. Once again the receiver is rather less the isolate implied by the mass society conceptions.

The importance of these social and cultural factors carries over to the levels of personality and organism. Not much needs to be said here. Evidently culturally derived attitudinal factors play their part in communication through internalisation into the personality. Theoretically, attitudes belong to both culture and personality. I am not aware of any really clear studies of the effects of different personality characteristics on the communications process, though there are some rather loose psychoanalytic formulations, but the interaction between film and personality is a common theme where the larger significance of the cinema is in question. Wolfenstein and Leites, for example, look at the cinema as a playing-out of psychological fantasies.[17] Inevitably the commercial cinema has tried to minimise the variable appeal of its product as far as different personality characteristics are concerned. To survive film must sell widely, but this does not mean that personality factors can be neglected in the analysis of communications. Similar considerations apply to the organism. Here the most interesting factors appear to be those concerning the physical conditions for high emotional receptivity. Experimental researches have suggested, for example, that factors like posture, focusing of information sources in the physical environment (the screen in a darkened cinema), and the like, are important elements in determining intensity of emotional response.[18] For many purposes such factors may be taken as constant; but they are nevertheless constituent elements in cinematic communication.

The fourth, and last, of the untoward compressions is really a summary statement of the others. It is the crux of the hypodermic model. People are effected, the argument runs; the message is pushed in and the direct effect comes out the other end. Man is a passive recipient rather than an active participator. All the arguments of the past few pages suggest the opposite. They suggest that the receiver does play some significant part in the process; that he *inter*acts rather than simply *re*acting. That he also has a creative role. Now this image of the creative audience has become something of a media cliché. I do not invoke it here as rhetoric or even as argument. To put it bluntly it is presented as fact. Although communication through the mass media is different to interpersonal communication this is not a qualitative difference. The receiver plays the same role in the process in almost every circumstance. To prevent him from so doing, it would be necessary to remove him from his social and physical world, deprive him of his personal and cultural history, and reduce him to a simple stimulus-response machine. Whatever else they may have done, mass communication processes are not guilty of this truly amazing achievement. It has been a tragically common distortion to imply that they are.

ONLY CONNECT...

Forster's dictum is apt.[19] I have tried to argue that in studying the communicational aspect of the cinema we are best served by looking at it as a particular sort of interaction. To 'connect' is to creatively participate in the complex of meanings which constitute our social life. For many people in modern societies processes of mass communication provide one important arena for such interaction. In trying to understand these processes it is necessary to understand the way in which *all* the elements of the communication process combine together to form the whole. This is why it is important to start by discussing communication in general. Once we know where to look, only then can we judge the value of what we do know and the need for what we do not know. Processes of communication are typically arranged in a pattern, some closer to the 'pure' form than others. It is with the pattern that we must begin.

In going on to discuss the detail of cinematic communication we will find many gaps. One heritage of the 'great tradition' in mass media research has been to direct attention to certain questions at the expense of others. A consequence of arguing that communication must be seen very positively as a *social* process is to ask slightly different questions for which we may have no well-established and coherent answers. We have questions without answers, and answers without questions. Where communication is concerned the latter is especially the case: we have quite a few answers but not very many sensible questions to go with them, and in one area in particular there is an enormous gap – the area of media languages. As we have seen this is the one crucial focus of the communication relationship, the link between microscopic components, communicator and receiver, and macroscopic components, culture and social structure. The most important questions we can ask about communication process are questions about language.

Beside the language and medium nexus the picture is most usefully filled out by identifying empirical characteristics of communicator and audience in the terms provided by the communications model. This inevitably spills over into larger issues, in part because the crucial 'external' environments of the participants derive from larger contexts. It does so also for a rather more important reason. The very process of communication itself creates and recreates the contexts in which it exists. The predominantly microscopic analysis with which I am immediately concerned is not designed to deal with this 'emergent' characteristic; but it is this emergence that is finally so important. What is created by accident or design through communication today becomes the partially given culture of tomorrow. It is reified; it takes on an 'objective' existence.[20] From the static categories advanced in this chapter we must try to progress to some attempt at understanding these dynamics. How we connect now will have a great deal of influence on our future social lives.

References

[1] Hugh Dalziel Duncan, *Communication and Social Order*, O.U.P., London, Oxford, New York, 1968, p. 438.

[2] The most elaborate attempt to explicitly reach such a synthesis in recent years has been that advanced by Peter Berger and Thomas Luckmann in *The Social Construction of Reality*, Penguin, Harmondsworth, 1967. Their advance seems more imagined than real. Their Schutz-influenced objective reality/subjective reality distinction serves only to give a slight difference in organisational emphasis to their otherwise fairly orthodox sociology. In mass communications studies a similar tactic is employed by David Chaney with similar marginal payoffs in organisation. See David Chaney, *Processes of Mass Communication*, Macmillan, London, 1972.

[3] M. Janowitz and D. Street, 'The Social Organization of Education', in P. H. Rossi and B. J. Biddle (Eds), *The New Media and Education*, Aldine, Chicago, 1966, p. 209.

[4] In this context see the analysis of the play 'Who's Afraid of Virginia Woolf', in Chapter 5 of Paul Watzlawick, Janet Helmick Beavin and Don D. Jackson, *Pragmatics of Human Communication*, Faber, London,

1968. This fascinating book is too often dismissed in inapplicable anti-behaviourist slogans.

[5] Increasingly a further term is being added: ecological attributes. In this context it seems reasonable to omit them from immediate consideration.

[6] This is a rather more general version of the figure presented in A. Tudor, 'Film Communication and Content', (p. 98) (see Selected Bibliography).

[7] Blumer was important here. As well as his work for the Payne Studies see his famous paper: 'The Crowd, the Public and the Mass', in Wilbur Schramm (Ed.), *The Process and Effects of Mass Communication*, Univ. Illinois Press, Illinois, 1954.

[8] In fact the development was in some respects prefigured in the discussions of the inter-war years which were themselves responses to the spread of radio and cinema. In the main the discussions were concerned with the possible dileterious effects of the movies, especially on the young. The Payne Fund Studies grew from this concern. Other writers were concerned with the potential good to be derived from the new media, most notably John Grierson (Selected Bibliography). The negative side received more attention in later developments, especially in the 'mass society' thesis. See, among others, David Reisman, the *Lonely Crowd*, Yale Univ. Press, New Haven, London, 1950; C. Wright Mills, *The Power Élite*, O.U.P., New York, 1956; William Kornhauser, *The Politics of Mass Society*, Free Press, Glencoe (Ill.), 1959.

[9] One example of this, with the media as the 'arm' of the power élite is to be found in C. Wright Mills, *op. cit.*, especially Chapter 13.

[10] See Harold D. Lasswell, 'The Structure and Function of Communication in Society', in B. Berelson and M. Janowitz (Eds), *Reader in Public Opinion and Communication*, Free Press, New York, London, 1966.

[11] See L. A. Handel, *Hollywood Looks at its Audience* (Selected Bibliography).

[12] H. J. Gans, 'The Creator – Audience Relationship in Mass Media' (Selected Bibliography).

[13] See H. J. Gans, *ibid.* See also A. Tudor, 'Genre: Theory and Mis-practice in Film Criticism' (Selected Bibliography), and the slightly different discussion in his *Theories of Film* (Selected Bibliography). See also Chapter 8 of this book.

[14] See P. Kendall and K. Wolfe (Selected Bibliography); see also E. Cooper and M. Jahoda (Selected Bibliograhpy).

[15] E. Cooper and H. Dinerman (Selected Bibliography).

[16] See E. Katz and P. Lazarsfeld (Selected Bibliography).

[17] M. Wolfenstein and N. Leites, *Movies* (Selected Bibliography).

[18] For discussion and summary of some of these factors see G. Mialaret (Selected Bibliography).

[19] From flyleaf of E. M. Forster, *Howards End*, Penguin, Harmondsworth, 1969. I understand the phrase here in the context of the novel.

[20] The terms made familiar in recent years by Berger and Luckmann. Their discussion of the process is lucid and provocative. See P. Berger and T. Luckmann, *op. cit.*

Chapter 3

Movie Communicators

The hypothetical 'movie communicator' is nothing if not complex. Under that one expression I subsume a variety of activities. Production crew, actors, director, producer, studio executives, front office, writers, distributors, financiers, and the endlessly proliferating parasite roles which are found in so many highly successful enterprises, all these have some case for inclusion. Indeed it is this collective claim to importance which has militated against a serious understanding of film. Western culture traditionally values the lone artist above other forms of aesthetic endeavour. Much of the desire to demonstrate that the cinema is a director's medium has derived from this conviction. If only it can be shown that films are really the work of a single artist, it is argued, then they will be recognised as serious Art. For this reason a good deal of criticism, history, and analysis has focused on whatever cinema could best be pressed into this traditionally legitimate mould. The European cinema in preference to the American; 'artistic' films in preference to commercial. Whatever would not fit was ignored.

This is not to deny the value of the so-called *auteur* principle. In fact its modern versions draw attention to precisely those cinemas which were traditionally neglected as entertainment rather than art. Any methodological device which leads in this direction must have something in its favour. But the old arguments about art or not, single author or not, are best buried. An axiomatic belief that the cinema is a director's medium can only be misleading if we are trying to come to grips with the process of film communication. Here we must deal with no single communicator as such, but with a hypothetical communicator constituted by the collectivity of individual film-makers. The characteristics of this communicator are usefully considered in the general terms suggested in the preceding chapter: in particular, in terms of culture and social structure.

The focus, then, is on the characteristics of the collectivity of movie-makers rather than on them as individual personalities. Of course it is possible to make glib generalisations as to the typical personality characteristics of different figures in the movie industry – producers as ego-maniacs, writers as neurotics, or actors as infantile – but such thumb-nail sketches remain extraordinarily unsatisfying, mainly because we lack information more reliable than rumour and stereotype. Generally one would only expect personality (and organismic) characteristics to be especially revealing in a detailed case study of a specific communication process. No doubt, for instance, the personality attributes of John Huston, Gottfried Reinhardt, and Dore Schary would play a significant part in any detailed analysis of the making of the ill-fated *Red Badge of Courage*. This much is clear from Lillian Ross's illuminating account.[1] But the problem is to transcend these particularities; to understand the social processes characteristic of the creation of movies independent of the twists and turns deriving from the quirks of the individuals involved. Only in this way can we arrive at a socio-cultural picture of our movie communicator.

The problems are similar to some of those faced in the sociology of science. There we have a social institution operating in a wide variety of social contexts but nevertheless exhibiting a range of common characteristics. Although individual scientists vary in their personality characteristics, and although they live and work in different societies, there is a great deal to be learnt about scientific practice by studying them *as if* they constituted a society of their own.[2] Similarly with movie-makers as a part of the communication process. They can usefully be thought of as constituting their own society, with its own aims and problems, its special strains and conflicts. By so conceiving them we can begin to isolate the socio-cultural factors which seem to be repetitive elements in movie-production.

There is inevitably a further complication. Although the movie-making system has only grown up in this century it has undergone considerable change. We have not yet seen the end of these changes, nor is it entirely clear what that end might be. Rates of change have not been uniform. Whereas the originating institutions of Hollywood have largely declined, the Hollywood model is still to be found. The Indian, Japanese, and Egyptian systems, for example, still variously approximate the classic form. The Soviet Union, on the other hand, appears to be retaining a form of state capitalist film-making first developed in the Stalinist period, while the Western European industries, though not yet as segmented as the French and American, stand somewhere between the traditional and the new: nobody is really sure where it will all lead.

Obviously this sets us a problem of analysis. The contemporary state of affairs is so incoherent that one can only develop provisional suggestions and guesses. And to do this requires a fixed point against which contemporary change may be viewed. This seems best provided by analysing the classic Hollywood system, a system which in its outline has been repeated in an endless variety of contexts. Of course Hollywood itself was an extreme. That hardly needs repeating. But its very extremity makes it useful as a case study of the movie making process. Whether by deliberate aping, or universal constraints of film-making, Hollywood has been very much the model for many other industries. Even more than that, in the thirties and forties it was, in a very real sense, a society unto itself. The strategy of seeing the film community as some sort of social system is given additional force by virtue of the fact that its members also saw it in this light. It had a subjective reality to them which dominated their lives. As a consequence, the rules, the beliefs, the power structures which underlay its operations are fairly close to the surface. We do not have to dredge so deep for them, nor are they confusingly overlaid with 'outside' factors. Allowing for admitted variations from society to society, Hollywood can be used as an illuminating paradigm case. Hence the detailed discussion which follows, based on

Hollywood in its peak era. I shall look first at basic role structure; then at the patterns of power and authority relating to these roles; finally at the culture which underwrites this system.

HOLLYWOOD: BASIC STRUCTURE

Most accounts of Hollywood in the 'great days' are bitter. This is hardly surprising. Many of them were written by men who at one time or another worked as Hollywood writers, the least favoured limb of the production process. From them come so many stereotypes, not always consistent. Schulberg's Sammy Glick – amorally ambitious and compulsively philistine – is to be contrasted with the same author's Manley Halliday, a thinly disguised portrait of Scott Fitzgerald. Fitzgerald himself provides the memorable and tormented Monroe Stahr, and writer-turned-producer/director Richard Brooks, in *The Producer*, offers a telling if sour reflection on the Hollywood of his experience.[3] Even the self-centred movies that Hollywood allowed itself to make had a fair share of this bitterness. The portentious *Barefoot Contessa* exudes the traditional stereotypes, and the best of them all, Billy Wilder's *Sunset Boulevard*, is far from complimentary. However, without impugning the motives of the authors of these books and films, it should be recognised that Hollywood itself was not unwilling to encourage the Hollywood legend. As the trade-paper *Variety* might have put it, it was good for b.o. (box-office, not body odour!).

It is not easy to decide where the myths begin and end. No doubt Hollywood deliberately created some and then came to believe them. And apart from the endless interviews with leading figures in later life, there are really only two major sources which try to probe the social process behind the myth. Both are accounts of Hollywood around its peak period. Rosten's study was published in 1941 and researched in the three years previous. Powdermaker's in 1950 on the basis of a year in Hollywood in 1946–7.[4] The former is a combination of impression, received statistics, and an extensive survey. The latter is anthropological, and rests on participant observation and anthropological sensitivity. Because of this it is probably the more revealing; Powdermaker gets beneath the surface where Rosten is weighed down by the minutae of income, education, nationality, and the like. Nevertheless, they both give the lie to some widespread misconceptions about Hollywood life. Rosten demonstrates, for example, that salaries *in general* are far below the levels suggested by myth; only the few are truly extravagantly rewarded. Powdermaker maintains that sexual promiscuity was not as common as the publicity departments sometimes liked to maintain. And although Rosten sometimes reads like an apologia, they both do reinforce one of the traditional Hollywood stereotypes: they blame commercial interests for obstructing the progress of a properly creative cinema.

So much that is written about Hollywood shares this distaste for the commercial strictures placed on the artistic spirit. Again, of course, this is a reflection of the traditional view that art should be free of such constraints; the artist should create in solitary splendour. Yet it is arguable that this very combination of commercial and aesthetic elements has allowed the American cinema to produce so many great works of art free of the pretentiousness common elsewhere. Which is not to say that great works have not been destroyed by the same hand. There are endless examples, from *Greed* right on through to *Major Dundee*. But one should not take commercial philistinism as *the* characteristic of the system. There are plenty of creative film-makers who have found themselves more than able to survive in the Hollywood system. For instance, it is difficult to imagine Fritz Lang rising to the culminating heights of *The Big Heat* outside the Hollywood context, while the superb westerns of John Ford or Anthony Mann and the striking thrillers of Don Siegel all clearly benefit from the restraints imposed by the commercial system. Their self-control and richness of characterisation is partly a product of the context in which they work. It is too easy to take the commercialism–aestheticism dichotomy as the whole story and leave it at that. Things are not that simple.

Even so, the contrast between commercialism and aestheticism is a sort of *liet-motif* of the Hollywood system. Not only is such a potential conflict of interest intrinsic to the structure of movie production, it is also part of Hollywood culture. In their various ways the film-makers expect, even relish, this seeming contrast of goals and standards. Not that they always react in the same way. Although all but 15 per cent of Rosten's sample of directors complained of 'stupid supervision', unsympathetic producers, thwarted craftmanship, and the like, they remained totally involved in their art.[5] For every one that complains there may be one to congratulate. Take two, both widely thought of as 'artists'. Tony Richardson:

'I'm thrilled I went there because I know I never want to make a film in Hollywood again. It is impossible to make anything that is interesting or good under the conditions imposed by the major studios in America. It is a totally impossible creative set-up: even after the film is made, so much mutilation goes on, and it becomes the product of many different people.'[6]

By way of contrast, the French director Jean Renoir:

'As far as I am concerned, commercial requirements and the different censorship regulations are in many ways in my favour, because they force me to look at things with a more subtle eye. And I am not the only one in this situation: the history of art is full of artistic development in the midst of the worst tyrannies. If I were absolutely free, I probably would make the same kind of films I do now.'[7]

Both of which reflect the fundamentally economic character of film production. For various reasons – some grotesquely out of proportion – film-making requires very large commercial investment. Some form of economic restraint is almost unavoidable. Exactly what form remains to be seen.

This comes well to the fore in the basic structural patterns of the Hollywood community. Occupational structure is inevitably an important element in any social structure. But

in Hollywood it is occupational role which almost completely *defines* the normally more diffuse social role. Social
role here depends overwhelmingly on an individual's
identity in the occupational division of labour. Like many
of the 'professions', movie-makers make no clear separation
between their occupational and private lives. As Rosten
remarks: 'They are paid for doing things which other
people would like to do without being paid.'[8] Their elaborate
differentiation of working roles is faithfully reflected in the
norms, expectations, and constraints of everyday social life.
Hortense Powdermaker offers some sense of this carefully
structured community:

'The atmosphere of Hollywood both resembles that of a
village and differs from it. There is the same extroverted
cordiality, but more stress on status as determined by income
and power. This is reflected in the use of first names. Those
in the upper brackets call everyone beneath them by their
first name, but this is not always reciprocal. Mr Very Important will be addressed by some as "Mr Important, sir," by
others as "Mr Important," as "VI" by those earning over
$1200 a week, and as "Very" by only a few close associates.
But Mr Very Important calls everyone by his or her first
name. As in villages the same people are at the same parties,
the same restaurants, the same clubs, and the same week-
end resorts. But again there is more emphasis on financial
status. With rare exceptions the people at a party are all in
the same income bracket, and there is very little association
with private people. The stimulus of contact with those
from other fields of endeavour, which is so accessible in most
big cities, is lacking in Hollywood. For the most part
people work, eat, talk, and play only with others who are
likewise engaged in making movies. Even physical contact
with the private people is exceptional. . . .'[9]

This sort of occupational dominance and consequent social
insularity is not unique (academics are another example),
but it is rarely this extreme.

It means that an analysis of the basic occupational structure is more than just that; it is also an analysis of the social structure in general.

At its most general Hollywood organisation is based on one gross division of labour: that between 'commercially' and 'creatively' specialised roles. Both are essential. Movies are cultural products of a heterogeneous nature. They require enormous creative imputs as well as the familiarly large financial investments. Their very nature is a source of instability in that their potential value as commercial and aesthetic products is very unpredictable.[10] Goals are not clearly defined and fixed. Although the organisational chart might suggest that the commercial experts do the commerce and the movie experts the movies, it rarely works out that way. The system does not function this smoothly, and for two main reasons. For one thing there are no really clear bases of legitimacy for the distribution of power. The elaborate vertical differentiation of the Hollywood system – its stratification – is too often seen by its members to be fortuitously exploitative; we shall shortly see in what manner. More immediately, there are problems built into the role structure of the community. Roles are blurred by virtue of the ambiguities in the creative-commercial distinction, and, as a consequence, role occupants tend to spill out of their roles.

We can begin to see this in terms of a *rough* picture of the Hollywood occupational structure (fig. 3.1). First, simple vertical differentiation. Reliable assessments of the financial rewards offered by Hollywood are notoriously difficult to come by, concealed, as they are, by a curtain of exaggeration and wild conjecture. Both the main sources provide information, although Rosten's materials (based on studio accounts, tax figures, and survey research) are much more extensive. Although there are specific exceptions the pattern offered here does probably reflect a rough ranking. Certainly financial rewards are crucial in defining the structure of social relations. All the sources are replete with accounts of this dependence on income as a symbol of social position. Consonant with this, Rosten divides Hollywood into three concentric circles. At the outside are all the many employees

D

who are not part of the Hollywood community. In the middle circle, the large majority of movie-makers (including most of the roles in fig. 3.1). And, at the centre, a movie

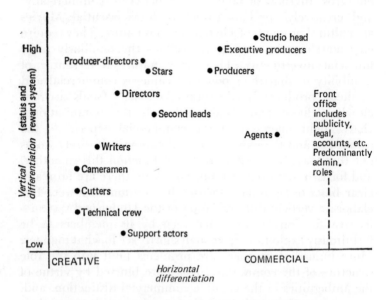

Figure 3.1   HOLLYWOOD OCCUPATIONAL STRUCTURE

élite, for Rosten roughly delineated by taking those earning more than $75,000 in 1938. For that year this élite had the following composition:

80 actors and actresses
54 executives and producers
45 directors
17 writers
4 musical directors[11]

However for most positions in the hierarchy, from directors on down, there is considerable variation in status and rewards. For the most part income levels are far below those of the élite. Powdermaker quotes a distribution of income obtained from the Screen Actors Guild for 1948. Although the top bracket is headed by Humphrey Bogart on $432,000 (figure for 1946), the Guild figures show that some 61·2 per cent of their members earned less than $7,500. This is the very bottom of the system.[12]

The horizontal axis differentiates roles as between 'commercial' and 'creative' specialisations. Of course any individual on the creative side may be motivationally involved for purely financial reasons. Nevertheless, their role in the production system is creative rather than commercial. Certain roles, above all, stars, producers, writers and directors, are open to considerable contradictory pressures. They are the most likely to find themselves caught between conflicting sets of expectations. It is no accident that writers and directors have been among the most vociferous objectors to the Hollywood system; the structure of that system puts considerable pressure upon them.[13] But the role with the most potentiality for segmentation and strain must be that of producer. His is the crucial linking function between the two major strands of specialisation. Demands are placed on him from all directions. He must contend with Executive Producer, Director, Writer, Stars, who may well be at loggerheads. He must find some way to resolve these endless conflicts, balance creative and commercial budgets, and adopt an overall integrative role in the production system. Which elements he chooses to emphasise varies from case to case; producers have historically adopted all sorts of strategies. Some have made a straight decision: they deal with the more commercial aspects while the rest is left in the hands of the director. This is rare. More common is the situation wherein the producer plays some part in the creative process. This may be by mutual agreement (in which case he is a 'creative participant'), or he may use his position to swing certain decisions (in which case he is 'interfering'). It is clear from the terms in which Hollywood people speak of producers that they are not conceived by those in 'creative' roles as 'creative participants'. 'Interfering' is the common term. It is equally clear that many do see themselves as playing a crucial role in integrating disparate creative elements. In other words, their self-conceptions are frequently at odds with the images others hold of them. Their roles are ambivalently defined and they find it difficult to 'fit' into them.

Faced with this the producer must find a way of restructuring his situation so that he can operate within it. Some do find such ways, especially the independent producers who are at least out of the immediate reach of the studio front offices. The director Don Siegel speaking of Walter Wanger:

'*Riot in Cell Block 11* was a project that was entirely Walter Wanger's. He himself was imprisoned and he was the inspiration for the picture. He was also an educator. I knew nothing about penology and he instructed me. He took me to various prisons and I think it was because of his instruction and supervision that the picture turned out as well as it did. Walter Wanger is one of the very few producers who reads. He's enormously well-read. Reads everything. He's a very young man in spirit and enthusiasm. He's one of the very few producers who, I feel, actively contributes. Not actively contributes in the manner of some idiotic producers. He's never on the set and he would never presume to tell you where to set the camera. A good man. A good producer.'[14]

But the Walter Wangers are as rare as the evil ogres of Hollywood myth. More often than not the elaborate hierarchical structure of Hollywood, with its confusion of specialisms, gives rise to accident, inefficiency, excessive politicking, and apparently uncontrollable peculiarities. Gottfried Reinhardt, producer of *The Red Badge of Courage*, gave a gently cynical picture to Lillian Ross:

'"Where you have your office is a sign of your importance," Reinhardt told me as we sat around talking. "I'm on the first floor. Dore Schary [Production Executive] is two floors up, right over me. L. B. [Mayer, Executive Head] is also two floors up. I have a washbasin but no shower in my office. Dore has a shower but no bathtub. L. B. has a shower *and* a bathtub. The kind of bath facilities you have in your office is another measure of the worth of your position." He smiled sardonically. "An important director is almost as important as a producer," he continued, getting up and straightening one of the prints. "John's [Huston] office is a corner one, like mine." '15

Not surprisingly the producers tend to 'solve' their problem by falling in with the executive side of their situation. They cannot easily redefine their roles, so they adopt the attitudes and values of the traditionally more powerful side of the dichotomy.

Other roles present obvious problems, but none as seriously as that of the producer. For most of them the principal difficulty lies in the fact that they are somewhat demeaning to those with high ambitions and self-images to match. Writers, for example, are simultaneously claimed to be highly valued but blatantly exploited. Several writers may be employed on a film (often unknown to each other) such that they are continually rewriting each others work. Those who are recruited from outside with 'outside values' are placed under considerable and unproductive strain: Scott Fitzgerald is an extreme case. Directors face similar difficulties. Apart from the commonly reported problem of direct commercial interference, there may also be widespread sources of strain even for a director of talent placed in a situation free of the worst elements of crass commercialism. Arthur Penn is reportedly very unhappy about *The Chase* because he was unable to control the various *creative* inputs of producer, writer, and star (Spiegel, Hellmann, Brando). As the status of directors increases, as it appears to be doing in the contemporary cinema, this will no doubt become more common.

Roles other than producer, director, and writer seem less problematic. For cameramen, editors, and the rest of the highly specialised technical staff, their very specialisation acts as a buffer to the system. Only in their higher reaches (some cameramen, a chief cutter such as Margaret Booth at MGM) are the technical staff open to the familiar conflicting blasts.[16] Executive producers and studio heads will be considered shortly; they are primarily interesting in the context of the authority structure of movie-making. Where producers, directors, and writers have problems, they have power! For actors (stars or otherwise) the prime difficulties lie in their contractual position. In Hollywood at its peak they were described as the 'best paid slaves in history'. Effectively they were signed over lock, stock, and barrel for seven years, abrogating all control to the studio. In certain respects they were, as Alfred Hitchcock described them in another context, cattle: but cattle with emotional responses, and pursuing one of the more peculiar specialisations in the world. It is not entirely clear what the consequences are of spending every day simulating various emotional states in the brief bursts dictated by the exigencies of film-making. But whether it encouraged catharsis, neurosis, or neither, it does seem that it is the *substance* of the role which is likely to cause problems here rather than its structural position. It is the *acting* rather than the organisational position of the *actor*.

One thing clearly emerges from this brief sketch of the basic Hollywood role structure: there are a number of built-in instabilities and conflicts central to the movie-making situation. Now if this is the basic skeleton of the system, if the general social interaction of Hollywood people depended on this structure, how was such a potentially unstable system made to operate? In any system as hier-archical and as functionally specialised as this one such a question is crucial. How do the élite maintain their positions? How does the system survive the strains created by its own structure, its internal contradictions? Why do those in the 'middle ranks', for instance, tolerate the treatment meted out to them? How do the bits and pieces fit together to produce the final social process? Not in the mechanical sense of who, what, or when. The basic pattern of production is commonly available knowledge, but what oils the wheels, what enables this rather peculiar system to 'get things done'?

HOLLYWOOD: CONTROL STRUCTURE

There are two things involved in answering this question. First there is the structure of decision making and control itself. This needs little said of it here since it is largely that embodied in the vertical differentiation of fig. 3.1. Second there are the *bases* on which this structure of control rests. In effect, how it is that the large numbers at the bottom of the occupational pyramid allow themselves to be exploited by the few at the top, where the 'bottom' can be anything from the director role down. Now questions of this sort are not uncommon; starting with Marx, sociological theory has offered a range of answers to this question. We must very sketchily digress into some of them.

The first and most obvious 'exploitative' mechanism has been straightforward coercive power: the ability to *force* an individual to do as you wish. But this is rarely satisfactory as a solitary explanation – it is too unstable a method to exclusively bring about extended survival of heavily exploitative situations. A second level of analysis must be introduced through the concept of *legitimation*. This reflects the situation in which the participants see it as *only correct* that they should be controlled, manipulated, or exploited by particular ruling groups. Marx rightly saw religion as playing a crucial role in this process: hence the much quoted 'religion is the opium of the people'. Weber conceptualised the process in terms of a distinction between power and authority. The exercise of *authority* was, in effect, the exercise of *legitimate* power. Participants in the process conceived it as justified, as being the right way in which things should be done. It is readily apparent that exercise of authority is a more 'efficient' basis for exploitation than straight coercion. This crucial power/authority distinction does not exhaust the possibilities. Etzioni, in his important analysis of complex organisations, slightly alters the terminology and adds a third component. He speaks in terms of *compliance* relations and sees them as based on coercive (power), normative (authority), and renumerative factors. That is, he adds the possibility of utilitarian inducement as a basis of control; above all, money rewards. Finally, this is made even more complex in the 'media of control' conceptualised by Parsons. He speaks of money, power, influence, and value-commitments, leaving force as a residual category. The differences are basically differences in type of legitimation.[17]

Although by no means complete these theoretical suggestions can be of some help here. In particular, Etzioni's tripartite division provides some empirical leverage. Reduced to a slogan it suggests that people 'obey' because they are forced, because they are paid, or because they think they ought. Etzioni sees one or another pattern dominating different forms of complex organisations. In societies at large, however, and in the 'mini-society' of Hollywood, all three mechanisms of control operate. Some may be more important than others in different sectors of the system. For instance, it is widely believed that the oil on the Hollywood bearings is money. In Etzioni's terms, that the Hollywood system is basically one of utilitarian compliance relations. This seems to be true only at the worst paid levels. That is, in Rosten's outer circle. It has been remarked that Hollywood technicians are the best paid workers in America. Thus, although they are near the bottom of the Hollywood income pile they remain sufficiently well rewarded to maintain participation on a remunerative basis. But it also seems the case that this 'working class' is largely outside the much observed Hollywood system. Rosten, as we have seen, is quite explicit about this. Hollywood as anything more than a business organisation exists in his two inner circles. Powdermaker holds the same position by default, in that the Hollywood she discusses is made up only of the 'upper' and 'middle' classes who live, eat, and sleep the movie colony. Those involved in a purely utilitarian capacity are those who treat Hollywood as a place of work rather than the whole social context of their lives.

With this exception the myth that everyone is in it 'for the money' is indeed a myth. Of course Hollywood salaries are very high, if not as high as popular culture puts them. Of course this must have some importance, especially in recruiting for certain roles such as writer, and, to a lesser extent, director. Anyone who has shown talent elsewhere may well be drawn by high financial rewards. But once captured, the money is as important a symbol of one's authority position as anything else. As writer Mary McCall has it:

'I look forward to the day when my salary will be very high. I want that big salary not because I need it... there's nothing about a $2,000-a-week salary which is at all relevant to my way of life except this one thing – it will give me authority. Then when a producer says, "Look, sweetheart, I have a terrific angle on this opening, we fade in on a bed," I can say, "That's silly," and he will listen to me because I will be so very expensive. I say "That's silly" now, but he rarely listens to me.'[18]

It should be repeated that Miss McCall is a writer. Of all the Hollywood groupings it is the writers who are most marginal and least experienced in other fields of movie-making. If any group was likely to be much concerned with remuneration this would surely be it.

Salary payments, however, are not the only way of ensuring compliance through material inducement. There is another obvious sense in which money can oil the wheels. The large financial resources needed for making films also constitute some sort of reward for those whose involvement is above all in making movies. Control of facilities is a basic power factor in the Hollywood situation, and one which is especially pertinent to directors. Almost all information suggests that it is the directors who are most personally involved with the film-making process as such. 'You're only as good as your last movie' takes on more than just a suggestion of redundancy to someone in this position. The creative–commercial conflict has its roots firmly located in this material base. Without resources, the director's 'creative' life is destroyed.

Allowing for these economic base-lines, there still remain the various imbalances intrinsic to the commercial–creative dichotomy. Not everything can be dealt with in terms of direct remuneration or control of scarce resources. Now the most efficient way of dealing with such difficulties would be to transcend them through a set of shared beliefs. An opium of the people. If, for example, all participants believed that they were collectively attempting to reach the same goal – let us say, good movies – then this would at least provide a basis on which to handle the strains. Indeed, studio heads have sometimes tried to articulate such collective claims, generally to the disbelief of all. Occasionally one finds such a level of shared commitment in a producer–director relationship – Siegel's comments on Walter Wanger for instance – but generally the control system breaks down at this point. Instead of successfully appealing to shared commitment, the studio chiefs, production executives and producers have to fall back on a mixture of coercive and utilitarian techniques, none of which work very well. The creative process is, of necessity, highly personalised. Making movies requires the complex interaction of creative people. Yet the Hollywood system is clearly not structured in such a way as to maximise this possibility. In some respects it is totalitarian rather than co-operative. The production élite is largely set on getting its own way, which it believes to be correct, i.e. the way to good profitable films. The fact that they are frequently shown to be wrong in their judgements is dealt with in other ways to which I shall return. Now such a system could operate relatively smoothly – and has done on occasions – either if the 'lower participants'[19] are devoted to a particular figure because of his personal charisma, or if they are normatively involved. The first is rare at the higher production levels, though David Selznick and Irving Thalberg seem to have had some such capacity. In any case, as a basis for control it presents all sorts of long-term problems; the process Weber spoke of as 'routinisation of charisma'[20] does not appear to have operated in the Hollywood situation. Glory has not rubbed off very successfully. The second alternative (normative involvement) has not operated on a system-wide basis. Crews working on specific movies may have involved themselves in this sense, but there is no general institutionalised legitimating machinery to deal with the situation in which so many desired goals are divergent.

In these circumstances the production élite frequently find it necessary to use more 'naked' mechanisms. Indeed, the very fame of these processes is an indication of how little the Hollywood system is able to depend on normative involvement and the exercise of authority. Hence the paradoxical situation that, although many participants are not involved primarily for utilitarian reasons, the production élite are willing to treat them as if they were. This is the sort of incongruency between power and involvement which Etzioni suggests is unstable.[21] So runs the adage: everyone has his price. At the very top levels this clearly had some effect. Thalberg was allegedly *given* $250,000 to prevent him resigning over an internal dispute. But further down the system the actuality and the threat of coercion become more likely. Harry Cohn, studio head of Columbia, is one much quoted case. As Philip French puts it, he

'. . . delighted in humiliating his employees, estranged many of his best artists, and was dubbed "White Fang" by Ben Hecht. "I don't have ulcers. I give them," he once boasted. The director Charles Vidor unsuccessfully attempted to break his Columbia contract on the grounds of Cohn's notoriously foul language; Cohn had sound stages wired so that he could listen to employee's private conversations; at one Christmas party in his studio he put a secretary in his swivel chair and invited her to point to anyone in the room – and Cohn would fire him as a Christmas present to her.'[22]

All the serious Hollywood accounts make some mention of this sort of behaviour. Powdermaker reports the case of a director (Mr John Mighty) currently sleeping with the star of the movie he was directing. She arrived on set half-an-hour late, with apparently good reason, whereupon he publicly reprimanded her, and continued by making her repeat an apology to those on set:

'"I apologise because I am late, and because I have caused loss of money to the studio, and more particularly because I know I am an actress without ability." At this point she broke down and, crying, said, "But please, John!" She got no further. The director bellowed," 'John' in bed, you bitch; 'Mr Mighty' on the set!" Humiliation as a technique for maintaining authority is not confined to big people: assistant directors often show the same pattern in their treatment of extras.'[23]

Of course these are the extremes, the points at which the basics are revealed. But both threat and practice of coercion seem well institutionalised in the Hollywood system, the strongest legally established arm being the ill-famed contract system.

The control structures of complicated social systems generally depend on a range of mechanisms. Highly specialised organisations may depend on one particular form much more than others. Total institutions, for instance, depend mainly on coercion: prisons, mental hospitals, and the like.[24] It can be argued that systems which attempt to harness a variety of creative talents to produce a complex cultural object are best served by control structures based on normative commitment. Otherwise, too much energy is expended in uncreative directions. This is especially true in a case such as Hollywood which is so much more than a commercial organisation which happens to be producing films. Stable social intercourse requires that there are clear bases of legitimacy underlying the structure of social relations. If there are not, such intercourse ceases to be stable and varies according to any minor fluctuations in the external symbols of position. All becomes flux. In fact this is partly true of Hollywood. Most observers remark on the transitory nature of social relationships in the colony. Power structures are not directly legitimated, so people create various buffers against them. Transient personal relations is one such; fatalism, as we shall see, is another. The context in which we find these 'buffers' developed is that of Hollywood culture.

HOLLYWOOD: CULTURAL CONTROLS

Hollywood culture is many things, but one thing, frequently noted, is immediately significant. Powdermaker quotes from an article in *Variety*:

'It isn't that we like such crises. Existing as we do on the people's hopes and making films evocative of these hopes, we just can't let a crisis effect our creative efforts. We have to function in our own atmosphere of crisis. Betting

$400,000,000 or so a year that the pictures will please is what we term a crisis *ab initio*.

'When someone says, "Bergman, you look worried," I always answer by saying, "No wonder; I worry all the time."

'. . . Let's remember that crisis is the backbone of our business.'[25]

Powdermaker goes on to claim that this is a representative view, in effect that it is part of the character of Hollywood, part of its culture. Whatever the source of such a pheno-menon (Rosten suggests 'self-punishment for obscure and disturbing guilts')[26] it does have odd consequences. One of the things which stands out in most accounts of the movie-making process is the difficulty of provoking extreme conflict. For all the conflict potentiality in the *Red Badge of Courage* situation, it hardly ever surfaces in such a way as to destroy the whole enterprise. Nor is this simply a question of power and authority relations, though this is an element in Schary's 'victory'. It is more as if the participants are so accustomed to thinking and talking in terms of perpetual crisis that a genuine crisis is indistinguishable. Hence it is treated in the same fleeting way. As Sam Spiegel remarks to Huston: 'Beneath this facade of worry is worry.'[27]

This is what might be termed a *crisis culture*. Its language, its style, its imagery, are cast in terms of a pattern of perpetual crises. The tiniest events are blown up to vast proportions. Claims are outrageously exaggerated. Everything is carried on at a somewhat larger than life level. This applies right through from the wild excesses of the publicity departments to the characteristic modes of everyday discourse. The memoes and letters quoted in *Picture* are revealing here, suggesting a continuous need for mutual reassurance. Head of Production writes to Producer on the first day of shooting. Producer writes to Director. Later the Chief Cutter writes to them both to say how good the rushes are. The air-waves hum with cables, letters, and notes filled with congratu-lations, good wishes, and terms of endearment. In this way capital is borrowed against open conflict. Once every minor difficulty is seen as a major crisis, then a major crisis becomes little more than a minor difficulty. Besides, as Powdermaker suggests, '. . . the atmosphere of continuous crisis helps create the illusion of everyone's and everything's being of the greatest importance'.[28] This helps to play down the wide differentials which we have already seen to be structured into the system. Whatever the actuality in terms of decision-making and control, the crisis culture can make everyone feel that their contribution (or its absence) is as crucial as everyone else's.

In a way this sort of culture is a 'second line of defence' for the system. The hypothetical 'first line' is that in which participants are normatively involved; the culture – widely adhered to by definition – specifically justifies the state of affairs. Whether it does so in terms of a god or just producing great movies is immaterial here. Such a stable situation does not characterise the Hollywood case. The 'second line', the crisis culture, does not shore up the structure *directly*. Rather it provides indirect mechanisms which shift attention away from the realities so minimising potentially destructive consequences. It has its price in terms of organisational efficiency; Hollywood is far from efficient as a commercial institution. But an organisation of such mixed goals can hardly pick and choose. If this second line fails, then there are always the possibilities that we have already discussed: withdrawal of facilities, income, and general threats of coercion. Continual use of such techniques is probably subject to diminishing returns as well as consequent alienation. This too contributes to the ephemeral character of Hollywood social relations; interpersonal trust does not come easily in such a context.

The *crisis* element does not exhaust Hollywood culture, though it does provide the major features. Many other factors are closely related to it. There is, for example, a peculiar optimism. Rosten sees the two as implicitly related: 'Optimism and insecurity run through the movie colony side by side.'[29] Powdermaker, drawn to anthropological analogies, sees this as fundamentally magical. Instability and uncertainty (incarnated in the crisis culture) give rise to compensating tendencies. The situation is analogous to primitive uses of magic to 'deal' with the strains attendant upon unpredictable situations. One finds more complex versions in cultures which do not formally offer any security as to the afterlife. In peasant Buddhism, for instance, there are all sorts of astrological elements although they are specifically renounced in the formal doctrines of Buddhism.[30] The Hollywood situation is doubly unpredictable. Not only is the success or failure of the product itself indeterminate, the lack of a clearly *legitimated* structure of social relations makes much social interaction equally unpredictable. Social relations are thus emptied of their normal emotional invest-ment; terms of close endearment, normally reserved for intimates, are used in all situations; superstitions are invoked as ways of controlling this apparently uncontrollable environment; great faith is placed in the predictability of other essentially unpredictable events, for instance, in gambling and horse-racing. Without attempting to sort out a causal pattern, it is clear that all these elements make some sort of sense as a cultural configuration.

These are the norms of Hollywood culture. Beyond them it seems peculiarly empty. Although writers and directors commonly value 'creativity', this evaluation remains rela-tively diffuse. There is no clear specification in the culture as to what would indeed constitute a creatively acceptable movie. The definition remains, understandably, at the level of 'creativity' versus 'commercialism'; each individual makes his own interpretation. Of course there are endless narcis-sistic myths, formulae for success, achievement stresses, and a collection of confused and confusing 'audience-images',[31] but like magical systems these are primarily formulae to be used to counteract 'evil spirits'. There is no distinct sub-cultural morality, unless a belief in finding ways round a difficult issue could count as such. Morality is what the Code provides, and though the movies may stick to the letter they can usually manage to avoid the spirit. At points of serious crisis – the 'Red' scare and the treatment of Chaplin for example – Hollywood seems to lack a moral and ideo-logical centre which could sustain it in defence of its members.[32] Alison Lurie has written of Los Angeles as the 'Nowhere City'; the term is just as apposite to Hollywood.[33]

Hollywood, then, is a peculiar mixture incapable of adequate summary. It is an elaborate structure without any clear legitimation. Its self-conceived goals are often inconsistent with one another. Although it requires enormous commercial investment, its members like to see themselves (with various degrees of justice) as basically creative. Although virtually a 'society', the normative involvement of its members is drastically attenuated. Its culture thrives on crisis and exaggeration; yet in the end it will ruthlessly alter its own images to get them into line with its perception of its audience. And the movies are a product of this set-up. Somehow they emerge, the results of as elaborate a set of social processes as one is likely to find. One wonders how it, and we, survived. Yet survive it did until finally brought low by outside changes rather than internal strains. Less income meant contraction; and contraction meant a greater potential for adaptation. The classic system – long bolstered by the social machinery I have described – finally, and significantly, fell to a commercial decline.

THE LAST PICTURE SHOW

Peter Bogdanovich's film is set in the early fifties when so many picture shows had to finish in America, Britain, and parts of Western Europe. Hollywood hardly noticed it happenings until it was too late to respond rationally to the crisis. They had been expecting it since the thirties; it was a perpetual part of Hollywood culture. When it finally came Hollywood wriggled desperately, but largely in vain. Change was well on the way, how widespread is another matter. The commercial detail has been widely documented; there is no need to enter that discussion here.[34] While Spraos' famous title overdoes it a bit – *The Decline of the Cinema* – it is partially true. Relative to the "golden age", audiences and receipts have declined. DeFleur presents a diffusion curve which exhibits the classic pattern of obsolecsence.[35] Consequently the whole financial structure of film-making has undergone change. In particular, the big studios have gone while the low-budget movie has gained ground. Instead of risking all on the big production (Hollywood's first response to the crisis – witness the string of failed block-busters), it is possible to diversify risks for the same price. Standard estimates for America have it that for the price of one traditionally financed movie, four low budget quickies can be mounted. Only one has to be a hit; if it's another *Easy Rider* a fortune is guaranteed.

Predictably the commercial structure has altered most obviously. The independent producer has come into his own, the producer-director is much more common, the enormous front office system has declined, and the percentage-of-profits system of payment has become more common. Financing has changed in original ways. For instance, in 1972 Paramount set up a new deal with three of the most startlingly successful young directors: Peter Bogdanovitch (*The Last Picture Show, Whats Up Doc?*); Francis Ford Coppola (*The Godfather*); William Friedkin (*The French Connection*). Together these three form a Directors' Company to be floated on the New York stock exchange, and Paramount's agreement is with the company.[36] So, though a great deal of the commercial and legal superstructure of the Hollywood system has wasted away new variations may yet replace them. Change has not been the same everywhere. It seems to have begun in the French industry with the '*nouvelle vague*', and has spread outwards from there. With it has come a new pattern of recruitment. In France film-makers have come from film criticism. In Britain from TV and the theatre and more marginally from criticism. In America from no single clear source, although a number of directors moved in from TV. Not that things are now a bed of creative roses. There are still many of the usual constraints, especially at the distribution end. Nor is it entirely clear that the breakdown of the old hegemony is as automatically beneficial as some have claimed. Tony Richardson (whose arrogant comments on Hollywood have already been noted) is a good example of the failure of the new to produce

E

'good art'. *Sailor from Gibraltar* and *Mademoiselle* could do with a little of the traditional Hollywood constraint!

Such changes are easy to recognise. How the socio-cultural context of film-making has changed is more obscure. Parts of Hollywood society survive, although rather attenuated. Hitchcock, always somewhat apart, has remarked:

'My interests outside the movies? House and Garden, I'd say. Home Lover. A few paintings collected. We live a very suburban life here. We're in bed by nine o'clock every night.'[37]

The division of labour, too, is less significant. Of course there is still a need for the full range of technical specialisms – more of them, if anything. And in Britain and America particularly there are still union regulations which ensure large crews. But movies can no longer support the vast range of activities they once underwrote, and, besides, the locus has shifted. For many reasons films are shot increasingly on location, and increasingly in other countries, especially Spain and Italy. The social system of film-making is more and more segmented. There are still many recognisable elements of the old ways; but there are as many examples of the new.

The whole process remains incomplete. In one important area, for example, the film-makers have not yet stabilised their image of their potential audiences. They have recognised that the audience is composed of discrete 'sub-cultures of taste', but they are not too sure of their specific character.[38] They are still taking shots in the dark in the wake of every new success. *Easy Rider* inspired a string of weak imitations. Political issues such as the Vietnam war and race conflict have led to some reasonable movies (*Summertree*) and some abysmal ones (*Welcome to the Club*). In the bigger budget area film-makers have been looking into cinematic history for inspiration, sometimes with considerable success. Peckinpah's 'evening westerns' (*Ride the High Country* and *The Wild Bunch* especially) have inspired a mixed bag of imitations. The cycle of Don Siegel thrillers from *Madigan* through to *Dirty Harry* successfully invoke the forties idiom, and Bogdanovich's *Whats Up Doc?* may yet provoke a new cycle of classic Hollywood comedies. In some sectors the film-makers have long ago settled down in recognition of their audience. The Hammer films horror cycle is an excellent case. Their understanding and control of the conventions of the genre is now so well developed that they can let their younger directors produce experiments as well as the perfect genre movies. Peter Sasdy, for example, can try and fail with *Countess Dracula*, and go on to produce a classic in *Hands of the Ripper*. No doubt other groups will find other niches.

This combination of an increasingly speculative field of independents and the need for cultural selectivity may draw new structures into crucial roles in the system. Hirsch has argued (in relation to publishing and record production as well as movies) that this speculative element increases reliance on 'gatekeepers',[39] that is, on those individuals who occupy opinion leader roles *vis-à-vis* specific audiences. Output is mediated through disc-jockeys, film and book critics. It is not a question of direct selling but of selling to the gate-keeper who in turn 'sells' to his particular sub-culture. Hirsch is rightly least confident of the thesis in the movie industry, and it is difficult to identify gatekeepers who are genuinely independent of the business and who must therefore be specially approached. Power seems more vested in the organisational structure of distribution than in any autonomous world of film critics.

So the picture is confused. In some areas something like the Hollywood system still prevails. Elsewhere it barely survives. For the most part it is somewhere in between. But there is a real sense in which the industry is becoming an 'international' one. As Guback shows in detail the European and American industries are more and more intimately related; economic and cultural uniformity looks more and more likely.[40] To that extent a 'global village' is just around the corner.

THE COMMUNICATOR

Quite obviously there is no typical film-maker. There is as much personal variation in the movie communities as there is in any other diversified social context. To construct *the* film communicator, in this sense, would be a pointless exercise, but there may be some important characteristics which film-makers do share in common. As individuals they may come from rather similar social and educational backgrounds. More important, as film-makers they are likely to share a socio-cultural situation in common, the situation I have been analysing here as a movie community. Both these things may be constant factors impinging on the production of movies. In addition, of course, there are endless sources of variation. Movie-makers are bound to be open to external influences; events in the wider world, currently fashionable topics, and such like. A community such as Hollywood can, and did, act as a filter to such influences, but in other contexts – the Italian post-war cinema for example – outside events might outweigh all else. Whatever the world may be doing it is certain that the collective and creative activities of the movie-makers will be largely unpredictable. This is the character of creativity by definition. So what can we conclude *in general* about the cinematic communicator?

Quite a lot and not very much! A lot in the sense that we can develop an image of the constant characteristics, particularly of the movie-maker's social system. Very little in that to make any sense of such a portrait as part of the social process of cinema requires it to be fitted into an even larger jigsaw. There is no simple way out of this situation, nor should there be. We may learn a little from some individual factors. It is suggestive, for instance, that the directors involved in the Soviet cinema (1920s), German expressionism, and Italian neo-realism were largely middle class and pretty well educated.[41] Their American counterparts had rather less formal education, though the legend definitely exaggerates how much less. One rather suspects, however, that as the German, Soviet and Italian industries 'settled down' after their social crises (two world wars and a revolution) then

film-makers were increasingly recruited from similar contexts as in America. Or again it might be that the social
backgrounds of the original big figures in Hollywood (mainly
lower middle class with little formal education) played a
considerable part in the developing style of Hollywood
society. It is certainly a tempting way to account for some of
the more extravagant excesses.[42]

A lot here depends on the complexity of the movie-making
system. Where technological facilities are primitive, budgets
low, and commercial pressures (however temporarily)
distanced, in this situation *individual* characteristics of film-
makers can be expected to be important. With a medium like
the cinema such situations have been rare; commercial
pressures are much too well founded, and when they have
arisen they have done so as a result of crises. In the cases
mentioned, much larger social crises which have successfully
undermined whatever cinematic institutions already existed.
Elsewhere similar changes have flowed from internal difficulties, especially those of declining audience. Once the
'tried-and-true' ways are found to be commercially wanting
then the gates are open for innovation, experiment, and a
different body of film-makers. This has happened in France
in the modern period, and to a lesser extent in Britain and
America. Usually the orthodox pattern has returned;
slightly altered but not radically so. Indeed, except for the
very special case of the Soviet Union, they never really
vanished. But contemporary changes may well be more
permanent. This time the precipitating crisis is fundamental
to the operation of the industry. Even the heralded 'cassette'
revolution seems unlikely to push things back up to earlier
levels.

Still, for much of the movies' history, and for a significant
part of modern production, the Hollywood pattern is *the*
factor. In this situation individual characteristics become
less important. Of course creative figures are not expunged,
though they do not have the control found in some other
contexts. They become a highly specialised sort of artist.
They find ways of imposing themselves on their materials
through the system rather than without it. A list of examples

(margin note, top left: as opposed to Director AUTAS the film.)

would be endless, especially among directors. John Ford, Alfred Hitchcock, Howard Hawks, Anthony Mann, Don Siegel, Sam Peckinpah, Arthur Penn, William Wyler, Jack Arnold, and so many more. But however great, these men *are* the exceptions. The commercial exigencies of film-making create the system; the system creates the films. The whole becomes greater than the sum of its parts. However peculiar, talented, or plain stupid the individuals who make the movies, the movies themselves survive. They are a function of the conflicts, strains, and patterns which we have partly explored.

It is not possible at this stage to precisely stipulate this relation. It may never be possible. Perhaps there are too many imponderables. We may understand particular cases; *The Red Badge of Courage* makes a lot more sense after reading *Picture*. We can learn where to look. Hollywood is an unstable authority system, but at least it is a system. We can locate seats of power; we can try to trace the mechanisms whereby such power influences the product. The fact that power lies with the commercial élite, however unstably, means that their evaluations must be considered. The fact that their goals are mainly commercial draws our attention to their audience-conceptions. They are there to sell. In such a situation one finds an asymmetry quite the opposite of that suggested in mass society theory. Here the communicators are dedicated to discovering 'what the public want' rather than wielding some insidious power. It is this that has led to the view that the cinema has evaded its responsibilities to influence and inform. It has participated in the communication process only for gain, not for the benefits of the communication itself.

(margin note, left: Midnight Express !)

As we have seen, this stereotype, like all the others, stresses only one element in a complex situation. Movies are produced by many people, related to one another in a variety of ways. They have mixed motives for what they do and they are not always aware of how little they are able to control their actions. Hollywood, in particular, is a good example of a system of social relations constraining its members. So much of Hollywood activity is designed to deal with the problems of the system that one is tempted to conclude that in Hollywood at least the people exist to serve the society! Making movies is such a peculiar goal. It makes such unique demands – though it is no longer unique – that the movie-makers have had to develop makeshift forms of society to deal with it. It throws together personalities, values, goals, and practices which in most contexts are 'safely' insulated from one another. Hollywood has 'invented' ways of dealing with these problems. They have not been highly efficient ways, but they have worked, and that is fascinating in itself. They may well be constants in the situation of the movie communicator.

References

[1] L. Ross (see Selected Bibliography).

[2] See, for example, the sort of treatment in Norman Storer, *The Social System of Science* (Holt, Rinehart & Winston, New York, Chicago, San Francisco, Toronto, London, 1966). The widely read work of T. Kuhn is also relevant here; one could employ an analogous concept to 'paradigm' in application to movie-makers. See Thomas Kuhn, *The Structure of the Scientific Revolution*, Chicago Univ. Press, Chicago, 1962, 2nd ed., 1970.

[3] Budd Schulberg, *What Makes Sammy Run?*, Random House, New York, 1941, and *The Disenchanted*, Random House, New York, 1950; F. Scott Fitzgerald, *The Last Tycoon*, Penguin, New York, 1960; Richard Brooks, *The Producer*, Simon & Schuster, New York, 1951.

[4] H. Powdermaker, *Hollywood, the Dream Factory. An Anthropologist Looks at the Movie-makers*, London, 1951. L. Rosten, *Hollywood the Movie Colony, the Movie Makers* (Selected Bibliography).

[5] See L. Rosten, *ibid.*, pp. 297–300.

[6] Tony Richardson in *Films and Filming*, June 1961, reprinted in H. Geduld, pp. 145–6 (Selected Bibliography).

[7] In R. Hughes (Ed.), *Film Book 1*, p. 57 (Selected Bibliography) also in H. Geduld, *op. cit.*, p. 288.

[8] L. Rosten, *op. cit.*, p. 53.

[9] H. Powdermaker, *op. cit.*, p. 19.

[10] cf. P. Hirsch (Selected Bibliography); also L. Rosten, *op. cit.*, pp. 38–40.

[11] For these and other figures see L. Rosten, *op. cit.*, Chapters 3 and 4.

[12] H. Powdermaker, *op. cit.*, p. 209.

[13] Cf. Jarvie's summary of the vital factors in the situations of film workers in I. Jarvie, *Towards a Sociology of the Cinema* (Selected Bibliography). If anything, he seems to underestimate the range of factors in the situation of producers and writers.

[14] Quoted in Paul Mayersberg, *Hollywood the Haunted House*, Penguin, Harmondsworth, 1969, p. 61. Siegel also talks of Wanger in an interview in *Positif*, translated and reprinted in A. Lovell, pp. 8–9 (Selected Bibliography). However, his relations with Wanger did not prevent Allied Artists from seriously altering their next (and excellent) production, *Invasion of the Body Snatchers*.

[15] L. Ross, *op. cit.*, p. 20. For an excellent fictional account of the trials and tribulations of the producer role see R. Brooks, *op. cit.* On the official self-image of the independent producers see D. Nelson (Selected Bibliography).

[16] This area is largely unstudied except as a by-product of other work. See, for example, Murray Ross, *Stars and Strikes*, the same author's 'Labor Relations in Hollywood' (Selected Bibliography). For further indirect information see the lengthy and fascinating interviews with major cameramen in Charles Higham, *Hollywood Cameramen*, Thames & Hudson, London, 1970.

[17] The theme runs right through Marx's work. The full phrase on religion is: 'Religion is the sign of the oppressed creature, the heart of a heartless world, just as it is the spirit of a spiritless situation. It is the *opium* of the people', 'Contribution to the Critique of Hegel's Philosophy of Right', in this case quoted from Karl Marx and Frederick Engels, *On Religion*, Moscow Pub. Hse, Moscow, 1955, p. 42. The best source for Weber's discussion of power and authority is Max Weber, *The Theory of Social and Economic Organization*, Free Press, New York, 1947, Part III. Etzioni's discussion appears in Amitai Etzioni, *A Comparative Analysis of Complex Organizations*, Free Press, Glencoe (Ill), 1961, especially Part I. The Parsons material is scattered over a number of essays, some of which can be found collected together in Talcott Parsons, *Sociological Theory and Modern Society*, Free Press, New York, London, 1967, Part III.

[18] Mary McCall, Jr., 'Hollywood Close Up', *Review of Reviews*, May 1937, p. 44. Quoted in L. Rosten, *op. cit.*, p. 81.

[19] Etzioni's term. See A. Etzioni, *op. cit.*

[20] See M. Weber, *op. cit.*, pp. 363–73.

[21] A. Etzioni, *op. cit.*, Part I.

[22] Philip French, *The Movie Moguls*, Penguin, Harmondsworth, 1971, p. 58.

[23] H. Powdermaker, *op. cit.*, p. 330.

[24] See A. Etzioni, *op. cit.*; also see Erving Goffman *Asylums*, Penguin, Harmondsworth, 1969.

[25] Maurice Bergman, *Variety*, 17 January 1948. Quoted in H. Powdermaker, *op. cit.*, p. 32.

[26] L. Rosten, *op. cit.*, p. 39. There are a number of such peculiar mock psychoanalytic suggestions in his study; they are not usually very plausible.

[27] L. Ross, *op. cit.*, p. 130. The phrase is used in a situation where Huston and Agee clearly deliberately set out to play on Producer Spiegel's worries.

[28] H. Powdermaker, *op. cit.*, p. 32.

[29] L. Rosten, *op. cit.*, p. 39.

[30] Apart from the standard anthropological discussions of magic see the fascinating paper by Gananath Obeyesekere, 'Theodicy, Sin and Salvation in a Sociology of Buddhism', in Edmund Leach (Ed.), *Dialectic in Practical Religion*, Cambridge Univ. Press, Cambridge, 1968.

[31] See H. Gans 'The Creator–Audience Relationship in the Mass Media'; also see L. A. Handel, *Hollywood Looks at its Audience*. (See Selected Bibliography.)

[32] For some of the basic material see Gordon Kahn, *Hollywood on Trial*, Boni & Goer, New York, 1948. Also see Charles Chaplin, *My Autobiography*, Bodley Head, London, 1964, pp. 440–507.

[33] Alison Lurie, *The Nowhere City*, Pan, London, 1967.

[34] The literature is very extensive. For some idea of the magnitude and direction of change consult the following: S. Rowson; H. E. Browning and A. A. Sorrell; J. Spraos; W. A. Belson; PEP; J.-C. Batz; T. H. Guback. (See Selected Bibliography.)

[35] See Melvin L. DeFleur, 'Mass Communication and Social Change' in J. Tunstall (Ed.), *Media Sociology*, Constable, London, 1970, p. 71.

[36] See Michael Pye, 'Hollywood Stars Plunge into the Old Routine', *The Sunday Times*, London, 3 September 1972.

[37] Quoted in P. Mayersberg, *op. cit.*, p. 167.

[38] See H. J. Gans, 'The Creator–Audience Relationship in the Mass Media', see also H. S. Becker, *Social Problems: a Modern Approach*, pp. 459–620 (Selected Bibliography).

[39] P. Hirsch, *op. cit.*

[40] T. Guback, *op. cit.*

[41] See G. Huaco, *The Sociology of Film Art* (Selected Bibliography).

[42] For detailed breakdowns of Rosten's Hollywood sample see L. Rosten, *op. cit.*, Appendixes C, D, and E.

Chapter 4

Movie Audiences

'Audience' is not a satisfactory term. Even its everyday use has overtones of passivity: to be a member of an audience is to be a non-contributing recipient. Traditional uses of the expression in mass media studies simply underline this common-sense meaning and takes it as a definition. We study an anonymous, mass, aggregated body within which all individuals are similarly placed. Detailed analysis of the 'situation' of the audience member is replaced by a set of definitional characteristics; and by implication any medium associated with such an audience is, at the least, disturbing, and, at the most, an insult to traditional values.[1] There seems to be a classic mistrust of anything which apparently provokes the same response in so many different people. So, having observed the widescale popularity of the cinema, negatively disposed critics tried to contend with it in terms of audience uniformity. Having correctly observed that many popular movies were basically uncomplicated, they went on to assume that the audience must be responding unselectively to this simple stimulus. Popular culture thus became mass culture.

However, a member of a movie audience is not usefully conceived as a typical unit within a mass, or as a passive recipient of media messages. In the term that Perkins aptly steals from social science methodology, movie audiences are 'participant observers'.[2] In their various ways they *participate* in the world offered to them by the movies. Precisely how they participate depends on the individual, his mood, his situation, and endless other factors in his everyday experience. Going to the movies (or watching TV, or listening to a concert) is part of a person's social interaction. It offers him experiences which he enjoys, hates, learns from, and believes. It extends his world. In a very real sense he may *interact* with the characters of a fictional film. He certainly identifies with them and uses them to project his emotions, needs, and pleasures. He is not brainwashed as some critics of popular culture like to suggest. Like everyone else, he uses culture as part of the fabric of his social life. No more and no less.

So the problem is to somehow reconstitute an image of a movie audience which does not start from a mass media prejudice. One which includes the sorts of factors our general model of communication suggests as relevant. Obviously, the absolute base-line must lie in the one thing which all movie-audiences share: their physical environment. This does not necessarily mean a cinema, which context already introduces a social dissension. More fundamental is the situation of nearly total darkness dominated by the proximity of a large, projected, sound-synchronised, moving image. This much is basic to any audience situation and clearly has consequences of its own. For example, experiments have suggested that the simple act of isolating a single source of information strengthens the bond between source and audience. Without other things to capture wandering attention, the movie experience has even been likened to a pre-hypnotic state. But this is an obvious point. A moment's reflection on the difference between the movie and television situation confirms it. Television, viewed in the home and in some light, operates in a familiar and visible physical environment which carries with it connotations of our everyday experience. In the cinema this bond is broken. Our awareness of context is minimised, and as a result we may be much freer to respond in otherwise unacceptable ways. Extremes of emotion for instance: more people must weep in the cinema than in any other 'public' place.[3]

So many of the technological developments of film have served to extend this monopoly of the individual's senses. The sound and colour revolutions moved in new directions; the development of wider screens and better sound systems enlarged on what there was. Either way the nature of the experience was altered.[4] It is instructive, for instance, to view *2001: A Space Odyssey* in Cinerama, in 70 mm, and in 'normal' wide-screen. In Cinerama, the medium of which it is the best product, it is enormously compelling. Viewed from the focal point of the curved screen it is an assault on the sensations impossible to avoid. As screen size and sound quality drop, so too does involvement. Narrative problems are increasingly apparent. It becomes clear that certain 'difficulties' are 'papered over' by Kubrick's skill with Cinerama. Return to the Cinerama version and the difficulties once more seem insignificant.

This whole area of technological developments merits more study than it has received. But for present purposes we can safely assume that most technological change has led to an increasing capacity for stimulating emotional involvement. Indeed, if the medium can be said to have any characteristic in and of itself it is surely this high dependence on a predominantly emotional effect. This should not lead us where it has led others. It does not follow that the movies are therefore an outstandingly powerful medium of persuasion. Long-term attitude change is very different to short-term emotional involvement. But the history of media studies demonstrates the dangers of this jump. The Payne Fund Studies, for example, stemmed partly from concern over the potential effects of such a seemingly powerful medium. Yet most evidence suggests that people are not directly affected in the suspected ways. To understand why we must also look at the social and psychological context of the audience situation.

'LET THE SUPPORTING CAST DO THE DRINKING'

The basic psychological machinery through which most people relate to film involves some combination of identification and projection. As we have seen, the whole character of the audience situation encourages high levels of immersion. With 'distraction' minimised the audience is almost compelled to enter the world of the film. Primarily, of course, this applies to the fiction film and to those documentaries which rely on 'fictional' techniques: *Louisiana Story* and *The*

War Game would be suitably different examples. Other cinematic forms develop their own specialised techniques of involvement, but for most audiences the fiction-film exhausts the pattern of consumption. This discussion will be confined to this most familiar example.

There are different points at which the identification-projection pattern can apply. Two stand out from the rest: the performer and the story-type. In the days of the so-called mass audience the former was very much the focus. The star system provided the basic leverage for audience involvement. More recently, along with a clearer emergence of 'sub-cultures of taste', story-type may have increased in importance.[5] In any case the two are not independent. Particular star figures often developed an affinity for particular story-types. And very clearly defined forms, such as the horror movie, constituted their own film worlds with their own specialised stars. Boris Karloff, Bela Lugosi, Vincent Price, Peter Cushing, and Christopher Lee all developed, and largely remained, within their one very specialised area. Nor is this a reflection of limited acting talents. With the possible exception of Lugosi they are all performers of considerable abilities. But their role as stars was understood by the audience in a specific context; they formed recognisable 'signals' through which an audience could easily re-enter the familiar terrain.

Which leads us to a definition of 'star' for these purposes. Film acting is technically rather different from other forms, especially from the theatre. Above all it is the acting of understatement; where the stage requires a gesture, the camera needs only a tiny movement. This no doubt helped to create a body of successful film actors who 'played themselves' to varying degrees. They developed a relatively fixed persona in the minds of their audience, and this pre-established persona could then be fed into their subsequent movies. This does not mean that they were bad actors. It is merely that the demands of film acting are very different to those in other media, partly because of technical constraints, partly because of star-identification. Intuitively this is easily recognised. Some of the most noted of stage actors have not seemed entirely at ease in the transfer to the screen. However virtuoso their abilities they have not fitted the medium. Olivier and Gielgud are cases in point. Alec Guinness has only excelled where he has been able to apply modified stage techniques in fairly caricatured parts: *Kind Hearts and Coronets*, *The Ladykillers*, *Tunes of Glory*, *The Bridge on the River Kwai*. Those who are exclusively film stars have different qualities. The bland sophistication of Cary Grant; the blunt honesty of John Wayne; the neurotic self-doubt of James Stewart; or the attractive aggression of Katherine Hepburn. Film makers, recognising the relatively fixed audience conception of these personae (and in some cases consciously creating them),[6] can build on them as elements in the communication process. At its crudest this led to the star vehicle; the movie created purely as a frame within which the star could be profitably exhibited; but more subtle uses blended the stars into the overall pattern of the film. The best directors of the Hollywood system have always excelled here. John Ford carefully counterposes the Wayne and Stewart personae in *The Man Who Shot Liberty Valance*. Anthony Mann made a series of westerns which leaned heavily on the James Stewart image: *The Man From Laramie*, *Winchester '73*, *The Naked Spur*, *Bend of the River*, and others. In fact one of his best films is marred by the simple fact that the 'Stewart character' is played by Gary Cooper (*Man of the West*). Much of the pleasure in Hitchcock's *North by Northwest* derives from the various attacks on the smooth Grant character, and, in a devious and inverted way, Howard Hawks' crazy comedies *Monkey Business* and *Bringing up Baby* also use the Grant persona. Even lesser films than these are lent some credibility from such a stable foundation: James Stewart, again, in a pot-boiler like *No Highway*.

This star system is obviously a crucial part of film language, and we shall have occasion to return to it. For the moment it is sufficient to recognise what the film-makers themselves saw – that the relatively fixed persona of a star, created through the movies themselves and through the publicity machine, was a central element in audience involvement. The audience is able to identify with its favourite in a range of different story circumstances, and project its desires and frustrations into this intimately accepted character; it is this, of course, that gives rise to the familiar finding that audiences are attracted to stars of their own sex. But there are variations. Handel began to develop a rudimentary classification of different star identification processes by asking his sample of 100 movie-goers why they preferred stars of their own sex. He met with five classes of response. In descending order of frequency they were: conscious self-identification; emotional affinity; own sex claimed to have better acting ability; idealisation, idolisation; admiration of fashions, styles, etc.[7] The first three are rather difficult to distinguish from one another. It seems likely that the claim that one's own sex has greater acting ability is part and parcel of conscious identification, emotional affinity, or both; and the latter two are distinguished from each other only by virtue of self-consciousness. A large group of movie-goers explicitly recognise that they 'put themselves in the place of' the star. A slightly smaller group prefer to talk in the more distanced terms of their own sexual role conceptions fitting into those projected by the star. The basic pattern is the same; it is the presented rationale for it which varies. Thus it seems reasonable to collapse these three distinctions into the straightforward category of 'identification'.

Idealisation and idolisation are the characteristics of a rather smaller group, most typically young and female. The link with the star extends beyond the immediate movie context and informs a range of aspects of the fan's life. This much wider involvement is commonly found in the reported interview material, though there is no question of its being representative of the audience as a whole. Its frequency derives from the fact that much research has been carried out on the young, often with self-selecting and therefore biased samples.[8] For this reason interpretation must be carefully qualified. Handel's final category – rather more widespread – is also probably related to the idealisation pattern: the star as a source of fashion, style of dress, smoking, lovemaking, and the rest.

By slightly altering this terminology we can reformulate

these ideas into a simple classification. The dimensions of variation are quite clear. The distinction between diffuse

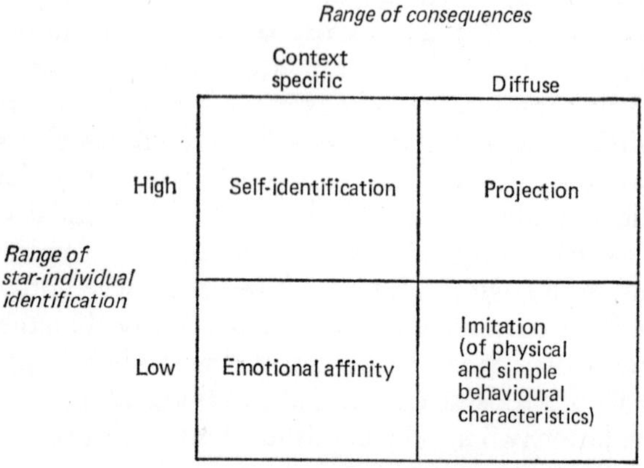

Range of consequences

		Context specific	Diffuse
Range of star-individual identification	High	Self-identification	Projection
	Low	Emotional affinity	Imitation (of physical and simple behavioural characteristics)

Figure 4.1   TYPES OF AUDIENCE–STAR RELATION

and specific consequences tries to tap the difference between identification which is limited to the watching-the-movie situation, and identification which has consequences for a diffuse range of aspects of the fan's life. Of course, the absolute division is artificial; it helps discussion to dichotomise in this way. Similarly with the vertical axis which dichotomises the degree of involvement with the star image.

Of the four consequent types the weakest is '*emotional affinity*' (not employed in Handel's sense). By the same count it is probably the most common. The audience feels a loose attachment to a particular protagonist deriving jointly from star, narrative, and the individual personality of the audience member: a standard sense of involvement. There may be complications, however. It is always possible to obtain strange results from particular combinations of narrative situation and star: the one may overcome the other, for example. Margaret Thorp quotes a revealing case in which emotional affinity to a star is undercut. She reports the comments of a cinema manager in Minnesota:

'I don't know how you or your patrons feel about scenes dealing with the stars getting intoxicated, but I do know that about 76 per cent lose a lot of interest in any star who has the misfortune to be so cast. It may seem like a small matter, but any feature we have played with any such scene has taken a tremendous box-office drop after the first day. Irene Dunne lost all draw here after the drinking scene in RKO's *Joy of Living*. . . . Let the supporting cast do the drinking.'[9]

Treating the '75 per cent' with circumspection does not impugn the general argument. The fundamental but weak link of 'emotional affinity' is subject to rapid and extensive variation. As such it is the 'normal' response.

The stronger case, still specific to the immediate cinema-going context, is *'self-identification'*. Involvement has reached the point at which the audience-member places himself in the same situation and persona of the star. This can reach extremes of self-consciousness. There are endless anecdotes about *The Magnificent Seven* enthusiasts returning repeatedly with the expressed intention of identifying with each of the seven in turn. One avid fan of my acquaintance refused to continue after six – he could not bear the thought of identifying with Horst Bucholzt! But with lesser degrees of self-consciousness this sort of identification is quite common; Handel claimed it as empirically the most frequent. It is aptly summarised in the words of one interviewed cinema-goer, a middle-aged woman:

'These actresses I mentioned are great. They make me feel every emotion of their parts. I feel as if it were myself on the screen experiencing what they do.'[10]

The third category, *'imitation'* seems to be common primarily among the young. Consequences are no longer limited to the immediate cinema-going situation, the star acting as some sort of model for the audience. 'Imitation' merges into 'projection' at the point at which the process becomes more than a simple mimicking of clothing, hairstyle,

F

kissing, and the like. This point cannot be easily placed; we are dealing with a continuum not a dichotomy, and simple imitation is no doubt part of the more general projection pattern, but it does also appear to exist independently. Apart from the much publicised cases (for example, the danger to factory workers who imitated Veronica Lake's 'one-eyed' hairstyle) the available interview materials are replete with examples. Take the following nineteen year old girl reported in Mayer.

'The settings of the love scenes always held my interest and I've always noted little tricks (which I've put into practice) such as curling my boy-friend's hair in my fingers or stroking his face exactly as I've seen my screen favourites do in their love scenes, one of the first things I noticed was that an actress always closes her eyes when being kissed and I don't need to add that I copied that too.'[11]

Wider ranging influences, much nearer to *projection*, are to be found in yet another of Mayer's cases. A twenty-two year old girl speaking of her love of Deanna Durbin:

'She became my first and only screen idol. I collected pictures of her, & articles about her & spent hours sticking them in scrap books. I would pay any price within the range of my pocket money for a book, if it had a new picture, however tiny, of her in it. I adored her & my adoration influenced my life a great deal. I wanted to be as much like her as possible, both in my manners & clothes. Whenever I was to get a new dress, I would find from my collection a particularly nice picture of Deanna & ask for a dress like she was wearing. I did my hair as much like her as I could manage. If I found myself in any annoying or aggravating situation, which I previously dealt with by an outburst of temper, *I found myself wondering what Deanna would do, & modified my own reactions accordingly.* She had far more influence on me than any amount of lectures or rows from parents would have had . . .'[12]

The more extreme the projection, the more the person lives his or her life in terms bound up with the favoured star. This is not a case of simple influence; a wielding of media power. The star-conception is a product of both the projected image of the star and whatever characteristics specific individuals project into their own conception. So, although partly independent, the star also becomes a receptacle for the projected desires, frustrations, and pleasures of the fan. In asking themselves what the star might have done in this situation the star-struck are using the star as a way of dealing with their realities. At the extreme the whole range of life experiences are mediated in this way. The 'real world' becomes constituted in terms derived from the 'star-world'.

This projection pattern seems very much associated with age. It is during adolescence that audiences are most likely to grasp at the models provided by the star-system as a way of forming a sense of identity and a social reality. It is not uncommon to find such apparently extreme responses labelled as somehow pathological. Rosten, for example, makes one such suggestion, but with little amplification. He merely continues by listing some of the strange requests made of two movie stars in their fan-mail, a list which includes: soap, lipstick tissues, a chewed piece of gum, 'piece of (your) horses tail or a lock of (your) hair', cigarette butt, autographed pair of shorts, blade of grass from the star's lawn, etc. etc.[13] But as his own figures demonstrate most fan mail comes from adolescents, and a very large proportion (80 per cent and above) from girls. Unless one is to claim that all the other oddities of adolescence are pathological, the term hardly seems useful. The fact that projection appears to be a largely feminine trait suggests at least three possibilities. First, that boys are less willing to admit such behaviour to the researchers. Second, that girls are 'naturally' different in this respect. Third, that our societies provide a very different socialisation experience for girls than that offered to boys, and this makes the pattern more probable in one than the other. This last seems the only really plausible possibility.

It should be stressed that, even allowing for the youth of the cinema audience, the extremes of projection are easily exaggerated. The studies have invariably looked at the most avid of fans, and would hardly claim their samples to be representative. Nor does the phenomenon appear strongly sexual, though sexuality must surely play some part in such a significant aspect of adolescence. Although a large proportion of fans appear to admire stars of their own sex, this is only occasionally explicitly homosexual. Some researchers have also reported a willingness on the part of boys to use the term 'love' in relation to male stars. What significance can be attached to that must depend on the cultural context of the expression. Of course, once adolescence is past, projection generally loses its force. Self-identification and a loose emotional affinity are then the main mechanisms through which the audience–star link is promoted.

The star-system, then, is a central factor in the psychology of the movie-audience. It demonstrates a pattern which is also found, in diluted form, at other levels of involvement. The story-type, for instance, although involvement here is largely limited to emotional affinity. Of course it can be argued that certain sorts of narrative meet certain deep-seated needs of their audience; in that sense they act as vehicles for audience projections. But even at its strongest such a link does not match that provided by the star system. It is not projection in that a film would be utilised as a *central* element in defining the audience's reality. Story-type is rather more limited.

In fact the most interesting characteristic of audience responses to story-type is that they come to conceive things in this way at all. The patterning of story preferences (women liking love pictures, men liking war pictures, etc.)[14] is uninteresting compared to the fact that audiences clearly do ascribe meaning to labels like war movie, horror movie, love story, musical-comedy, and the rest. That is, that they see the movies through the lens provided by such genre labels. A picture of this process would be very much more useful than all the random pages of audience preference statistics classified by age, sex, or chronic astigmatism! The

very fact that such labels exist suggests the principal mechanism through which story-type acts as an element in the
audience situation: familiarity. To see a movie made
within a clearly recognised genre, such as the western or the
horror movie, is to participate in a familiar locale and
development, and this familiarity facilitates easy and
immediate involvement. The first sight of decaying castle
and ghoulish aristocrat; the first long shot of the mesas of
Monument Valley. In these the spectator is offered a land-
mark. He knows exactly where he is. Of course, his attention
is not necessarily retained by a formula reproduction of the
standard clichés. But rather like the 'Once upon a time. . .'
of fairy tale the process of transition from one world to another
is accomplished with the minimum effort. We shall return to
this again and again in pages to come.

GOING TO THE MOVIES

These direct links between individual personality and movie
are only one part of the cinema-going situation. Members of
audiences are also involved in a larger social life. For the
most part this larger context is exactly that: a context. A
person fits his movie experiences into it along with all the
rest. But there are some parts of the sociocultural world
which bear directly on the business of 'going to the movies'.
We are dealing with a social institution as well as an individual experience. And as such we find a discernible structure,
a pattern among its elements. An invitation to go to the
movies is an invitation to participate in something more
than a few hours watching a flickering screen in a darkened
auditorium.

There are enormous regional and temporal variations in
the detail. In the thirties, for instance, 'going to the movies'
had much more of a ritual flavour attached to it. Affluence,
familiarity, and an increasing range of leisure activities have
changed that, though by no means evenly. Within England
there is differentiation between north and south. As late as
the sixties a northern city centre Odeon was still the scene
of a Saturday ritual. The cinemas themselves, decorated in

that heavily plush style favoured by earlier generations of cinema designers, provided a suitable setting for the self-consciously dressed-up audience. Second house Saturday was packed. The over-carpeted foyer crowded with patrons. The whole thing suggests a peculiarly distorted reflection of the theatre-going activities of another class at another time. The flavour of the ritual, the sense of occasion, the gilt and plush environment, the clothing, all contributed to that experience of which the film was centrepiece. In the days before television changed our patterns of cultural consumption this ritual quality was that much more pervasive. It was part of the cinema-going process, matched by the architectural extravagances of the nineteen-thirties' picture palaces.

But it was transient. In many parts of the world (though not yet all) it has become yet another stage in the history of the cinema. It was a sort of superstructure of movie-going which was practicable only for a brief period. Only its vestigal remains survive now. However, there is a substructure to movie-going which has remained fairly constant. The crude audience statistics suggest some part of it,[15] and its most blatent characteristic is the dominance of youth. Even though recent years have seen the film industries laying claim to a 'new' youthful audience, it is clear that the movie audience has always been youthful. It could be little else. With increasing age come all the material restraints which tie the individual to a more domestic life. Even without the more subtle psychological pressures, this crude limitation goes a long way toward keeping movie-audiences young.

This constancy of pattern is readily seen in most cross-tabulations of age and frequency of attendance. Compare, for instance, two sets of British data, one from 1946 (table 4.1) and the other from 1968 (table 4.2). Although overall attendance has declined, the audience remains predominantly youthful.

The specific figures in these tables are not comparable since the age groupings and attendance categories are different, but they do display a strikingly similar relation between youth and attendance. Statistical estimation of this association confirms what is obvious on inspection: although the overall audience declines, the relation between youth and attendance is very stable.[16]

	Age						
	16–19	20–9	30–9	40–9	50–9	60+	All
Cinema-going	%	%	%	%	%	%	%
Once a week plus	69	57	35	28	22	11	37
Less than once a week	28	34	46	52	43	28	38
Never	2	9	19	20	35	61	25

Table 4.1. From *The Social Survey 1946*

	Age						
	16–24	25–34	35–44	45–54	55–64	65+	All
Cinema-going	%	%	%	%	%	%	%
Regularly	19	5	2	2	1	2	5
Occasionally and Infrequently	70	67	57	45	31	19	49
Never	10	27	41	54	70	79	46

Table 4.2. From *JICNARS 1968*

This, then, is one popular belief which is true. Others – that women attend more than men, that audiences are typically comprised of the poorest and lowest educated sector of the population – are not. Most surveys over a long period have found that the sex distribution is pretty even, and that, although there is a tendency for movie-going to be inversely correlated with class, income, or education, such correlations are fairly weak.[17] Most people go to the movies in company, though more women appear to do so than men. Olsen has tried to argue that '. . . the greater the social isolation, defined as a lack of close personal friends, the higher the movie attendance', on the basis of the more general supposition that '. . . to a large extent people go to the movies because they cannot find more personal forms of recreation'.[18] This general supposition seems implausible, as does Olsen's claim to provide empirical substantiation for this thesis. Since his measures are defined at an aggregative level (Standard Metropolitan Areas) his is a good case of the ecological fallacy.[19] His correlation between inter-city mobility, intra-city mobility, and urbanism, with attendance could arise for all sorts of reasons having nothing to do with

social isolation. Social isolates may indeed go to the movies;
but by no means all those who do go are social isolates.
Children are quite the opposite, attending very much as
part of their peer-group activity. As they progress through
their teens they attend more and more frequently with
friends rather than with the parents and siblings of earlier
years. Going to the movies becomes that important
part of adolescent socialisation with which we are all so
familiar.[20]

As well as these rather obvious characteristics, there is one
very important social structure attached to the institution of
movie-going. This surrounds the role that Lazarsfeld and
his colleagues christened the 'opinion leader'. In contrast
to the familiar stereotype of the 'mass' audience this role
develops out of the group structure of movie-going. Katz and
Lazarsfeld document the incidence of opinion-leadership
in movie-going; basically, the characteristics of people filling
the role of adviser on matters cinematic. Primarily on
matters of attendance, though evaluation and understanding
must also figure. They report the peculiarly fascinating
discovery that movie opinion-leaders are disproportionately
young women.[21] Within kin relations the child tends to be
adviser to the parent. Such a flow of influence, whatever else
it may do, must surely serve to reinforce the importance of
movie-going in the lives of those accorded this 'expert'
status. Thus, in the case of the child–parent relation the
child will be encouraged in his movie-going, gaining the
double reward of pleasure in the cinema and esteem outside
it. So, unlike other elements of youth culture the movies
have straddled the age boundary in a very special way. Not
only do older groups attend, though in smaller numbers than
the young, but in the period of the Katz and Lazarsfeld
research they also sought the advice of the young on their
patterns of consumption, an inversion of the standard
authority relations between generations. The decline of this
possibility, with the general decline in popularity of the
cinema in the last two decades, may thus have contributed
to the crystallisation of a much more explicitly separate
youth culture defined as antagonistic to the parental genera-

tion. Certainly, opinion leadership in cultural matters has become increasingly age-specific.

The social structure of the movie-audience is basically simple. It is predominantly youthful, rarely solitary, and encompasses an authority structure different to those found elsewhere and in some respects the opposite. But beneath this 'face-to-face' level there is a further layer of more distanced social relationships. For instance, the film critic occupies a formally defined role as opinion-leader though in practice he may lead no opinions. Such research as there is does not suggest that the film critic is a crucial figure in this more amorphous social structure, though he clearly does have some authority. Falewicz, reporting some Polish research, claims that the popularity of films (in terms of attendance) is only weakly influenced by critical opinion, although there is some tendency for critics to influence the pattern of evaluation once the film has been seen. The more educated and the more interested movie-goers adopt views closer to those of the critics.[22] Thus for some sectors of the movie-going population opinion-leadership is located in the critical establishment. It may also be that these more enthusiastic film fans act in turn as opinion-leaders for others, thus allowing for more than the 10 per cent critical influence reflected in Falewicz's data. This multi-step chain could have a considerable indirect impact on the evaluation and understanding of any particular movie.

At the extremes this is obviously so. The British critical response to Sam Peckinpah's *Straw Dogs* is a case in point. Meeting with widespread critical condemnation (including a rather hysterical collective letter from the critics to *The Times*) the film then had to play to audiences whose expectations had been conditioned by this critical fuss. Fuel was added by the distributor who chose to publicise the film using adverse quotations from the various reviews. As a result one common comment to be heard from the large crowds leaving after a performance was that it was not as 'bad' as was expected. That is, it was not as evilly violent as the histrionic critical establishment claimed. In fact the various spot researches carried out by interested parties at the time suggest that the audience was in some disagreement with the critical evaluation. Nevertheless, they clearly had been influenced seriously in that they attended the film with very specific expectations. Thus, although in disagreement over judgement, they are still bound in a perceptual framework set by the initial critical response, and it therefore becomes impossible to see *Straw Dogs* outside the context set by the institutional opinion-leaders.[23]

Besides recognising the importance of these authority structures, surveyed audiences generally agree on one other important factor which we have already briefly mentioned: story-type or genre. This can be a complex subject but, for the moment, we will consider only one aspect of it. If audiences claim that they are influenced by whether a film is a 'weepie', a war picture, or a western, then by carrying the categorisations over we can begin to get at the phenomenon of audience culture. To employ Gans' expression, we can see 'subcultures of taste' corresponding to the genre divisions. Such sub-cultures are not mutually exclusive and some may be more clearly defined than others, but they do provide a basis for analysis.

As a more discernible case than most, take the art-house phenomenon. As audience numbers have dropped, the more affluent of Western societies have produced an increasing body of movies widely claimed as 'art'. For the most part the Anglo-American variant operates by screening foreign language movies which, apart from their sub-titles, share a distinctively 'intellectual' approach. A taste for such films has become a clearly distinguishable subcultural trait in contemporary movie culture. How such a taste becomes established need not concern us now; undoubtedly it is through a complex process of innovation, reinforcement, and reiteration, mediated by the commercial requirements of movie production. Like the market in skin-flicks or horror movies, art-films are economically sufficiently stable to support an ongoing sub-culture. A specialised sub-cultural 'language' develops as the audience becomes accustomed to the conventions by which the films operate. Its members share this understanding rather as a juvenile gang or an extended family have a common conception of their world. In the case of art-films this is reinforced by three main factors. First, there are cinemas which specialise in these movies and virtually nothing else; unlike most film genre, then, there is some concrete embodiment of separate status. Second, art-films by their very nature demand a fairly articulate and educated audience. They are very much a middle-class 'intellectual' genre.[24] Thus the audience is better able to articulate its sub-cultural speciality than are other similiar groupings. Lastly, the films themselves promote a cinematic self-consciousness by their implicit claims to superiority as serious Art.

By these means the art-film sub-culture has become one of the most crystallised in the contemporary cinema, though there are others which are similarly distinct. Most obviously, skin-flicks. Generally they too have a specialised place of exhibition, sometimes for legal reasons, but often because the sub-cultural taste is sufficiently widespread to merit such specialisation. Most large cities in contemporary Britain have one such cinema; some have more. Like art-house audiences, the skin-flick audience is aware of its 'deviant' status, though the former would no doubt make claims to superiority. Slightly less self-conscious in contrast, is the sub-culture revolving around a taste for horror movies. Here there is partial specialisation at the exhibition end. 'Double Horror Bills' are screened on particular nights (often Sundays in Britain) or at special but regular late night shows. And less distinct again are those genres without special exhibition facilities, though having some degree of audience specialisation: musicals, thrillers, westerns, and the rest. They also act as a core for an audience sub-culture though these are rarely self-conscious groupings. They share only an understanding of the particular genre language, of the typical situations and characteristics of their chosen taste.

So, apart from the culture an audience may bring with it from 'outside', it is also enveloped in some sort of 'film culture'. This set of expectations and beliefs about movies, and about the individual's relation to them, has both general and specific components. The large majority of the audience has some general movie experience to draw upon, though the most specialised of the sub-cultures may dominate their own audiences. Built on these general film culture foundations there is a range of specialised taste sub-cultures with variously cross-cutting membership. All this provides the audience's cultural context. Superimposed on this we find the more materially apparent factors: the authority relations of opinion leadership; the distribution of socio-economic characteristics; the simple distinguishing factors like sex and age. And within these the variations in identification and projection which characterise the individual's response to the movie-going situation. All these, varying together and separately, characterise the movie-audience. Quite clearly they will effect the process of movie communication in such a way as to render the 'hypodermic' image untenable. From some points of view the audience may be a 'mass', but it is also made up of personalities, groups, and cultures. It should be treated as such.

THE BLUNTED NEEDLE

So far I have said little about 'effects'. Yet most audience studies have wanted to deal with this issue; to show in what way the movie audience was indeed affected by the movies it saw. In fact, from the first spread of the new and extra-ordinarily successful medium, such questions dominated popular discussion. Understandably, the major focus of attention was on the growing child who was rapidly substituting the cinema for more traditional sources of socialisation. The popularisation of the Payne Fund Studies called them 'our movie made children'. Movies offered to them a world of experience even wider than that provided by the extended peer groups of adolescence. A new dimension had been added to the process of growing up.

By the end of the twenties American public discussion had reached the point where it seemed justified to mount a series of ambitious researches on the effects of motion pictures upon youth. Financed by the Payne Fund, and based on research conducted between 1929 and 1932, they applied the newly respectable weaponry of experimental, statistical, and survey analysis to a range of topics. Social attitudes, delinquent behaviour, patterns of sleep, and all sorts of other factors were exhaustively investigated. The results appeared to confirm the worst expectations of worried parents. The Chairman of the Studies, W. W. Charters, put it this way:

'We have concluded a description of the studies which essayed to measure the influence of the motion picture as such. We see that as an instrument of education it has unusual power to impart information, to influence specific attitudes toward objects of social value, to affect emotions either in gross or microscopic proportions, to affect health in a minor degree through sleep disturbance, and to affect profoundly the patterns of conduct of children.'[25]

This is rather strong by virtue of being a summary statement; even Charters's own lengthier discussion is more qualified. But the Payne Fund Studies do come out quite firmly on the side of the 'strong effects' school.

Of course they had their critics. Adler's study *Art and Prudence* devoted considerable energies to a rebuttal.[26] In retrospect their methodology does seem too crudely devoted to interval measurement to be trusted as an accurate reflection of relations of cause and effect. Some of their materials retain a certain fascination—the interview reports in the Blumer studies, or Peterson and Thurstone's attempt to test persistence of attitude change and the cumulative effects of more than one movie.[27] One must be struck, for instance, by their finding that *Birth of a Nation* significantly shifted children's attitudes toward racial prejudice, and that this attitude remained after eight months. Or that *All Quiet on the Western Front* shifted children's attitudes toward pacifism, a change which did not survive the longer period. To make sense of these and other such differences one must obviously consider other factors. Having been made consciously aware of some form of racial prejudice (to which he may have been predisposed) the child goes on to find reinforcement in his social environment. In the case of pacifism he does not, with the inverse consequence. A whole socio-cultural context has to be invoked. The ultimate problem of the Payne Fund Studies is not their devotion to statistical analysis, but their largely 'hypodermic' image of the communication process. They look at movies as if these were the only source of influence on children.

Most research since the Payne Fund Studies, both experimental and survey, has claimed rather less in the way of direct effects. Of course this varies according to what sort of effects are postulated. It goes without saying that movies have emotional effects on their audiences; that is at least part of their purpose. What the Payne Fund Studies call 'emotional possession' is an essential part of the cinematic process. Their suggestion that children should be taught to distance themselves from the movies is an odd denial of the nature of the experience itself. Even odder is their touching belief that adults already see the movies in this distanced way:

'To adults the picture is good or bad, the acting satisfactory or unsatisfactory, the singing up to or not up to standard. To them a picture is just a picture.'[28]

This claim, in itself an attempt at defining adulthood, lays bare the values fundamental to the studies. The adult has a 'real' world rich in experiences. He therefore does not respond to movies in this characteristically childish way. They are merely play and not part of the serious things of life. Childish things must be put aside. The general tone of their warning about movies is reminiscent of nothing so much as the Victorian moralists warning of the dangers of masturbation.

'Emotional possession' is the normal order of things cinematic. An audience has to be emotionally caught up in the unfolding drama if the medium is to work at all. Indeed, moviegoers themselves have ways of dealing with such short-term consequences. There are endless interactive mechanisms for marking off the boundary between the imagined world of the cinema and the 'real' one outside.

'Who do you think you are . . . John Wayne?' and 'Well, of course, it was only a film, wasn't it?' are only two of the most obvious ways in which we locate our 'emotional possession' and so render it socially acceptable. But later researchers have tried to focus on more specific 'emotional' effects on experimental audiences. For instance, the many studies of film violence and subsequent aggressive behaviour, especially those conducted under the direction of Leonard Berkowitz.[29] These experiments are variations on one basic form using three main elements. An experimental audience who are shown a violent film clip, a seven minute prize fight sequence from *Champion* in the course of which Kirk Douglas is badly beaten. An accomplice to the experimenter who treats some members of the experimental group neutrally but deliberately insults others. A situation in which the subjects can give socially sanctioned electric shocks to the accomplice. Out of these basic materials the experimenter tries to assess the effect of the violent film on the subject's aggressive behaviour *vis-à-vis* the accomplice. Obviously, the design allows for a series of different 'control' groups: those who did not see the film and were treated well by the accomplice; those who did not see the film and were treated badly; those who did see the film and were treated badly, etc. Berkowitz and his colleagues have developed several variations. They tried to discover whether the violent clip offers a means of catharsis and, by and large, they find that it does not. They show the ways in which certain 'cues' modify the effect. Thus, when the accomplice is introduced as a boxer and the subjects have seen the prize fight sequence, strong aggressive behaviour is recorded. There is similar cued variation if the accomplice is introduced as 'Kirk'. But the most general finding running through all the experiments is that the violent scene does have some capacity to promote subsequent aggressive tendencies.

It is some way from the social psychology laboratory to the normal social situation within which movies are viewed, and it would be a foolhardy student who was prepared to make that jump without a long list of qualifications. Even then it would not follow that violent films breed aggression since the experimental results apply to the short term only. Over longer periods we have no evidence to suggest a straightforward link of this sort. As one might expect, this sort of emotional arousal is very much an immediate affair. Nor is it independent of the sort of contextual factors which 'interfere' with any simple effects chain. Various sorts of predispositions, for instance, would be one type of mediating factor. At this roughly 'emotional' level experimenters have tried to explore this phenomenon. Maccoby, Levin, and Selya, for example, look at the effect of previous emotional arousal (by frustrating the subjects) on retention of aggressive movie content. Their results are inconclusive in that one experiment confirmed the frustration-aggression hypothesis while a replication did not.[30] But their general supposition that emotional state at the time of viewing is an important factor seems eminently reasonable. No one has come up with convincing evidence to the contrary.

Although the violence issue is important in terms of changing cultural patterns, the study of these simple individual effects is very limiting as it is their cumulative consequence which is likely to be most significant. We shall return to the possibility in a later chapter. But as far as individual effects are concerned much more attention has been directed at areas other than this. Most commonly, studies of film as a communicator of knowledge and film as an attitude changer. Both figured in the Payne Fund brief and both are prominent in the later history of experimental and survey analysis. As far as the former is concerned, film has been claimed as everything from saviour to satanic lier. One strand of social criticism, now enjoying some vogue in reference to television, has seen the information transmitting function as socially crucial. John Grierson, who founded the documentary movement, argued that film's ability to show us our fellow man in his everyday life would act as a cement for the building of democratic society.[31] Others, less ambitious, have seen film as an invaluable aid to the process of learning, still others as an instrument of control: a medium to lend untruth the status of fact.

The researchers have generally looked at these questions

in terms of film as teacher and film as propaganda. The latter spills over into the general issue of attitude change. The former suggests that film is neither saviour nor sinner; it can be both useful and useless. The 'American Soldier' experiments are interesting examples.[32] Hovland and his colleagues suggest three important limiting factors. They found that those of greater intellectual ability learnt more on a given exposure, a relation which held regardless of the difficulty of the material. There was little support for the view that film makes it easier for those of lower intellectual abilities to learn, though used strictly as an *aid* it can have some effects. They also found that learning from film varied with motivation. Advance announcement of a test increased learning by some 15 per cent, though whether such an effect would persist in a situation where tests were a regular factor is an open question. Lastly, active participation in the learning process had variable effects. Participation seemed to help more when other conditions were less favourable; the relatively unintelligent, unmotivated men learnt more by participation.

Like all such experiments these dealt with a captive audience, in an educational situation, watching explicitly instructional films. As ever the path from experimental particularity to sociological generality is strewn with hazards. Was the relative failure of these films a characteristic of the movie situation as such, or something to do with the specifically educational context? Do the stronger claims of the Payne Fund Studies reflect different susceptibilities on the part of adults and children, more sophisticated methodology, situational variation, or all three? Is an audience more likely to believe a 'fact' proffered by a favoured character in a thoroughly involving fiction film than the same information presented by a 'neutral', non-fiction, teaching film? Undoubtedly there is a residual area of information which is ideally conveyed by an audio-visual medium such as film. Some things are better grasped by being seen. What has concerned the researchers more has been the possibility that information channelled through film is more believable (whether true or not) than information communicated in

G

other ways. From control of knowledge, to control of attitudes, to control of actions.

This has always been the crunch of the effects studies, and also the rock on which they have foundered. It can be stated at the outset that *most* evidence is against movie-induced attitude change. At various times considerable effort has been expended in exploring the propaganda possibilities of film. As the rise of Nazi Germany should suggest, propaganda must completely blanket a culture if it is to work. One *Triumph of the Will* does not make a Third Reich, though slotted into a larger pattern it can play its part. Limited to analysing the discreet item, the 'American Soldier' researches found some change in opinion on *specific* factors dealt with in the films, but very few or no effects in relation to general opinion items or to the motivation of their subjects to serve as soldiers. As propaganda these movies failed. Around the same time the issues of anti-semitism and Nazism occasioned research into the dramatised propaganda of *Tomorrow the World* and *Crossfire*.[33] No dramatic changes were discovered, though the researchers make claims for the films as 'confirming devices' and as initiating 'a learning process'.

The experimental studies were not alone in finding no dramatic changes in attitude. Hulett explicitly tried to escape the limitations of this 'social psychological' approach by exploring the net effects of the movie *Sister Kenny* on community opinion.[34] Again the results are hardly striking, and Hulett concludes that *Sister Kenny* was poor propaganda. Interestingly, he suggests 'propaganda sophistication' as one of the reasons for this 'failure', a suggestion also reflected in the 'American Soldier' finding that a film which obviously appeared to be propaganda was the least likely to be accepted. The most efficacious combination was that in which the new attitude was demonstrated as somehow superior to the old. It was not slipped in under the carpet but presented with a *semblance* of rational argument. This property seems hardly encouraging for the makers of those laboured 'message' films which most film industries intermittently produce.

To shorten this already overlong summary, there is no doubt that most research is little help in understanding the general effects of film. Because they deal with an atomised and socially isolated situation there is rarely any safe route for generalisation. They do demonstrate that the images on the screen have some effects, especially on the emotions. But that needs little demonstration; if it had no such effects the cinema could hardly have survived this long. In other respects they waver. Although some influence on beliefs and conduct can hardly be denied (the cinema-goers themselves have often documented it),[35] its depth and pattern remains undiscovered. The best one can say is that the experimental studies are inconclusive. They serve only to demonstrate that there is no simple one-to-one relation between the movie and any effect it may have, that there is no simple pattern to mass media effects.[36]

Yet few institutions can have angered, delighted, or moved as many people. In understandably trying to break this process down into easily manipulated pieces, the effects analysts have lost sight of the larger process. For many years they conveniently avoided recognising that the audience was a social entity. It took the work of the Lazarsfeld school on selective perception and the 'two-step flow hypothesis' to recover the simple insight that communication takes place in a socio-cultural context not a mass cultural vacuum. Perhaps the next advance will be to forget the expression 'effects' entirely. Just as natural scientists have learnt that the penalty for an atomised view is pollution, media researchers may yet act on the recognition that the long-term cumulative factor is potentially the most important. The fact that the traditional methodologies cannot handle it should not be allowed to obstruct its discussion. To look at the audience as part of the communication process is incomplete unless we also look at the media as part of our culture. Having seen that the hypodermic needle is blunt we can hardly go on pretending that it is not. And it is just that pretence which characterises the study of effects and the related study of the audience.

References

[1] Whatever the varying detail of his own position Blumer has a lot to answer for here. See H. Blumer, 'The Crowd, the Public and the Mass', reprinted in W. Schramm (Ed.), *The Process and Effects of Mass Communication*, Univ. Illinois Press, Illinois, 1954; H. Blumer, 'The Moulding of Mass Behavior through the Motion Picture'; H. Blumer and P. M. Hauser; H. Blumer, *Movies and Conduct*. (See Selected Bibliography.)

[2] See V. F. Perkins, Chapter 7 (Selected Bibliography).

[3] For a general discussion of some of the experimental work on the physical context of movie viewing see G. Mialaret (Selected Bibliography).

[4] For an illuminating discussion and polemic see C. Barr, 'Cinemascope: Before and After' (Selected Bibliography).

[5] For example, in the survey reported by Falewicz 20 per cent of the respondents gave 'cinema genre' as their main guide in choosing a film to see. See J. Falewicz (Selected Bibliography).

[6] The techniques for creating images are common property in the film industries. For a case discussion see T. Harris (Selected Bibliography).

[7] L. Handel, *Hollywood Looks at its Audience*, pp. 145–50 (Selected Bibliography).

[8] There is a great deal of such material. Amongst others see: L. Handel, *ibid.*; M. Farrand Thorp; E. Morin, *The Stars*; J. P. Mayer. (See Selected Bibliography.) See also the various Payne Fund Studies.

[9] M. Farrand Thorp, *op. cit.*, p. 64.

[10] L. Handel, *op. cit.*, p. 147.

[11] J. Mayer, *op. cit.*, p. 42. Blumer's contributions to the Payne Fund Studies also provide many such examples; H. Blumer and P. Hauser, *op. cit.*, and H. Blumer, *Movies and Conduct, op. cit.*

[12] J. Mayer, *ibid.*, p. 90 (my italics).

[13] L. Rosten, *Hollywood the Movie Colony, the Movie Makers*, p. 411 (Selected Bibliography). Part of the list is also reprinted in E. Morin, *op. cit.*, p. 93.

[14] See L. Handel, *op. cit.*, Chapter 8, for this and other similar information.

[15] See for example the summary tables in I. Jarvie, *Towards a Sociology of the Cinema*, Chapter 8 (Selected Bibliography).

[16] The values of Kendalls Tau for the two tables are 0·43 and 0·46. In other words the association between ranking by age and by cinemagoing is very similar in the two cases.

[17] There have been many surveys of such material and there is no reason to reproduce them here. A brief impression can be gained from I. Jarvie, *op. cit.*, Chapter 8, and L. Handel, *op. cit.*, Chapter 7.

[18] M. E. Olsen, p. 108 (Selected Bibliography).

[19] The problem is given its first major discussion in W. S. Robinson, 'Ecological Correlations and the Behaviour of Individuals', *American Sociological Review*, **15,** 1950. It is a problem based on differing levels of analysis and is reflected in the fact that correlations established on data at one level *may* not reflect any correlation among the individuals who together make up the aggregate. In the case of Olsen's study one would have to interpret the macro-correlations before claiming that isolated individuals tend to go to the cinema. It may only be that in areas where there are many isolates there are also many gregarious people who go to the cinema. For an illuminating general discussion of the ecological correlation see Adam Przeworski and Henry Teune, *The Logic of Comparative Social Inquiry*, Wiley, New York, London, Toronto, Sydney, 1970, especially Chapter 3.

[20] Again see L. Handel, *op. cit.*; also see Edgar Dale, *Children's Attendance at Motion Pictures*, Chapter 4 (Selected Bibliography).

[21] See E. Katz and P. Lazarsfeld, Chapter 13; and P. Lazarsfeld. (See Selected Bibliography).

[22] See J. Falewicz, *op. cit.* Also W. D. Smythe, P. Lusk, and C. Lewis, pp. 35–6 (Selected Bibliography).

[23] For a perceptive and entertaining discussion of the *Straw Dogs* affair read C. Barr, '*Straw Dogs, A Clockwork Orange* and the Critics' (Selected Bibliography).

[24] For material quite early in the development see W. Smythe, P. Lusk and C. Lewis, *op. cit.* Their position is re-examined in K. Adler (Selected Bibliography). On the phenomenon in general see J. Twomey (Selected Bibliography).

[25] W. Charters, p. 43 (Selected Bibliography).

[26] M. Adler (Selected Bibliography). Since I have been unable to consult this book I can only go by the standard secondary comment: Adler attacks the Payne Fund Studies principally because of their pseudo-scientific inadequacies.

[27] H. Blumer and P. M. Hauser, *op. cit.*; H. Blumer, *Movies and Conduct, op. cit.*; Ruth C. Peterson and L. I. Thurstone, *Motion Pictures and the Social Attitudes of Children*, Macmillan, New York, 1936.

[28] W. Charters, *op. cit.*, p. 39.

[29] There are a number of papers on these experiments. The following selection will give some idea of the range: L. Berkowitz, 'Some Aspects of Observed Aggression'; L. Berkowitz and R. G. Green; L. Berkowitz and E. Rawlings; L. Berkowitz *et al.* (see Selected Bibliography).

[30] See E. E. Maccoby *et al.* (Selected Bibliography).

[31] See J. Grierson (Selected Bibliography). For a brief summary discussion see A. Tudor, *Theories of Film*, Chapter 3 (Selected Bibliography). For a longer discussion of Grierson see A. Lovell and J. Hillier (Selected Bibliography).

[32] C. Hovland *et al.* (see Selected Bibliography).

[33] M. J. Wiese and S. G. Cole (see Selected Bibliography), L. E. Raths and F. N. Trager (see Selected Bibliography).

[34] J. E. Hulett (see Selected Bibliography).

[35] See, amongst many others, H. Blumer, *Movies and Conduct, op. cit.*; J. P. Mayer, *Sociology of Film* and *British Cinemas and their Audiences, op. cit.*; W. D. Wall and W. A. Simson. (See Selected Bibliography.)

[36] The best summary – much longer and more far-reaching than this brief discussion – is by A. Gluckmann. Originally published in French in *Communications*, it is now available in book form (see Selected Bibliography).

Chapter 5

Movie Languages

The medium is obviously central to any communication; it both forms and carries the messages which are the very stuff of the process. Whatever one's primary focus, be it on communicators or audiences, the medium, and its content, inevitably claims attention. Thus the common belief that Hollywood's commercial structure demeans creativity is founded as much on inference from the films themselves as on direct and documented accounts of the perversions of the production process. Even the 'effects' debate is argued in terms of abstracted movie content as well as through self-professed claims of influence: the Payne Fund Studies tried to look at content as well as conduct.[1] If we are to begin to understand the forms of modern culture, then what the movies say, and the way they say it, is crucial. Culture is about meaning.

This conceptual centrality always forces the content question upon us. Yet it has not been satisfactorily handled. Although resources have been poured into 'content analysis' obtained results remain disproportionately unimpressive. This is partly a confirmation of Berelson's famous injunction that the energy input to content analysis frequently exceeds its reward in usable results. But it is also one consequence of rampant *scientism*: the ritual pursuit of a misplaced rigour so that finally the rigour replaces the research. The possibility of utilising sophisticated methods becomes the main criterion for choosing research. As a result of this bias content analysis has focused on cognitive content at the expense of other forms, and on the quantitatively manipulable at the expense of the qualitative, thus narrowing its area of potential application. What it may have gained in complexity it has lost in relevance.[2]

There are, however, more basic reasons for the difficulties encountered by content analysts. Problems in the nature of the task itself, not just consequences of academic insularity or scientific pretension. The whole formulation of the method makes things difficult. George Gerbner, a notable in the field, has claimed that content analysis arose as a response to '. . . the need for *systematic* and *objective* determination of various types of communication significance'.[3] An 'objective' assessment of message content independent of the 'subjective' claims of communicator or audience. What can this mean in practice? Put crudely it might simply mean that the analyst claims *his* view as objective; what others see is false. Such bluntness is not common, and claims to infallibility are usually a little more elliptical. Besides, modern sociology is too embroiled in issues of value and meaning to permit such a simple and misleading 'solution'. Most approaches are more circumspect. Take Gerbner again. In making some fundamental definitions he sees communication as '. . . a specialised, formally coded or representative social event which makes possible inferences about states, relationships, processes not directly observed'. In the light of this he goes on to define the content of communication as '. . . the sum total of *warranted inferences* that can be made about relationships involved in the communication event'.[4] We understand a communication by making inferences from it. Whether it is a string of words or a dramatic scene we try to make sense of it, to give it meaning, by interpretation. Out of the combination of communication event and audience predispositions comes the 'meaning'.

Obviously this leads to relativism. If understanding is inferential, then who is to say that A's inference is any closer to the content of the communication than B's? There are as many contents as there are audiences. Some researchers have taken this too literally and tried to reduce content analysis to an analysis of the professed understanding of an audience. But extreme relativism does not often hold. There is always *some* pattern, *some* common agreement on the meaning of a range of communication events. There are implicit rules by which people make sense of particular acts of communication: there is a shared 'language' in which the communication is cast. It is this relatively constant element that permits of Gerbner's 'warranted inferences'. By knowing the rules on which such inferences are made *among the users of the language*, the analyst is able to distinguish among all possible interpretations of the communication event. This is the *only* way in which he can claim any 'objectivity' for his account. So, implicitly, any content analyst postulates a rule-governed 'language' which provides the rationale for each act of concrete analysis. He may not be aware of it, but provided he keeps up with any changes in this language he continues to have some basis for making 'warranted' inferences.

Content analysis, then, leans inevitably on the idea of language. This is unavoidable the moment we recognise that communication is inferential. Whether in a film review, or in a computer programme for content analysis, any claim to understanding is based on that same proposition: knowledge of the language. That is, the sociologist's claims to understanding are just the same as anyone else's. That they may be taken more seriously is a reflection of our social structure not of their validity. Unfortunately, the only language that we know much about is speech, a limitation reflected in the extant techniques of content analysis. The field is understandably biased toward the written or spoken word; effectively it is parasitic on linguistics. Since our understanding of the language of music, film, bodily gesture, or clothing, is rather limited, so content analysis of these media remains highly speculative.

This is further complicated by the fact that some media may be inherently more ambiguous than others. 'Warranted inferences' might vary greatly according to time, place, and audience. It does seem likely, however, that any medium widely institutionalised will develop a considerable body of rules of inference. Even if this is not true the very recognition of our 'language dependence' must have consequences for our methods. In cases where we do not know the detail of the medium-language (which seems likely of the cinema) then the 'impressionistic' methods of the critic are just as useful as the 'sophisticated' methods of the social scientist. For any claim to validity in a situation of limited knowledge must be based on a subjective understanding of the language in question. Nothing else is possible. We can only appeal to intersubjectivity. Premature scientism serves only to reduce a complex language to a simpler one that we already happen to understand. So, in studying film there are two clear tasks: a long-term attempt to extend our knowledge of the language of film; a shorter-term need to inject a little more method into the 'subjective' techniques we borrow from the critic. This two-pronged attack structures the remainder of this chapter.

LANGUAGES OF FILM

It is one thing to recognise that we urgently need to understand film language; it is quite another to know where to begin. The term 'language' has not been uncommon in discussion of film, and 'the grammar of film' is almost a cliché. Loosely used, this terminology can be stimulating. It carries with it the connotations of a shared and structured framework of interpretation. But it also carries other connotations, less useful, and sometimes positively disadvantageous. There are strong pressures toward analogy with spoken or written language; toward identification of equivalents to words and sentences; toward predominantly linear language structures. Obviously no one could sensibly carry through a full blown analogy; the excercise would rapidly become futile. But more sophisticated attempts, such as Worth's, also reveal the limitations of their origins. His attempt to identify units in terms of *cademes*, *edemes*, and *videmes*, and to structure them together, remains an exercise with little apparent pay-off.[5] In limiting itself to cognitive elements such an approach to film language cannot contend with the full range of the phenomenon. Any beginning analysis must at least be capable of conceptualising differences in ways of communicating, from the simple image up to the most complex thematic structure. Technical and formal elements (such as montage, camera movement, composition, etc.)

are only one part, albeit an important part, of this process.

This is in line with our image of communication as a process of inference. People watching movies make inferences from the patterns of light and shadow on the screen; from the particular combinations of sound and image; from the actions that they see; about the 'meaning' of these events; and about almost everything else that is set before them. As anthropologists have been fond of remarking, men imbue everything with meaning. At every level they try to make sense of the barrage of information with which they are faced. There is no reason to suppose that they behave any differently in the movies. Quite the opposite; this is expected to be a 'meaningful' experience, and the range of potential 'meaning-elements' in a movie is vast indeed. Now, in speaking of a language of film, we can either delimit the concept drastically by only using it in application to formal factors, or we can apply it inclusively to the whole range of potential sources of meaning. In the end it does not matter where the label begins and ends, only that all the elements find their place. But at this primitive stage an over-emphasis on the formal simply emasculates our analysis.

This is further complicated in the case of film because our images of film language are enmeshed in a number of aesthetic disputes. Traditional film aesthetics saw the distinctive mark of cinema in *montage*. This they derived from Eisenstein, vulgarising it not a little along the way.[6] What was presented in Eisenstein's mature work as a *part* of the filmic process thus found itself elevated above all others. This tradition is still with us, and even studies which would claim independence of such aesthetic bias find themselves repeating the old propositions. Pryluck's analysis of the symbol system of film, for instance, is deeply imbued with such sub-Eisenteinian aesthetics. He approvingly suggests that 'juxtaposition, it is widely believed, lies at the heart of filmic communication.'[7] He then goes on to produce an analysis which corresponds fairly closely to Eisenstein's generalised concept of montage. As far as it goes there is nothing wrong with this – Eisenstein's work is frequently quite brilliant. It is the suggestion of centrality, the 'heart of filmic communication', which is disturbing. What of involvement in the narrative situation of a fiction-film? What of the 'meanings' we ascribe to particular objects in the films' world? What of those movies which display little in the way of juxtapositional techniques: do they therefore have no filmic heart? These premature claims to having discovered the central element of film can only foreshorten our understanding.

Because of this aesthetically induced myopia we must step back a little. If we can find some way of sorting out the various ways in which films communicate, then we can both place what we do know and methodically list what we do not. Under the influence of structural linguistics, semiology, and structuralism, contemporary film theorists have tried to do just that. Not surprisingly the result has been something of a taxonomic nightmare. In trying to develop our understanding of film language, theorists have begun by classifying, by trying to methodically distinguish among the various components of film. Thus, Christian Metz, heavily influenced by Barthes and Saussure, has tried to define a set of syntagms of the fiction film.[8] His work is a welcome contrast to the more traditionally based ideas of 'film grammar'. Others, similarly inspired, have taken other lingusitic sources and applied them to the cinematic sign: Peter Wollen has invoked Pierce in this context.[9] Whatever the merits of such attempts they do grapple with problems beyond the Eisensteinian limits; in Wollen's case, while explicitly recognising Eisenstein's importance.

As well as the specifically Eisensteinian input, orthodox aesthetic argument has fed discussion of the language of film in another related way. Traditional approaches to the 'grammar' or 'language' of film have focused on *form* at the expense of *content*. That is to say, they have taken an *analytic* distinction, claimed it as real, and tried to single out form from the matrix in which it is embedded. The 'language' of film is thus limited to the ways in which formal characteristics (again montage) convey certain sorts of meanings. Narrative meanings, meanings derived from substance, from content, from the combination of the various elements of film, these all remain outside the scope of such analysis. The classic reaction to this imbalance has been to deny any validity to distinctions of the form/content type. But this also leads to distortion. Provided that we recognise it to be solely an *analytical tool* the form/content distinction can be useful. And provided that we also recognise that form is not identical with structure, and content with meaning, it may be possible to construct a general classification of the different methods by which films communicate.

As they stand these terms are too loaded; they have been weapons in too many aesthetic battles. In one of his less polemically disposed papers Metz tries to clarify the issue.[10] In so doing he is indebted to Barthes and, in turn, to Hjelmslev. Following them he analyses the basic nature of the sign system in terms of a distinction between 'signified' (*signifié*) and 'signifier' (*signifiant*) on the one hand, and between form and substance on the other. Let us first take signifier/signified. These are the two components of the sign: that which does the signifying and that which is signified. In any body of signs, then, there is a *plane of expression* (signifiers) and a *plane of content* (signifieds).[11] Each of these planes may be sub-divided in form/substance terms, i.e. there is a *substance* of content and a *form* of content, a *substance* of expression and a *form* of expression. Substance of content refers to the 'human content' of the body of signs, in this case the film(s). Form of content refers to the formal structure within which this diffuse human content is constrained; Metz speaks of a 'thematic structure' here. Substance of expression includes what has traditionally been called the 'materials of the medium', the moving image, sound, speech, and music. Form of expression encompasses the traditional interest in the patterning of these basic elements. Metz does not specify it too closely:

'La forme du signifiant, c'est l'ensemble des configurations perceptives reconnaissables dans ces quatre substances: ainsi, la recurrence reguliere d'une association syntagmatique entre telle phrase du dialogue et tel motif visuel, etc.'[12]

It is, of course, in this sector that traditional aesthetic discussion has focused. The taxonomy may be given diagrammatic representation (see fig. 5.1).

	Substance	Form
Plane of content (signifieds)	Human content or 'Reality'	Thematic structure
Plane of expression (signifiers)	Materials of the medium	Structures of technique

Figure 5.1   ASPECTS OF FILM

This taxonomy suggests the breadth of application of semiological analysis. What has normally been thought of as the 'linguistics' of film[13] focuses on the rules governing the 'form of expression'; permissible interrelations between the four basic elements of film. Semiological analysis claims that there is more to language than this, and that any analysis must be prepared to take in the full range of elements which make up the sign system. As Barthes points out, the *form* dimension is the area traditionally handled by linguistics. In the case of film, though, even the 'form of content' has been neglected. This neglect was one source of dissatisfaction with this tradition: it was 'formalist' in that it focused on 'form of expression' at the expense of 'form of content'. Semiological analysis suggests that this is not the only limitation. There are areas of film, conceived as a semiological system, which require 'extra-linguistic' consideration, most notably the areas of 'substance', and, in particular, that area which Metz refers to as 'human content'.

Particular films include a characteristic body of such content; a 'reality' on which they draw. It is not a single 'reality', for it must always be selective in picking out certain factors as constitutive of its film world. In film criticism some attempt is made to tap this element through the concept *genre*. When we speak of a genre we are above all thinking of a world common to a range of films which may vary considerably in the detail of their narrative. Their world is similarly constituted. The 'western', the 'war film', the 'gangster movie' have their own special human content on which a particular film may draw. We will look at some of them in detail in a later chapter. Of course, genre is not the only way in which human content can be conceptualised; indeed its traditional meaning encompasses more than this. Individual directors may also create 'worlds' which remain constant across very wide changes in thematic structure. And so-called film 'movements' may share a basic human content on which they build. One thinks most obviously of something like Italian neo-realism – their special version of 'reality' remained constant from film to film.

Out of these human, social, and natural materials the film-maker builds a 'thematic structure'. Events are ordered, narratives constructed, special emphases selected, and themes developed. So, where *all* westerns draw on one sort of reality, one range of human content, each film may differ in what it makes of these materials. Which is not to suggest that the two levels (form and substance of content) are independent. The distinction is analytic; the two contents are aspects of the same thing. Thus, particular sorts of realities may limit potential for variation in thematic structure. There may be only so many themes that can be successfully developed within a particular genre-reality, and genres themselves may differ in this respect. It seems likely, for example, that the horror movie 'reality' permits less variation in theme than the western. But besides this variation within genre, 'thematic structure' suggests the inverse: a communality of theme across genres. Where this lies in the work of one director – Siegel, say, in his westerns and his thrillers – lies the interest of the so-called *auteur* theory. Again, *auteur* does not equal 'form of content', though their focus has been very similar in practice. Generally an *auteur* is thought to utilise the available realities in a constant way; he develops the same 'world-view', the same pattern of interest, whatever the particular human content. As well as Siegel one might quote Howard Hawks's adventure films and comedies, or Antonioni's Italian and Anglo-American work.[14]

Although *genre* and *auteur* are not co-terminous with Metz's categories, their similarities are striking. It is significant that recent developments in film criticism have revolved around these terms. For many years there has been considerable dissatisfaction with the familiar film-as-art approaches, which, seemingly, prevented properly meaningful discussion. The initial response was to dismiss any analytic attempt to look at film as being unjustifiably formalist. But this was an overreaction. More recent interest in *genre* and *auteur* approaches suggests a growing recognition of the need for analytic machinery, and it is encouraging to find critical practice and abstract semiological schema coming together here. It now remains to find suitable techniques of analysis for the other semiological categories: substance and form of expression.

'Substance of expression' encompasses the raw material of cinematic communication: most basically the images and sounds which go to make up the film experience. If it is possible to imagine a 'pure' film – shapes, colours, and sounds – then this would exemplify the category, but, of course, there can be no such thing. There is always some structure; or, at least, we always impose some structure. Form and substance of expression are in fact indivisible. It is merely convenient to consider them separately. Metz himself puts forward the standard four categories of substance; picture, sound, speech, music. We, the audience, combine these elements, as they are presented to us, into more and more complex inferential structures. At the most primitive level we learn to make them intelligible as pictures and sounds. We see and hear people, houses, animals, space-ships, Triffids, and what have you. By referring them to a postulated 'human content' we make them make sense. So when a figure floats across the screen wearing a domed helmet and a pneumatic outfit we do not apply to it the reality of a western. If we know nothing of space-suits then perhaps we see him as some sort of esoteric deep-sea diver. But the pressures to fit him into some reality are enormous. Once we have got this far, of course, layer upon layer can follow. Content takes on form; we make narrative and thematic inferences. The elements combine to become meaningful at more and more levels. Expression takes on form and we are into the world of montage, composition and formal meanings.

As I have suggested discussion of film language has often focused here. This is understandable even without the historical pressures which directed it. These 'formal' ways of communicating meaning are the easiest to handle. And on some accounts of the term they would indeed be the true 'language' of the medium. They are unique to film, and they are easily accessible in terms akin to 'grammar', i.e. as a set of rules independent of semantic questions. The mistake is to claim that they exhaust our analysis of the language of film, for film is a highly complex medium, its communication many-levelled, its language multi-faceted. Metz's distinction among its elements is one start to the process of understanding. These elements must be analysed in their turn, and then the whole thing recombined. In the end we might have some sort of account of the language in which movies speak to us, and some rudimentary basis for actually analysing those movies.

ELEMENTS OF FILM

Let us take for granted the 'primitive' inference an audience must make from the audio-visual signal to a set of meaningful configurations. One must learn how to decipher a two-dimensional picture, but in modern societies most children receive early socialisation in this interpretive process. As the 'global village' grows there is less and less variation in this respect. But once the audio-visual materials have been resolved into intelligible configurations, potential variation increases. Movies have a 'reality' in which narrative develops, anything from outer space to an inner dream-world. Contrary to some aesthetic approaches there is no absolute reality which the cinema properly reflects.[15] There are

H

multiple realities which film itself makes plausible, and which we may (to some extent) accept or reject according to our predispositions. We learn to recognise these conventionalised film realities as we learn to recognise the various realities in which we spend our lives. We recognise actions, physical details, characteristic environments, as part of specific film worlds. They provide the diffuse context within which a film becomes meaningful to us.

As I have suggested the classic expression for dealing with this phenomenon is 'genre'. The term is very general: it is an umbrella concept. It shelters a variety of aspects of film communications. Film makers have genre conceptions; audiences become 'sub-cultures of taste' focused on particular genres; the genre-world is one important element in film language. So though not all film realities derive from genre, some of the best established and most popular are genre-realities. That is, they are realities which we recognise and 'understand' because a long series of movies (and other elements in our culture) have prepared us for them. For most of the time films offer us worlds outside our direct field of experience. They may make sense to us because we have read about them or seen photographs (outer space); because they live up to the images we have built up over the years (films set in historical eras); because we have seen many other films set in the same world (westerns, gangster movies, other genres); basically, because they are recognisable in some perspective or other that we bring to the cinema with us. Genre is thus the special case where a body of films is the prime source of definition of the specific film's reality. But whatever the source of the framework, the machinery is largely the same.

This 'film reality', Metz's 'human content', is invoked through series of audio-visual cues. We recognise a western, for instance, by its settings, its clothing, its horses and guns; by its language, by its sounds, by its music. In a couple of scenes we grasp a whole world. The outward signs of this familiar environment trigger off a whole series of resonances. They release a cumulative image in our minds. They tell us where we are, what sort of things to expect. They give us a basic spectrum of meaning in which the film is founded. This reality we are offered may be complex or simple; it may be rich in its associations or very limited. It may even fail to convince us, because it misuses the materials or because it is so far from our own store of realities that we are unable to see it as plausible. But it is part of the process through which we render a film meaningful, and, as such, it is part of the language.

Proper study of this area must presumably belong in the domain of iconography and iconology; or, at least, it must begin here. Panofsky defines iconography as '. . . a description and classification of images', while iconology is '. . . an iconography turned interpretive'.[16] In studying the cinema this procedure would have to be generalised to include elements other than the visual image: a classification of the images, sounds, and music which serve to cue an audience into a specific reality. Some of the cruder cases are disarming in their simplicity. Panofsky talks of the 'poor but honest' milieu traditionally suggested by the chequered table-cloth.[17] Even the black versus white clothing convention of the early westerns was still seriously utilised as far through as George Stevens's overrated *Shane*. Although these hoary icons may have faded into history, others can arise to take their place. The Colt ·45 Magnum, for instance, may be one such. Used to considerable effect by the heroes of *Point Blank*, *Dirty Harry*, *Hickey and Bogg*, and *The Getaway*, the enormous pistol may yet come to represent a set of characteristics imputed to its owner.

These are only individual images. The true creation of a film world undoubtedly lies in complex combinations of such elemental components. The classic gangster movie combines special lighting, a seedy urban environment, slightly grotesque versions of period clothing, cars, snubnosed automatics, sub-machine guns, and the rest, to create a nightmarish, violent, and fatalistic world. Whatever the different narratives this world remained a fixed context; the actions of its characters severely limited by virtue of it. Even the actors themselves become part of this conventionalising process. Besides portraying particulars character, their very

appearance becomes part of the iconography. In this way
the star system is made an adjunct to this process of reality
construction. Performers like Edward G. Robinson, James
Cagney, Humphrey Bogart, and Richard Widmark, define
a film-reality as much by their appearance as by their
acting abilities. The idea of the star-persona takes on
enormous importance.

Once the film world is defined, the potentialities for
inference multiply. Having invoked a particular reality in
the minds of his audience, the film-maker can try to direct,
constrain, and influence the specific meanings communicated. In some small part this is possible at that same general
level of reality definition. Invoking and then breaking conventions has become increasingly popular in recent years:
for comic ends in such parodies as *Cat Ballou* or *Support Your
Local Sheriff*; more seriously in the flush of 'evening westerns'
which have followed Sam Peckinpah's *Ride the High Country*.
But the major communicative weapon, of course, lies in the
narrative and thematic structure of the movie. This area
has a rich potential for elaborate inference. Indeed, if a
film is sufficiently ambiguous it may allow for several
systematic thematic accounts which are equally consistent
with the 'evidence'. Such a process can be carried as far as
any particular spectator wishes. The more one reflects then,
possibly, the more elaborate the consequences. Resnais'
L'Année Dernière a Marienbad gives rise to endless permutations and combinations, though the exercise becomes quite
arid in the process.

A film like Resnais' is an exception. Not because it is
open to such interpretations – all films are – but because it
treats the process as an intellectual game. It openly sets an
inferential puzzle, challenging the audience to *self-consciously*
make some sense out of it. It is a crossword of a film, and
very atypical. The large majority of fiction-films rely on the
audience's participation within their narrative as a basis for
communication. Through this participation the spectator
'receives the message'. He does not necessarily build *explicit*
inferential accounts of his understanding of the film, though
he may do so. Certainly the analyst must do so if he is to

reconstruct the range of meanings embedded in any particular narrative structure. But we have very little explicit knowledge of the workings of film language in this respect, knowledge which would direct us in the attempt to make our inferences 'warranted'. Yet we must make the inference. Otherwise we cannot study the films to discover their language. So, without the language we are uncertain about our analysis; without the analysis we are uncertain about the language. Catch twenty-two.

Much recent criticism has wrestled with this problem: how can we better base our thematic analyses? Obviously it is essential to be methodical, to try to take into account all the 'evidence'. But what makes one methodical thematic account better than another? False gods have been found to evade this issue of relativism. Most notably, some have seen the application of a structuralist methodology as a panacea for the ills of analysis. These implied claims to objectivity founder on a crucial point. They effectively deny that the analyst is also a person responding to a movie. This can be quite easily seen. When a critic, say, reflects on a movie, considers its meaning, writes his analysis, he is doing no more than producing a more or less ordered account of his own responses. If others share his understanding of film language then they will agree with his account. For them he would be right; in that sense, 'objective'. When he analyses the film, however, he is breaking it down into components on the basis of his preconceptions. He is (quite properly) imposing a structure upon the raw material he sees. Now if he is a social scientist, and his aim is to understand the meaning of the film *vis-à-vis* some audience or class of audience, then a 'warranted' inference will be one which would be intersubjectively agreed among this audience. He analyses in the light of their knowledge of the language. If he is interested in a body of film as part of a culture then the problem is more acute. He now needs to analyse out everything he can from the film that might be relevant to his interest, in defining the state of a particular culture, and, perhaps relating that culture to structural patterns in society at large. In other words there is no such thing as *the* inference. A 'warranted' inference depends on the purpose of the analysis, whether it is to study an audience or explore 'homology of structure'. This raises problems to which we shall return. But for the present it underlines the basically relativistic character of film analysis.

The crude structuralist critics retreat from this relativism. They seem unwilling to recognise the fact that their critical perception *necessarily* involves them in imposing categories on the material. Thus they claim that their methodology allows them to discover the objective, concealed structure of the piece. In effect, that a movie has a thematic structure strictly independent of their perception of it, and that structuralist methodology brings this 'deep structure' to the surface. In a phrase begged, stolen, or borrowed from Levi-Strauss (though he would be unlikely to approve), the thematic structure 'leaps out' at the observer. Of course it is true that a film-maker may impose his 'world-view' onto the body of his films. Whether this is 'revealed' to a spectator depends entirely on whether he speaks the same language as the film-maker. There is no magical formula whereby the secret is automatically yielded up, and it is a pernicious doctrine to claim that there is. Structuralist criticism, in its vulgar manifestations, by-passes the question of language. It dresses inevitably and rightly subjective analyses in the clothing of spurious objectivity.

Nevertheless, this emphasis on structure is helpful in terms of general semiology and specific analyses of thematic patterning. The approach is not to be necessarily identified with its vulgar version, and it does underline the need for *methodical* analysis based on the principles of classic critical method. It is essential that we focus on movies as structured wholes, a development which has been prevented by the familiar scientist bias. Terry Lovell sees structuralism as a response to this plea:

'In the absence of an alternative method incorporating contextualism, this plea would have fallen on deaf ears; as long as the alternative was merely the old 'Eng. Lit.' methods, intuitive, qualitative and unreliable, however much theoretical sense the plea made. With the advent of structuralism, the situation changes. We may forecast increasing application of this method in sociology of art-media. The coincidence of a prestigious new method with the self-confessed lack of success of the old, makes this development inevitable.'[18]

Only time will test the pertinence of her optimism. Thus far 'structural analysis' of thematic structure in movies has fallen into two classes: the 'naïve optimistic' and the 'pretentiously extravagant'. The former seems rather more realistic in its aims; it uses the simplest tools to discover the system of similarities and differences which characterise a film or a body of films. The omnipresent technique of dichotomisation is common here. Jim Kitses, in his study of the Western, invokes a set of such oppositions.[19] He outlines a series of sub-distinctions within a master dichotomy between Wilderness and Civilisation. In this way he hopes to define the basic thematic structure of the western. In so doing he remains explicit about the links between image and theme. The more elaborate the analysis then the more difficult it becomes to follow the chains of inference. In something like Willeman's discussion of Roger Corman's films the analysis seems almost to take on a life of its own.[20]

It should now be clear that structural analysis is a label for an area and a germ of an idea on method. There can be no doubt that we must look to the question. Films are meaningful wholes; they cannot be safely reduced to plot analyses. But quite how this thematic structure is to be apprehended is still a largely open question. In the present state of knowledge we seem likely to operate with one part description, one part careful and explicit inference, and one part guesswork. We are still very much in the dark. But an admonition made in another context is worth repeating here: 'a little theory goes a long way'. Some of the more extravagant proponents of structuralist analysis would do well to heed the spirit of the aphoriam. One should not disguise critical reflection as absolute truth by dressing it in overfine clothes.

We have now looked broadly at the questions of 'film reality' and 'theme'. Both are aspects of the meaning-system of film. The third major aspect is in some respects the best understood; it has certainly received the most methodical attention. It is concerned with the ways in which 'formal' or 'technical' elements may be patterned into meaningful configurations, and the genesis of its study is in Eisenstein. His theories of montage provide the basis for much later development, and it cannot yet be claimed that they have been transcended. He too has suffered greatly from vulgarisation, especially in the undue emphasis given his concept of 'intellectual montage'. This ill-developed notion is in fact the weakest and least necessary part of his analysis. It owes its fame more to the 'Film-as-Art' campaign than to any great intrinsic value. If there is a basic element to Eisenstein's thought it lies elsewhere, in the concept of *juxtaposition*. In the insight that particular combinations of the elements of film can communicate meanings above and beyond those understood on the narrative and literal levels. The theory of montage, which is much more than a theory of editing, deals with this question.

There is a great deal in Eisenstein's work which cannot be considered here. I have discussed some of it elsewhere.[21] The germ lay in the famous Kuleshov experiments, forceful demonstrations of the way in which combinations of images create meanings in the minds of the spectator. The idea is simple. An identical shot of a neutral face is spliced to various different shots (e.g. a child playing, a bowl of soup, a coffin) and the resulting combinations shown to an audience. In each case the audience reacts with the relevant emotion; they even praise the actor for his consummate expression of joy, hunger, and sadness. The combination of the elements creates the meaning. Eisenstein developed an increasing-complex analysis from this basic idea. At his most generalised he arrived at what he called 'vertical montage': the application of the juxtaposition idea to the major primary elements – film-image, colour, speech, sound, music. It is this 'cross-track manipulation' which Pryluck suggests is the kernel problem of this aspect of film analysis.

From the simple components he too tries to build up a picture of the 'serial' and 'lateral' juxtapositions which form the cinematic experience.[22]

Again, discussion is very much at a preliminary taxonomic stage. Even our systematic knowledge of the individual tracks varies. We probably know most about speech and least about 'raw' sound, with music and image falling somewhere in between. And since our knowledge of serial juxtaposition is limited in this way, any attempt to analyse the possibilities of lateral juxtaposition is far from easy. Guesswork and classificatory sketches are the order of the day. It is significant, for example, that the most developed discussion of the relation between sound and image in film remains that advanced by Kracauer, which is based on a simple typology of synchronism and asynchronism, parallelism and counterpoint.[23] The music-image relation has been given less systematic consideration although it is obviously a major weapon in the communications arsenal. Kracauer tries to apply his general analysis of sound-image structures to the music-image relation, but without much success. First, we need a semantic component for music. It is not the obvious, though highly effective, techniques which are really problematic (for example, those favoured by Kubrick in such films as *Dr Strangelove* and *2001: A Space Odyssey*); it is the standard, less prominent methods developed above all in commercial Hollywood. To pursue this interest we must still rely on the systematic educated guess.

The image track itself has understandably received considerable attention. It will bear a closer look here, if only as an example of the potential complexity of the formal component of film language. We can conveniently break it down into a series of abstracted elements. Each successive link in the chain marks a further level of structuring. Thus, the basic visual sign is structured into the image, the image into the frame, the frame into the shot, the shot into the sequence and the sequence into the film. Each link can be considered in turn. (It is important to note that these are only simple examples of formal, visual techniques, for communicating meaning: they are not full-scale analyses.)

Sign-image

This is probably the least interesting structure from the present point of view. The various blobs of light and shade are patterned into some recognisable form; people make sense of them. Of course, this is a learned process, and, of course, it can be ambiguous. Think for instance of the central plot device of *Blow Up*: we resolve the blobs of the pictures into a body and a gunman. It is possible that the formal patterning of light and shade, independent of any 'realistic' meaning we ascribe to it, may have emotional consequences – certainly this seems likely with colour[24] – but we are here concerned with processes which turn light into coherent image.

Image-frame

This is necessarily torn from context. 'Frame' is intended to suggest the structuring of images into the rectangular framework of the screen, initially skipping the question of movement. This is *not* to fall into the 'pictures-that-move' fallacy; it is an essential analytic simplification. The line between static composition and composition of a moving image is very blurred, but some principles apply to both. There are two broad categories here. There are those compositions which are 'meaningful' in the special sense that they are thought to be 'beautiful'. They correspond to some cultural expectation of beauty and so, presumably, modify the other meanings involved in some particular shot. The second and more important case is that in which compositional structure makes or underlines a point. The composition is part of the process. Its effectiveness does not rest on conscious recognition. There are plenty of simple examples. Preminger is fond of divided compositions which visually project (and thus communicate) the emotional relationships between his characters. Perkins analyses one such case in *Carmen Jones*: the steel strut on the front of a jeep separates Joe and Carmen until she breaks across it.[25] There is a similar example in *Advise and Consent* in which Brig Anderson's wife threatens to leave unless he tells her what is happening. Most of the dialogue is in medium shot from the front with no within-frame movement. Anderson on the right, his wife on the left. Down the middle of the screen, and in the background, is the slightly out of focus vertical strut of a window. It divides the screen in two. Only when his wife realised that she could not really leave him is the pattern broken. As in *Carmen Jones* two things happen: she plunges across the 'barrier' to throw her arms around him: in so doing she introduces movement into what had been a static scene. Then the camera shifts out as they are disturbed by the little girl. There are many other more and less elaborate examples. Tilted frames are sometimes used to suggest a disturbed situation, though this is no longer as common or as gross a device as it once was. A similar sense of unbalance may be created by particular ordering of the distribution of physical mass within the frame: the final moments of *L'Avventura* for instance, utilise such a technique, and the 'discovery' of deep-focus in the forties films of Orson Welles and William Wyler adds a further dimension to such compositional possibilities. Any account of *Citizen Kane* provides plenty of well-worn examples.

Frame-shot
Strictly the addition here is movement, an important factor in the two Preminger examples, *Carmen Jones* especially. Generally speaking this adds a further layer of complexity. We are now dealing with the visual patterns as images pass through shot and camera passes across image. This can both make a point about the substance of the relationships of the images in shot (reinforcing a 'meaning' already suggested in other ways), or impart variations in rhythm to the narrative flow. A good example of the first is to be found in the beach scene in Antonioni's *L'Amiche*. In a single long tracking shot the camera follows Rosetta right through the middle of the cheerful and flirtatious group. We experience her unhappiness and her isolation from the others as they flow in and out of the moving frame. The 'moving composition' offered allows us to appreciate the emotional relations between the characters. The second case is that of using a single shot movement to fulfil the task most commonly

reserved for editing – inducing variations in tempo. Welles' work is full of such skills, at its most brilliant in the opening sequence of *Touch of Evil*. An intense feeling of movement, of excitement, of tension, flows from the long tracking and craning shots which follow the car as it hurtles into the square. It is a tour-de-force of 'montage' without cuts.

Shot-sequence

Here we come primarily to montage with cuts, the much studied field of editing. Fundamentally, of course, the cut from shot to shot makes a narrative point. It is the machinery through which the whole film is carried forward. The fact that cuts are from one image to another may also make certain 'commentative' points, or they may simply be cuts of convenience. But the phenomenon which has interested so many students of film – greatly influenced by Eisenstein – is the way in which patterns of montage add 'emotional overtones' to a sequence. Take the crudest case; Eisenstein called it 'metric montage'. Shots are spliced together in a constant proportionate relation, while the *absolute* length of each shot is shortened. The consequence is a progressive and controlled increase in cutting pace which imposes a sense of 'building to a climax' onto the sequence. The classic example is the cross-cut chase, the true invention of which is generally credited to D. W. Griffith in *Intolerance*. But variations on the metric montage theme are very common throughout the history of film. Controlling shot length and angle is a standard means of controlling the tempo of a film. Eisenstein's other montage categories give us further applications. What he calls 'rhythmic montage' deals with combinations between cut and in-frame movement and composition. His favourite example was the Odessa Steps sequence from *Battleship Potemkin*. The marching and ordered troops are contrasted with the fleeing disordered populace, and the whole sequence cut together to build up to an emotional climax. He also suggested a further variation based on the relation between 'visual tone' and cutting. This 'tonal montage' is also a common technique in contemporary cinema.[26]

Sequence-film

This shift has received little attention, most discussion of overall structuring invoking narrative not visual considerations.[27] Nor is this unjustified. For most film narrative is the dominant consideration in ordering sequences. It is not easy to imagine emergent properties of the structuring of sequences which parallel those of the structuring of shots. Occasionally there have been attempts to extend montage ideas across the whole structure of a film – to create an essay in rhythm. Ruttman's *Berlin, Symphony of a City* has some such characteristics;[28] but such oddities are the exception rather than the rule. More interesting are those means whereby the sequence-structure of a film can reinforce or create certain patterns of meaning. Examples are difficult without being able to 'quote' the whole film, and usually inextricably intertwined with narrative structure. Yet some uses are fairly standard. Take the communication of a sense of time. The pattern of combination of sequences, and the range of actions they cover, can communicate different senses of passing time. In *Muriel*, for instance, we lose a sense of 'normal' time, participating instead in the subjective time experience of the characters. In *High Noon*, on the other hand, it is the 'real' time of the film which is accentuated by structuring sequences in ways analogous to the devices applied at the level of the shot. In both cases it is the tempo and range of the sequence shifts which control our impressions of experienced time. Other examples might play down the tempo effects of a pattern of sequences by giving the film a much looser sense of structure. This suggests a mosaic of sequences (and hence events) which finally combine together at the crucial narrative point. *The Wild Bunch*, loosely organised around three key sequences, is a good example. By the time we arrive at the final scenes the last elements of the seemingly disorganised pattern are falling into place. *The Searchers* and *Rocco and his Brothers* provide two further disparate examples. All of which does not encourage generalisation. While it is clear that these 'macrostructures' are important, they can only be properly demonstrated as part of a *full* analysis of specific films. These

brief suggestions are necessarily ambiguous and unsatisfactory.

As all these examples suggest, even the image track alone
is highly complex, making a full breakdown of lateral
juxtapositions almost impossible. Add to such an attempt the
problems of analysing 'human content' and thematic
structure, then try to combine them. The enormity of the
task is a reflection of just how complicated is the language of
film. We have only just begun to isolate its elements let
alone understand precisely how they combine together to
carry such rich variety of meaning. As far as constructing a
'linguistics' of film is concerned we are still trying to come to
terms with the preliminaries; we must now also come to
terms with that limitation itself.

A TEMPORARY PARADIGM

Standard sociological and psychological approaches to the
analysis of film content assume that recognition of available
meanings is non-problematic. Films are about this or that;
the real problem is to produce a quantitative assessment of
the distribution of such meanings. Sometimes this is unexceptionable but uninspiring. Dorothy B. Jones, for example,
uses straightforward categories like 'story locale', 'character
analysis', 'presentation of crime', and incidence of 'birth,
marriage and death'. She is quite openly concerned only
with those materials amenable to quantitative treatment.
Rather less reasonable, if more typical, are discussions like
that by James Fyock whose 'new slant on an old technique'
amounts to a few superficial suggestions as to the solution of
some practical problems.[29] Always the basic meaning is
assumed to be given. Nor is this specific to the stress on
quantification. In promoting qualitative analysis Kracauer
defines it as '. . . the selection and rational organisation of
such categories as condense the substantive meanings of the
given text, with a view to testing certain pertinent assumptions and hypotheses'.[30] In practice this seems to mean little
more than a methodical analysis of plot summaries, a
limitation reflected in Kracauer's own study of the German

cinema and Huaco's later comparative research.[31] All of which is based on a misconception of film language. To take basic meanings as given is to assume that understanding is non-problematic, but we have seen that film language is extraordinarily complex. If content analysis is not both explicit and methodical it is nothing; but it can be neither until we have some sort of theory of film language on which it can be based.

To this the researcher correctly replies; then we must have a second best. There are too many pressing problems to stop everything to focus on, say, semiology. We need a stop-gap. Traditionally this has involved the application of 'scientific' content analysis to a 'translation' of the film. If the film cannot be analysed, rewrite it as something that can. But this simply evades the problem of analysing *film*. Kracauer is on the right track when he speaks of 'disciplined subjectivity'. What can this mean in the present context? Basically it requires us to construct an explicit paradigm for film analysis. A list which tells us where to look and what to look for. As well as encouraging method, this will provide an explicit framework within which any analysis may be placed, and some sort of guarantee that selective interpretation will be minimised. We are trying to explore some highly variable terrain. A full-scale account of film language would be something approaching a decent map. In its absence we must work from rough sketches, some parts better mapped than others. This is the purpose of my tentative schema of analysis.

The dimensions of this map distinguish two different aspects of a movie's capacity to transmit meaning; *aspect of meaning* and *channel of meaning*. The classification of the channels through which meaning is communicated, the 'machinery' of communication, grows directly out of the discussion of this chapter. It is a threefold division into 'nature of film world' (human content), 'thematic structure', and 'formal structure'. These correspond to three of the general 'sectors' of film already discussed. The fourth 'materials of the medium', is not directly relevant to problems of practical analysis. The fact that film uses certain materials and not others has implications for film language as a whole (setting its limitations and capacities), but makes for little variation from film to film. For all practical purposes it can be omitted from this paradigm. The *aspects of meaning* dimension is based on the classic distinction between cognitive, expressive, and normative meanings briefly discussed in Chapter 2. A cognitive meaning is one which is, roughly, a 'factual' meaning within the domain of a film. It is that element of meaning which informs the spectator; actions, appearances, events and the like. In short, what is shown and what happens. Expressive meanings are those which appeal to the emotions. One is excited, saddened, aroused, or embittered by what one sees. Normative meanings are the ethical or evaluative inferences which we make from a film. It need hardly be said that these are all faces of the same process: a particular sequence of events on the screen will invariably have cognitive, expressive, and normative dimensions. Movies are laden with meaning.

We receive this meaning through the three familiar channels. By cross-classification we arrive at a 'map' of film meanings constructed according to the sort of meaning

		Channel		
		Nature of film world	Thematic structure	Formal structure
Aspect	Cognitive	Factual nature of film world 1	Events in thematic development, e.g. plot 2	Factual meanings conveyed by form 3
	Expressive	Emotional meanings associated with film world 4	Emotional involvement in thematic structure 5	Emotional consequences of formal structure 6
	Normative	Normative meanings implicit in film world 7	Normative meanings implicit in thematic structure 8	Normative meanings conveyed by formal means 9

Figure 5.2   CINEMATIC MEANINGS

involved and the channel through which it flows. This is our primary paradigm. The nine categories shown in fig. 5.2 direct our attention to the various sources of meaning in a movie. Analysis can focus on any or all of them, but a claim to deal fully with a movie, or a set of movies, would have to look at them all. It can readily be seen that the failing of much content analysis of movies has been its focus on category 2 to the exclusion of the rest.

Obviously this is not designed to replace the sensitive assessments of the critic. Critical acumen is still essential and will remain so until we have a complete working knowledge of film language. The paradigm merely provided a basis for ordering the materials which will be 'collected' by rigorous critical method. As Kracauer put it, by 'disciplined subjectivity'. Ultimately it should prove possible to build up a secondary paradigm which details the particularities of each type. Thus, type 6 would break down into a theory about, say, particular montage techniques and their emotional consequences. Eisenstein has taken us some way toward this goal. Type 8 would involve a theory about the way in which the patterning of themes creates particular ethical meanings. Type 1 would involve an iconology, a set of classifications of the images associated with different film worlds. And so on. As knowledge of these various processes grows so too will the detail on the map, and that growth will in turn accelerate our learning.

Let me enlarge on the paradigm by *briefly* taking each type.

1 Analysis of the simple factual nature of the world invoked by a film is often by-passed. At the level of large groups of films – genre is a good example – this is very important. The sort of world defined by a body of films may be a significant factor in understanding a culture.
2 The principal focus here must be 'plot', where that is seen as the sequence of events presented by the film rather than what is written down in the screenplay. This is a standard focus.
3 Here we are concerned with information carried by formal

I

techniques. This includes the full range of elements: speech, sound, music, and image. Their formal combinations and permutations can, to some extent, inform the spectator about the events and participants in a film. Thus, in the Preminger examples, the composition carries information about relations between characters.

4 Here we are again close to the issue of genre. A film world carries with it emotional overtones, and to invoke it is also to mobilise our emotions. This will no doubt vary from case to case and culture to culture. A similar possiblity holds in the emotion-inducing potential of the star-system as a constitutive element in a film-world. The very appearance of the star is a source of emotional involvement.

5 Thematic structure in general, and narrative structure in particular, provoke us to emotional response. We are involved, disgusted, moved, and diverted by such patterns. We see them as aesthetically pleasing or displeasing. In short, we derive expressive meaning from the experience.

6 This is the well-worked area of the classic theorists; the theory of montage focuses above all on the formal capacity of the medium to communicate expressive meanings. By combinations of editing tempo, composition, music, and the rest, this element of film reaches directly for the emotions of the spectator.

7 Any diffuse pre-narrative 'film world' has some sort of structure, both social and natural. If it has structure, then it also has a pattern of normative evaluation embedded in it. It has a characteristic form of 'ideology' which, in all probability, circumscribes any more specific normative meanings.

8 This is the standard focus for analysing the values of a film, and indeed most other narrative arts. The patterning of themes betrays an ordering relation which expresses an ideology. Structural analysis of a director's 'world-view' is usually concerned to make inferences at this level.

9 The formal elements of film can also communicate normative meaning. The crudest examples are those associated with 'intellectual montage', generally involving some sort

of ironic juxtaposition. More subtly the very style of a movie may suggest an evaluation. Thus, a camera style which lingers lovingly on the trappings of the aristocracy may communicate a sense of approval for those trappings, for their owners, and for the system which allows them to survive.

By using the paradigm as an analytic map we can do two things. First, we can know explicitly where to look and we can do so in some sort of order. An essential component of disciplined subjectivity is that the discipline is explicit. Then others have some chance of following the chain of inference which leads us to interpret a film in a particular way. Second, the paradigm acts to 'balance' our analyses. That is, it ensures that we do not pay too much attention to one focus of analysis at the expense of others. Instead we attempt to cover the whole range. Of course, we may single out some areas as crucial to our decision on the *aesthetic* value of a work. But where we are attempting an ordered analysis of the meaning of a movie, then the paradigm must control and direct our attention.

Many questions remain. A paradigm is only a first fumbling step not a final analytic leap. Although it gives us some idea of where to look in general, it is of little help in particular. There is still no substitute for a thoroughgoing understanding of the workings of film in each of the paradigm sectors, in short, an understanding of the language of film. So this is, very much, a temporary paradigm; an essential second best. I shall use it in the analyses of Chapters 7 and 8 in that the categories abstractly presented here underly that concrete process of analysis. I shall not, however, use the categories to *present* the analysis; this would be too clumsy, at least for these purposes. For however methodical we make it, without a full-scale account of the language of film, practical analysis must remain a 'subjective' critical process. The paradigm aims only to provide a basis of order and coherence for that essential subjectivity.

References

[1] See E. Dale, *The Content of Motion Pictures* (see Selected Bibliography).

[2] For an idea of these developments see Bernard R. Berelson, *Content Analysis in Communication Research*, Free Press, Glencoe, 1951; I. de Sola Pool (Ed.), *Trends in Content Analysis*, Univ. Illinois Press, Urbana (Ill.), 1959, especially Charles Osgood, 'The Representational Model and Relevant Research Methods' contained therein: George Gerbner, Ole R. Holsti, Klaus Krippendorf, William J. Paisley and Philip J. Stone (Eds), *The Analysis of Communication Content*, Wiley, New York, London, Sydney, Toronto, 1969.

[3] G. Gerbner, 'Preface', in Gerbner *et al., ibid.,* p. xi (my italics).

[4] G. Gerbner, 'On Content Analysis and Critical Research in Mass Communications', in L. A. Dexter and D. M. White (Eds), *People, Society and Mass Communications*, Free Press, New York, 1964.

[5] S. Worth, 'Cognitive Aspects of Sequence in Visual Communication' (Selected Bibliography).

[6] On this traditional development in film aesthetics see A. Tudor, *Theories of Film*, especially Chapters 1 and 2 (Selected Bibliography).

[7] C. Pryluck, p. 390 (Selected Bibliography).

[8] C. Metz, 'La Grande Syntagmatique du Film Narratif' (Selected Bibliography). On the concept of syntagm see Roland Barthes, *Elements of Semiology*, Cape, London, 1967, Chapter 3.

[9] P. Wollen, *Signs and Meaning in the Cinema* (Selected Bibliography). For an interesting general discussion of some of the issues see F. West (Selected Bibliography).

[10] C. Metz, 'Propositions Méthodologiques pour l'Analyse du Film' (Selected Bibliography). Since this chapter was written an English translation of this paper has appeared (see Selected Bibliography). Where my terminology has differed from that of this translation I have preferred to keep mine. For example: the *Screen* translation uses 'social content' for Metz's 'contenu humain' which I have translated as 'human content'. I think this justified in that this level of analysis is concerned with a wider range of phenomena than is suggested by the term 'social' – it must also include natural and technological characteristics of the film world.

[11] On this distinction see R. Barthes, *op. cit.,* Chapter 2. For the Metz classification see C. Matz, *ibid.* The terms *plane of expression* and *plane of content* are taken from Barthes; Metz does not employ them.

[12] C. Metz, *ibid.*, p. 117.

[13] A fairly orthodox idea of film 'linguistics' is to be found in C. Pryluck, *op. cit.*, and in C. Pryluck and R. E. Snow (Selected Bibliography). Worth calls the area *vidistics*. See S. Worth, *op. cit.*, and his *American Scholar* (Selected Bibliography).

[14] On Howard Hawks see P. Wollen, *op. cit.*, pp. 80–94, and Robin Wood, *Howard Hawks*, Secker & Warburg, London, 1968. On Siegel see A. Lovell (Selected Bibliography). On Antonioni see A. Tudor, 'Antonioni – the Road to Death Valley', *Cinema*, **6** & **7**, August 1970.

[15] The major representatives of this view are Kracauer and Bazin. See S. Kracauer, *Theory of Film*, and A. Bazin, *What is Cinema?* (Selected Bibliography). See also A. Tudor, *Theories of Film*, *op. cit.*, Chapter 4.

[16] Erwin Panofsky, *Meaning in the Visual Arts*, Anchor, New York, 1955, pp. 31–2.

[17] E. Panofsky, 'Style and Medium in the Motion Pictures', in D. Talbot (Ed.), *Film: An Anthology*, Univ. California Press, Berkeley, 1966.

[18] T. Lovell, 'Sociology of Aesthetic Structures and Contextualism', p. 330 (Selected Bibliography).

[19] J. Kitses, p. 11 (Selected Bibliography).

[20] Paul Willeman, 'Roger Corman: The Millenic Vision', in D. Will and P. Willeman (Eds), *Roger Corman*, Cinema Pubs & Edinburgh Festival, Edinburgh, 1970.

[21] In A. Tudor, *Theories of Film*, *op. cit.*, Chapter 2.

[22] These terms derive from C. Pryluck, *op. cit.*

[23] See S. Kracauer, *op. cit.*, Chapter 7.

[24] Colour remains only a partly understood aspect of the image. Eisenstein's essay on 'Colour and Meaning' must surely be an important starting point. See Sergei M. Eisenstein, *The Film Sense*, Faber, London, 1943, Chapter 3.

[25] See V. Perkins, pp. 79–82 (Selected Bibliography).

[26] See most of Eisenstein's writings but especially the essays collected in Sergei Eisenstein, *Film Form*, Dobson London, 1951. For a summary account see A. Tudor, *Theories of Film*, *op. cit.* For contemporary technical discussion of montage techniques see Karel Reisz, *The Technique of Film Editing*, Focal Press, London, 1959.

[27] See, for example, C. Metz, 'La Grande Syntagmatique du Film Narratif', *op. cit.*, and also his *Essais sur la Signification au Cinéma* (Selected Bibliography).

[28] See J. Kolaja and A. Foster (Selected Bibliography).

[29] D. B. Jones, 'Quantitative Analysis of Motion Picture Content'; J. Fyock. (See Selected Bibliography.)

[30] Siegfried Kracauer, 'The Challenge of Qualitative Content Analysis', *Public Opinion Quarterly*, **16**, 1952, p. 638.

[31] S. Kracauer, *From Caligari to Hitler*; G. Huaco, *The Sociology of Film Art* (Selected Bibliography).

Chapter 6

Patterns of Culture

Whatever it may be that we label 'culture', the label itself has had a chequered history in the social sciences. At one time or another it has been hailed as all-important and relegated to trifling adjunct. It has been lauded as the source of all that is meaningful and denigrated as a cheap dressing on otherwise unpalatable fare. Its very presence has been claimed to promote alienation; its absence to lead to anomie. In short, it has been a focus for very considerable disagreement. Yet we still use the term at almost every level of our discourse. It touches something in our everyday experience although its meanings are so various.[1] 'Culture' is a catch-all which taps something fundamental:

'The fundamental categories of cultural life are the same in all societies. In all the different strata of any given society, the effort to explore and explain the universe, to understand the meaning of events, to enter into contact with the sacred or to commit sacrilege, to affirm the principles of morality and justice and to deny them, to encounter the unknown, to exalt or denigrate authority, to stir the senses by the control of and response to words, sounds, shapes, and colors – these are the basic elements of cultural existence.'[2]

Out of the rich complexity of our social lives we single out some things, and call them culture. They are the collective property of a body of people. They transcend the individual though they must be articulated through him. Culture consists of people's beliefs, their ideas, their values, their very conceptions of reality. It is given concrete expression in the richly varied artefacts that men lovingly create. It is found in religion, in law, in arts, in sciences, in the simple party games that people play. Cultural things are indeed all-pervasive. A sociology which could not comprehend them would have little to recommend it. To understand culture is a major task.

But how we have chosen to understand it has varied enormously. Take that most prominent of nineteenth-century social thinkers, Karl Marx. For him, culture was *formally* epiphenomenal. It was part of the ideological superstructure, *ultimately* shaped by the material forces of the economic base. Yet against the apparent leanings of his theory, and in contradiction to the later development of 'vulgar Marxism', he recognised the vital role of culture. He saw that it could, and did, interfere with the pattern of historic change. Religion, especially, could act as an opium of the people. Marxist theorists still encounter this problem, though with increased analytic sophistication. Nor are they alone. Others, recognising the importance of things cultural, were tempted to the opposite extreme. They committed what David Bidney calls the 'culturalistic fallacy'.

'The culturalistic fallacy may be said to be committed when one defines culture as an ideational abstraction and then proceeds to convert or reify this *ens rationis* into an independent ontological entity subject to its own laws of development and conceived through itself alone. No fallacy is committed simply in abstracting cultural products or achievements from the context of social behaviour in which they originate; this is legitimate and often pragmatically useful. The culturalistic fallacy is committed only when this logical abstraction comes to be regarded as if it actually were a reality *sui generis*. . . .'[3]

Culture comes to be seen as entirely independent of man's volition. Now everything else is epiphenomenal.

Bidney's point about abstraction is important; it is a net in which to catch many a red herring. So much discussion has stumbled on this point. It is not a methodological original sin to consider cultural factors in isolation from the rest of social process. It does not necessarily imply 'idealism' or some such belief in the unique determining power of cultural phenomena. Such abstraction is essential to any process of knowing. Of course, culture does not have a life of its own. It is created by men, and it helps them define what is meaningful in their world. It can be manipulated by the unscrupulous, used as comfort by the desperate, and erected as a 'sacred canopy' over us all.[4] Movies are part of this process. They are cultural objects, purveyors of cultural fare. They may be abstracted from the total picture and classed as culture. The abstraction itself is legitimate; it is the claim that it exhausts the institution we call the movies that is unjustified.

Conflicts over the status of our abstractions have been especially virulent in the study of culture. The least suggestion of idealism has provoked understandable reaction, and much debate can be usefully seen in terms of an idealism – materialism polarity.[5] Abstractions are made real and become entrenched defences. Yet much of this theoretical self-consciousness has been by-passed in discussions of *popular* culture, though here too abstractions have been elevated into certainties. The idea of the 'mass', for instance, is a typical distortion. In it, an accurate perception of an *aspect* of modern media was converted into a total account. Popular culture could be labelled mass culture and we could safely think no more about it. 'High' culture and the accepted products of the intellect have been honoured with minute analysis – the sociology of knowledge has often been a sociology of intellectual fashion – while the popular arts have been accorded only the most cursory of looks. All this, in part at least, because their relative 'massness' was made a definition of their essence. It is no underestimate to suggest that this emphasis put the sociology of the media back a step and kept it there. It is revealing to trace a rough outline of the process.

MASS CULTURE TO MCLUHAN

There is a sense in which the mass culture idea is a weak excuse for a macro-sociology of the media. In focusing on microscopic processes, media studies completely failed to explore the multiple relations between the media and society. The culture of modern societies is enormous and complex. Labelling it 'mass culture' rendered it simple, and the process became self-confirming. The label ensured that those elements which did not fit were conveniently ignored. This is not to suggest that media researchers invented the mass culture thesis as a substitute for their lack of socio-logical perspective, though they may have adopted it for that reason. They did not invent it at all. It came from other roots, in particular from those who were critical of the 'new' society, its institutions and culture, and although these critics shared a certain mistrust of popular culture they made very odd bedfellows. Amongst them one would have to number T. S. Eliot, C. Wright Mills, F. R. Leavis, David Reisman, Edward Shils, Dwight MacDonald, and a host of others. There is some catholicity of social doctrine here!

Given this obvious disparity, they retain some surprisingly common characteristics. For instance, many of the critics share a tone of condescension in their attitudes to popular culture. This is to be expected in one with views as openly élitist as Eliot's. For him true culture could only be preserved by and through an intellectual minority. But it also turns up in those who are less absolutely panic-stricken at the onset of the 'mass'. Thus, Edward Shils feels able to talk of 'refined', 'mediocre', and 'brutal' culture as if there were a scale of fixed and settled standards. He too finally arrives at the need to oblige intellectuals '. . . to look after intellectual things'. 'Refined' culture is to be defended against these undesirable inroads.[6] The main source of disquiet for these critics is specific to culture; standards are threatened, the good and beautiful may be destroyed. David Manning White has correctly pinpointed some of the assumptions and fallacies of this position. In a spirited defence of mass culture he writes:

'In the minds of certain critics of mass culture the people will invariably choose the mediocre and the meretricious. This mixture of noblesse oblige and polite contempt for anyone outside of university circles, or avant-garde literary groups,

seems to me just as authoritarian as the anti-intellectualism
that the "masses" direct against the scholastics. . . . It is just
these mass media that hold out the greatest promise to the
"average" man that a cultural richness no previous age
could give him is at hand.[7]

No one could deny that the mass media produce much that
is of little value; the misconception lies in thinking that other
forms of culture are so very different. The oil painting, that
most accepted of 'arts', encompasses an enormous range of
hack work produced between the sixteenth and twentieth
century.[8] The creations of the élite have no automatic claim
to greatness, just as those of popular culture are far from
uniformly dreadful.

So far I have mainly discussed culture as artefact. In this
context critic and defender alike have been concerned with
the value of the cultural product as such, so resolving the
argument into a defence of the old against the new. An
exercise in the conservation of accepted 'great art'. A more
interesting case is made by those critics of mass culture who
see the media as vital agencies in the creation of our contemporary 'styles of life'. Their interest is more sociological
in that they see mass culture as one aspect of social action.
David Reisman's famous analysis of the switch from inner-
directed to other-directed attitudes, for instance, is concerned
with the consequences of this change for our patterns of
social interaction.[9] Discussion on this more 'socially'
concerned flank has generally revolved around the impact of
mass media on society as a whole, not merely on the store-
house of legitimated art forms. These writers have recognised
the magnitude of social change in modern society, correctly
diagnosing a potentially important role for the media. But do
the media have the wide-ranging anti-humanitarian consequences that have been attributed to them? We have seen
things change, certainly, but have the changes been so much
to the bad? The claims for the all-powerful media have been
somewhat overstrong. Mills, for example:

'(1) the media tell the man in the mass who he is – they give him identity; (2) they tell him what he wants to be – they give him aspirations; (3) they tell him how to get that way – they give him technique; and (4) they tell him how to feel that way even when he is not – they give him escape.'[10]

There is some truth in all these claims; most forms of culture are sources of identity, aspiration, technique, and escape, but the position is overstated at the point at which people are assumed automatically to follow these media prescriptions. As we have seen, this view has a corresponding 'hypodermic' picture of media effects, a picture which neglects the individual's potential for autonomy. The real issue here – and to his credit Mills was one of the few to properly see it – is not so much the contribution that popular culture makes, but rather, who controls it. It is bound to provide some sources of identity, aspiration, and the rest. When it does so as an arm of the power élite then we have an issue to be taken seriously.

For the most part, however, the stress on *mass* emphasises the anonymous, subservient character of the 'mass audience' at the expense of considering the larger implications of media control. Yet 'massness' is hardly *the* major characteristic; popular culture is not necessarily repressive in all its consequences. When Hall and Whannel distinguish between popular art and mass culture they are responding to this variation. They try to show how a popular art need not be repressive, but a positive part of human experience.[11] They analyse the subtle workings of particular popular cultural products so demonstrating their quality. Those who are blinded by the universal claim of 'massness' cannot begin to imagine such a possibility. The concept of 'mass culture' answers all the questions before we can even ask them. By definition popular culture becomes a mediocre and socially destructive part of society. In such a perspective no other role can be entertained. At its worst this vulgar excuse for macro-sociology saves us the trouble of actually looking at the materials. This is perhaps its most pernicious consequence: it prevents a serious and close consideration of the extraordinarily varied products of modern popular culture.

In one form or another the mass society thesis has dominated the macro-sociology of the media. McQuail does not
overestimate the unfortunate consequences:

'Not only have inappropriate questions been fostered and
alternative ones discouraged, but the very weight of intellectual and ideological force behind these theories has discouraged competitors, and forced opponents to appear in the
light of apologists for an existing social order, for capitalism
and commercial exploitation, for ugliness and incipient
totalitarianism.'[12]

The only prominent recent attempt to escape this strait-
jacket on exploring the relation between media and society
has been that of Marshall McLuhan. This is in itself a poor
reflection on the state of the discipline since McLuhan's work
is hardly a rigorous sociology. He does make sociological
claims, very considerable some of them. His '. . . print
created individualism and nationalism in the sixteenth
century' is bold if foolhardy![13] And his apocalyptic vision of
the 'global village' contains all sorts of unanalysed social
implications. But his work is enormously frustrating. It is not
systematic not does he wish it so. It is crammed with partly
digested ideas, suggestions, assertions, and guesses. In
elevating the medium itself to the centre of the stage he has
done us a service, though Lerner and Reisman made a
number of similar points some fifteen years earlier.[14] But
ultimately it seems no better than the mass culture analysis.
If it were to become as influential, which seems unlikely, it
would also prove just as sterile.

Formally, McLuhan has much in common with the mass
society theorists. He may to some extent celebrate what they
abhor, but his claims are similarly grandiose. Both substitute
rhetoric for detailed analysis of popular culture. For the
one, the major factor is the anonymous 'mass' character of
contemporary culture and society. For the other, the global,
electronic, and instantaneous character of modern media. Both
imagine the media to have enormous power, though they
differ in their attitudes to it. Both lump the elements of

popular culture into one amorphous category, though McLuhan does add his famous 'hot/cool' distinction. And both are very selective about the evidence they adduce in illustration of their theses. One wonders about McLuhan's popularity. After so many years beneath the yoke of the mass society idealogues, students of the media might be expected to resent such monolithic conceptions. Yet briefly this new devil has been substituted for the old. Perhaps this itself is a sign of the need for a coherent macro-perspective, if media sociology is to make any further progress.[15]

The net result of these doctrines has been a limited understanding of popular culture. The most revealing work has come not from sociology but from the more 'literary' tradition of cultural criticism. This tradition, which has produced Raymond Williams and Hall and Whannel, has said more of intelligence about popular culture than most sociologists.[16] They have not created a systematic understanding of the relations between popular culture and society, nor is this really their aim. But they have not been blinded to the subject by the enormous reification of the 'mass'. When one factor is singled out from a complex phenomenon and claimed to tell the whole story, then we have reification. In media sociology we have had it with a vengeance. But building on the understanding created by socially sensitive criticism might enable us to overcome this crippling defect. We need a macro-sociology of the media to fill in the outline of a picture for which we now have some of the detail. Such a venture is certain to remain tentative and even speculative – what else could it be? But at least it can no longer be shrouded in the mists of 'mass society'.

ANALYTIC PERSPECTIVES

It is one thing to require a macro-sociology; it is another to know what to put into it. So we need first some sort of loose, guiding perspective within which specific analyses may be placed, a classification of the sorts of factors likely to be important in a macro-analysis of cultural phenomena— specifically, a way of approaching the problem of understanding the relations between cinema and society. This given, we can better understand the simplifications traditional to the field. Roland Robertson has developed such a schema in relation to religion.[17] By slightly changing his terms we can usefully adapt his classification to give us a way of distinguishing among the elements of our potential macro-sociology. The technique is to apply a social structure/ culture distinction to the relations between cinema and society. The basic terms are straightforward. 'Culture' refers to patterns of belief, values, and ideas, as well as to the artefacts in which they may be embedded. Clearly it is an abstraction. It singles out relevant factors from a concrete social situation, thus making them available for analysis. 'Social structure', similarly an abstraction, refers to estab-lished patterns of social relations: stratification, role-structures, organisational patterns, and the like. Combined with 'cinema' and 'society' this gives a four part classification of the principal domains on which a macro-sociology of film may focus (note that Robertson does not use the term 'society' in his discussion; otherwise this terminology corresponds to his, given the substitution of 'cinema' for 'religion').

The details of each domain might be studied in and of their own right, leading to a micro-sociology of their genesis and operation. Thus we might build up a picture of, say, the structure of relations which exist between communi-cators and audiences; this would be one part of 'cinematic social structure'. Having singled out this element we might then go on to explore the detail of its genesis. But this is not the traditional interest of a macro-sociological analysis. Such a focus would be on the *relation* between cinema and society, the way in which variation in one relates to variation in the other. This simple classificatory scheme is a guideline for 'discovering' these variables. In any specific research, interest must lie in their empirical combinations.

This sort of large-scale sociology has frequently, and understandably, dealt in pairs of variables: the Protestant ethic and the spirit of capitalism; class conflict and social change; the division of labour and anomie. Following

Robertson we may note six such paired possibilities in fig.
6.1. One of them, that between general culture and social

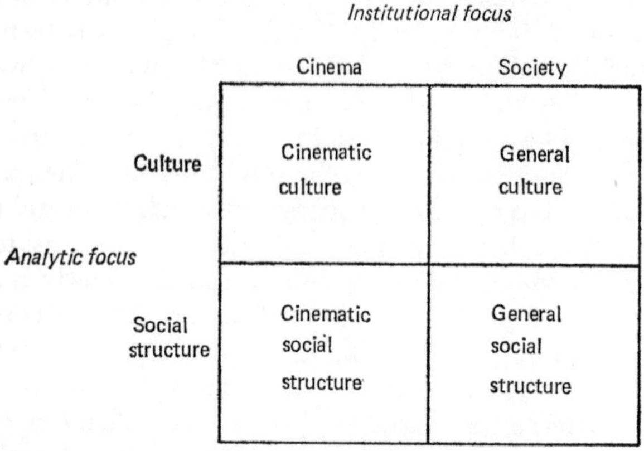

Institutional focus

	Cinema	Society
Culture	Cinematic culture	General culture
Social structure	Cinematic social structure	General social structure

Analytic focus

Figure 6.1   MACRO–SOCIOLOGICAL DOMAINS

culture, does not involve the cinema at all. It has been the
focus of much sociological interest and we may return to it.
Of the five direct links which do involve the cinema, one,
that between the culture and social structure of the cinema,
differs from the rest. It does so in that it requires no immediate consideration of the relation between cinema and
society. If anything it involves seeing the institution of
cinema as a society; analysing it into its socio-cultural
components. Communicators, audiences, and medium,
relate to each other in social structural and cultural terms:
they form an institution. Understanding this institution is
based on understanding the form of these relations.

A fragmentary beginning to such understanding occupies
the first half of this book. In discussing communicators,
audiences, and the medium, I have tried to show some of
the ways in which the cinema operates. The link between
the communication model and more macroscopic concerns
lies in the categories of structure and culture common to
them both. Traditional accounts have been oversimplified.
They see a superordination–subordination relation between
communicator and audience, a corresponding monopoly of

power on the part of the communicator, and so the communicator's consequent complete control of beliefs, attitudes, and values. In other words, a two-class social structure with a manipulative culture. However, we have repeatedly seen that audiences are not the subservient automata implied by this conception. Such analyses suffer from premature foreclosure. They simplify the link between the institution's culture and social structure into crude conspiracy. But as Gans suggested, the 'feedback' process between audience and communicator (and, we might add, between structure and culture) is crucial.[18] Whatever pattern there may be is produced as much by interaction as by domination.

The other four paired links invoke the traditional focus of a macro-sociology of any institution; they look at particular aspects of the relation between cinema and society. Take first a link at the purely cultural level, that between cinematic and general cultures. One aspect of this relation has received a good deal of attention and serious criticism: namely, the relation between the beliefs and values embedded in the films themselves and the beliefs and values of the larger society. One favourite subject for such analysis has been the German cinema of the inter-war years: Kracauer and Eisner have both looked at the 'elective affinities' between German culture and this particular film movement.[19] The focus is also found in the common claim that a particular group of films 'reflects' the values of the larger society. Obviously such claims are necessary simplifications; to discuss affinities solely at the level of culture is not to claim that cultural interrelations are somehow autonomous. One may explore the congruences between two bodies of belief in full awareness that such a relation is socially mediated, and without any commitment to 'idealism'. It is a valid *part* of a macro-analysis.

Similar considerations apply to the structure–structure link. In media studies (film being no exception) this area has been dominated by the mass society thesis. The social structure of the medium was seen as the social structure of the society in microcosm. The anonymous, isolated, and subservient mass audience was writ large into society as a

K

whole. Mills's 'power élite' found its reflection in the various media. This is also the form of orthodox Marxist analysis. The social structure of the institution reflects its larger and exploitative counterpart. Capitalism is all-pervasive. There is a good deal to be said for this view. Provided its claims are not elevated into total accounts it is a good starting approximation of the relationship between the two structures. The expression 'capitalist' is not uninformative applied to the cinema, nor is its application limited to the strictly commercial. At various points Marx's general account of the workings of capitalist society illuminates the workings of the cinema, though the vulgar Marxist commitment to crude materialism is far from adequate.

This last limitation is more apparent in discussion of the link between general social structure and cinematic culture, a simplification common to vulgar Marxist and vulgar sociologist alike. Huaco, for example, borrows the base-superstructure imagery and fills it out with a little Parsonian terminology. The resulting conceptual confusion does not, however, disguise the direction of his endeavour.[20] Generally, in this sort of analysis, cinematic culture is limited to film content; expectations, audience-images, and genre-images have received little consideration. For good reasons the culture is equated with the artefact. Thus, what little classic macro-sociology of film there is, most frequently focuses on the direct effects social structure has on the movies. It is only recently that this tradition has become more sophisticated, and much has been inspired by Goldmann's literary criticism and the general structuralist–Marxist tradition, with 'homology of structure' between artefact and society replacing the cruder determinism of old.[21] Even so, straightforward determinism is still not uncommon. The desire to demonstrate that the creations of the mind are circumscribed, directed, or even caused by the 'objective' social world is too well established to undergo rapid change. It is solidly based in the historic development of the sociologies of knowledge and art, and survives in such 'sociological' studies as Huaco's and Kavolis's.[22]

This 'sociology of knowledge' tradition focuses in one

causal direction: from social structure to artefact. What of the inverse? Take a simple if controversial case. Is there a link between the attitudes to violence contained in our cinematic culture and the apparently increasing institutionalisation of violence into our modern social structure? This is not sensibly argued at the 'violent films make people aggressive' level since the micro-research suggests serious limitations on the importance of this direct relation. But is there any macroscopic sense to the suggestion? An analogy with pollution is suggestive. Although scientists declared certain chemicals 'safe' on the basis of their microscopic researches, they later proved to have macroscopic consequences. Long chains of highly complex interaction effects, unanticipated on the straightforward, discrete cause–effect conception, led to large-scale pollution. So might it be with the media. If so, then the funds poured into research on direct effects have been wasted; the interesting questions are those of cumulative consequences. An appropriate strategy here must be some form of macroscopic analysis which tries to comprehend the whole as something more than the apparent sum of its parts. By exploring the cultures of the individual media we could build up a cumulative picture of a popular culture; given this picture, we might then go on to explore its potential effects on social structure.

This leads to perhaps the most interesting single area of macro-analysis – the complex of interrelations between particular cultural products and the larger social structure. All sorts of attempts have been made on this citadel. The 'theory of uses and gratifications', most functional analyses (including the opium-of-the-people variant), and the 'mass psychiatric' theories of escapism and wish-fulfilment are examples. They try to show how cinematic culture supports the given social structure, whether by sheer falsification or playing out collective strains. Although the actual evaluations may differ, this posture is common to analysts as varied as Kracauer, Wolfenstein and Leites, and Marcuse.[23] By providing even a partial definition of reality the media underwrite the larger social structure; media culture becomes a contemporary 'sacred canopy'. Indeed, there might be a case for a wholesale transfer of Berger's sociology of religion into media sociology.[24]

The final two-part link relates the social structure of the cinema to the larger culture. It is not uncommonly suggested that mass media structure, especially organisational structure, is a good reflection of the values of modern industrial societies. But this is little more than a claim that many characteristics of our most general beliefs manifest themselves in the structure of our institutions. In that sense, at least, some of us get the media we deserve! It is here that the poverty of the simple two-element analysis is most clear. This sort of suggestion can only make sense as part of a full analysis; having broken Humpty down we must put him together again. A macro-sociology which makes no such attempt falls all too easily into the trap of reification. But the elements cannot be pieced together at the conceptual level – this is only finally possible as part of empirical analysis of particular historical cases. We must begin to analyse the movies as patterns of culture firmly embedded in a complex social context.

Yet even with only four clusters of variables the potential range of analytic combination is large. Only through continuous interplay between our 'model' and the reality it purports to represent is progressive approximation possible. We might begin by exploring the effects of social structure on cinematic culture in some specified social setting. This might then be combined with a picture of the interaction between the two levels of culture. Then the internal dynamics of the institution. And so on. Ultimately we might arrive at a pattern, but 'ultimately' is a long way off. The process is slow and it does not admit of easy and premature answers based on gross and misleading assumptions. Rigorous guess-work seems as likely a strategy as any. We are seeking patterns which in the past we have wrongly imagined to be self-evident. We must beware of the same traps.

This said it is even more necessary to set limits on the rest of this book. This can only be a sketch for a part of a macro-sociology. The most likely focus is that shared by so much of the materials: the movies themselves. The reasoning is clear enough. One of the things distinguishing the cinema from most other social institutions is its explicit status as a 'culture-producer'. This it shares with the other media, with science, with religion, and with one or two others. Now, our rough analytic perspective applies equally to any sort of institution; they all have both social and cultural aspects. But in its major product the cinema externalises some part of its culture. The movies carry culture. They hardly exhaust the category, but they are surely the single most important element in it. The images, the reality conceptions, the values and beliefs, all are embedded in the films. They are the most tangible locus for analysis.

From the movies, then, we infer patterns of meaning, though this, too, is far from unproblematic. These patterns are one part of our raw materials; they substantially define cinematic culture. In some cases it is possible to go beyond specific movies, invoking the cultural conventions shared by communicators and audiences. The idea of 'genre' has value here: but it is with basic cultural configurations that we must begin. They may then be considered in relation to the other main categories of analysis: the social structures of society and institution, and the larger cultural context.[25] This task fairly naturally divides. The one relates the movies to the dynamics of the institution which produces them; the other relates them to the society in which they exist (consumption and production). The former theme has been implicit in much of this book, while the latter will predominate in what follows. When the two are combined – a distant prospect – then we have some approximation to an account of the relation between movies and society.

So the initial aim of a macro-sociology of film must be to see the movies as patterns of culture, as one element in a complicated cultural mix. There have been all sorts of views as to how these patterns actually fit into social process, how culture 'services' social life. If they were established theories then we might borrow them and apply them here. As they are, though, they can only suggest directions that our future theorising may take. Present purposes seem best served by taking various cases, variously documented, and trying to construct some order out of them. This I attempt in the two chapters that follow. It may lead to a sketch of a sketch and, in the end, to something resembling a theory. One article of faith must inform such a task: do not make premature assumptions about the direction and nature of the links between movies and society. The one thing we should have learned from the history of such studies is that we are dealing with interaction and not with simple cause and effect.

References

[1] For some idea of this variation see the 150 or so definitions discussed in A. L. Kroeber and Clyde Kluckhohn, *Culture: A Critical Review of Concepts and Definitions*, Cambridge (Mass.), 1952.

[2] Edward Shils, 'Mass Society and Its Culture', in N. Jacobs (Ed.), *Culture for the Millions?*, Van Nostrand, Princeton, New Jersey, 1951, p. 3.

[3] David Bidney, *Theoretical Anthropology*, Columbia Univ. Press, New York, 1967, p. 51.

[4] The expression originates with Peter Berger. The American edition of his *The Social Reality of Religion*, Faber, London, 1969, used the much superior title *The Sacred Canopy*. It aptly suggests the shelter provided by religion in particular and culture in general.

[5] For a perceptive discussion of the early development of these positions see George Lichtheim, 'The Concept of Ideology', *History and Theory*, reprinted in his collection of essays of the same name. On similar disputes in anthropology see D. Bidney, *op. cit.*

[6] See E. Shils, *op. cit.*

[7] D. Manning White, 'Mass Culture in America: Another Point of View', *Mass Culture: the Popular Arts in America*, Free Press, Glencoe, 1957, p. 17.

[8] For some amplification of this claim see John Berger, *Ways of Seeing*, Penguin, Harmondsworth, 1972.

[9] David Reisman, with Nathan Glazer and Reuel Denney, *The Lonely Crowd*, Yale Univ. Press, New Haven, London, 1961.

[10] C. Wright Mills, *The Power Élite*, O.U.P., New York, 1959, p. 314.

[11] See S. Hall and P. Whannel, *The Popular Arts*, Chapter 3 (Selected Bibliography). On the repressive culture of industrial society see Herbert

Marcuse, *One Dimensional Man*, Routledge, London, 1964, which makes a lot more sense in the context of his *Eros and Civilisation*, London, 1969.

[12] Denis McQuail, *Towards a Sociology of Mass Communications*, Macmillan, London, 1969, p. 35.

[13] Marshall McLuhan, *Understanding Media*, Sphere, London, 1967, p. 28.

[14] See for example, D. Reisman (Selected Bibliography); and Daniel Lerner, *The Passing of Traditional Society*, Free Press, Glencoe (Ill.), 1958.

[15] There are signs that this phase is over. One of the most recent media sociology collections betrays considerable interest in the macro-sociological issues concealed by the mass society thesis and McLuhanism. See Denis McQuail (Ed.), *Sociology of Mass Communications*, Penguin, Harmondsworth, 1972.

[16] See especially Raymond Williams, *Culture and Society, 1780–1950*, Penguin, Harmondsworth, 1961, and S. Hall and P. Whannel, *op. cit.*

[17] See Roland Robertson, *The Sociological Interpretation of Religion*, Blackwell, Oxford, 1970, pp. 65–8. For a similar classification see T. Lovell, 'Sociology of Aesthetic Structures and Contextualism', p. 332 (Selected Bibliography), in her case adapted from H. G. Martin's 'Sociology of Knowledge and Sociology of Science' (mimeo), 1970. An abridged version appears as 'The Kuhnian "Revolution" and its Implications for Sociology', in A. H. Hanson, T. Nossiter and S. Rokkan (Eds), *Imagination and Precision in Political Analysis*, Faber, London, 1973.

[18] H. Gans, 'The Creator – Audience Relationship in the Mass Media' *op. cit.*

[19] S. Kracauer, *From Caligari to Hitler*; L. Eisner; see also A. Tudor, 'Elective Affinities,' and Chapter 7 of *this* book. (See Selected Bibliography).

[20] G. Huaco, *The Sociology of Film Art*, especially pp. 18–19 (Selected Bibliography).

[21] See Lucien Goldmann, *The Hidden God*, Routledge, London, 1964. For an interesting summary discussion of structural thinking in relation to film see T. Lovell, *op. cit.*

[22] G. Huaco, *op. cit.*; Vytautas Kavolis, *Artistic Expression – a Sociological Analysis*, Cornell Univ. Press, Ithaca, New York, 1968, Part 1.

[23] S. Kracauer, *op. cit*; M. Wolfenstein and N. Leites, *Movies* (Selected Bibliography); H. Marcuse, *One Dimensional Man*, *op. cit.*

[24] See P. Berger, *The Social Reality of Religion*, *op. cit.*

[25] Since the movies are only one part of cinematic culture they should also be related to the rest of that culture. The characteristic beliefs and attitudes of the film industry is one such much mentioned relation.

Chapter 7

Cinema and Society: Film Movements

We have seen that there are various aspects to any conceptualisation of the relation between cinema and society. By and large two of them have predominated: the study of the consequences of movies for society, and the study of the consequences of society for the movies. Chapter 8 will look at the popular genres from, roughly, the first perspective. This chapter pursues one of the best loved simplifications of all sociological analysis: the reduction of a phenomenon to its social-structural base. The social-structure–cinema culture link. In its crudest manifestations this view suggests that society somehow 'causes' the movies, ignoring the fact that the relation between institution and society is one of complex interaction. However, we can still pursue the former in full recognition of the latter. Some part of the circle of causation must be abstracted, if only to be finally reconstructed into a fuller account.

It is rare to encounter such analytic problems in mass media studies, where attention has primarily been focused on consequences. The intellectual roots for studying the social-structural determinants of film are to be found elsewhere, in the European traditions of the sociologies of art and knowledge. These studies, in their turn, derive much of their emphasis from the corpus of Marxist materialism. The ultimate reduction – vulgar Marxism – is very crude indeed. It sees all things cultural as part of the superstructure, and the superstructure wholly determined by the base. Everything flows from the fundamental contradiction between means and relations of production via the concept of class.

The class structure determines art, knowledge, law, and the other superstructural phenomena. It is significant that although sociology has not inherited the rest of the Marxist apparatus, it has happily adopted the class structure/super-structure linkage. In so doing it has on occasion become a vulgarised version of 'vulgar Marxism', reducing complex social processes to the crudities of a survey research concep-tion of 'class'. Not that Marx himself was a vulgar Marxist. The subtle analyses of *The Eighteenth Brumaire of Louis Bona-parte* and *The Class Struggles in France, 1848–50* are very much aware of the complex interaction between base and super-structure, class and belief.[1]

In this context we can readily see how a roughly Marxist tradition has come to figure prominently in the sociology of art. From the aesthetics of Plekhanov or Fischer, through the elaborations of Lukacs or Goldmann, to Althusser's recent deliberations on 'overdetermination', runs a thread of interest in the determination of the superstructure.[2] All of them recognise that the superstructure in some way reflects the base, but their particular conceptions are progressively altered. While things are still fairly straightforward for Plekhanov, Goldmann is dealing with 'homology of structure', and Althusser with complex interaction determined in the *very* long run by the base. It is an interesting thread of development, though only one in the vast reaches of Marxist thought, for it is typical of a pattern found generally in the sociology of art. Nowadays it is less common for sociologists to seek straightforward causal links between social pheno-mena and art. Such interrelations are obviously more com-plex, and where we once sought causes we now try to conceptualise relations of pattern. Looser categories like 'reflection' have more currency.

This, of course, brings the tradition a little closer to the long-standing mass media studies; here 'reflection' has always been the name of the game. Though media conse-quences have received the most attention, some have also conceived popular culture as reflecting social relations and evaluations. Not that this has been constant or precise. Where popular culture could not be easily seen as a reflection it was hurriedly reconceptualised as a source of necessary catharsis. Media studies have found it too easy to shift between the two postures, an unfortunate flexibility which Lévi-Strauss has noted in another area. He makes the following comment on the anthropological study of myth:

'If a given mythology confers prominence on a certain figure, let us say an evil grandmother, it will be claimed that in such a society grandmothers are actually evil and that mythology reflects the social structure and the social relations; but should the actual data be conflicting, it would be as readily claimed that the purpose of mythology is to provide an outlet for repressed feelings.'[3]

The fact that the comment is equally applicable to media studies nicely suggests the potential confluence between the media tradition and the European structuralist analyses variously inspired by Marxism. Lévi-Strauss himself sees myth as both reflection and catharsis, though the terms are not really applicable. Myths, he argues, provide logical models for overcoming contradictions found in the socio-cultural world. They are both distorted reflections *and* ways of dealing with the contradictions they reflect.

'Structuralism', then, is a point of meeting. Catch-all that it is, it invokes Marxism, anthropology, lingusitics and semiology, in an attempt to grasp the intrinsic complexity of the relation between society and art. Not that there is a definitive structuralism. The categories of presumptive interrelation vary enormously, from reflection to homology, from affinity to transformation. But what all the various and contradictory suggestions represent is a shift away from the simple 'structural determinism' of other times toward a richer and more sensitive analysis. The sociology of popular culture and the media will do well to note this development. It does not assume that there are easy answers, and it wishes only to ensure that we remember that assumption. It demands that we understand the movies within a context, but without reducing them to that context: and above all it

looks for patterns. Of course such intellectual changes have
their penalties; 'esoteric structuralism' has been over-adopted
in some circles. Like vulgar Marxism such excesses belittle
the practitioners, not the practice. Structuralism is important
because it redirects our attention, and not for any ritual
formulae it may provide. It is a change of mood. In its light
I shall look at the particular case of the German cinema.
Though what follows *is not* a structura*list* analysis, some of
its inspiration derives from the 'paradigm for analysis' of
Chapter 5 and the analytic discussion of Chapter 6. For
reasons of style I have not gone out of my way to make these
influences explicit. Nevertheless, this analysis is founded
upon them.

THE FAMOUS CASE OF 'GERMAN EXPRESSIONISM'

There are several reasons for taking 'German Expressionism'
as a case study in the relation between society and film.
Above all it is well known and extensively documented.
For reasons which will become clear this cinema has positively
invited discussion of its relation to society. The major
studies – Kracauer's *From Caligari to Hitler* and Eisner's *The
Haunted Screen* – illustrate this fascination.[4] They both try to
probe the mass of relations between national culture,
historic event, and cinematic style. Both are in some ways
peculiarly mystic about the links; the one in psychoanalytic
vein, the other rather more traditional. Both persistently
refer to the German soul and its alleged propensities. Eisner
develops implausible 'explanations' in terms like '. . . the
German soul instinctively prefers twilight to daylight'![5]
Kracauer is less flowery though more tortured: 'the masses
are irresistibly attracted by the spectacle of torture and
humiliation' or 'the German soul . . . tossed about in gloomy
space like the phantom ship in *Nosferatu*'. But his real aim
is to see the early years of the German cinema as a *monologue
interieur* giving access to '. . . almost inaccessible layers of the
German mind'.[6] Because it was so distinctive, because it
arose in a highly unstable society, and because of the Third
Reich, the early German cinema has been *the* subject for

much generalisation. This account will try to reconsider certain of the assumptions of this received wisdom.

First, then, the materials themselves: the history, the films, and the patterns of culture contained therein. Various people have given various dates to 'German Expressionism'. Almost all of them agree on its real beginning, *The Cabinet of Dr Caligari* in 1919, though there are precursors of one sort or another. Its end is more difficult to place. The 'expressionist' film-makers continued working for many years, often in other societies, while the 'German style' diffused throughout the film-making world. Kracauer sees the shift from an open expressionist period into a 'stabilised period' around about 1924. Lotte Eisner, more interested in questions of stylistic continuity, traces distinct variations through to the coming of sound. Either way the peak seems to have been passed around the middle of the decade: 1926 saw *The Student of Prague, Faust*, and *Metropolis*, all important films in the idiom, while in the years that follow examples are rather more sparse. As the decade ended, the movement, if movement it was, lost its impetus.

Part of the difficulty of identification stems from the constant presupposition of a distinctly *expressionist* cinema. German movies from 1919 to 1926 display a range of styles and themes exhibiting some homogeneity. Critics and historians vary in their precise formulations, but the umbrella concept 'expressionism' is indeed the commonest description. Yet one must have some serious reservations about a term which lumps in a film like *The Last Laugh* with the very different *Cabinet of Dr Caligari* or *Raskolnikov*. Besides the few famous films designed to look like expressionist paintings brought to life, there are obviously other strong influences at work. Most notable is that deriving from the chiaroscuro tradition and Reinhardt's theatre, an element extensively documented in Eisner. This combines significantly with the expressionist input in ways which we shall shortly explore. Outside of this fairly coherent cluster we find other sorts of film: the 'costume films', for instance, largely dominated by Lubitsch, or the famous 'Mountain films' like *Marvels of Ski* or *Struggle with the Mountains*. Of course, the major money-spinners of the German silent screen were not exactly the elaborate products of expressionism. Yet there is some sort of core of films which displays some pattern. They include those usually labelled 'expressionist', those dealing with the super-natural and the epic, and the variously 'realistic' *Kammer-spielfilm*. The most prominent are listed here, year by year, to give some sense of character and variation.

1919 *The Cabinet of Dr Caligari*
1920 *Genuine, The Golem, Von Morgen bis Mitternachts*
1921 *Backstairs, Destiny, Shattered*
1922 *Dr Mabuse der Spieler, Nosferatu, Vanina*
1923 *Raskolnikov, The Street, The Treasure, Warning Shadows*
1924 *The Last Laugh, Die Nibelungen, Waxworks*
1925 *Chronicle of the Grey House, The Joyless Street, Variety*
1926 *Faust, Metropolis, The Student of Prague*

My discussion is cast within the terms developed in Chapter 5 and based largely on this group of films.

The most immediately obvious characteristic of these films – except for some of the *Kammerspielfilme* – is that they share a displaced setting. Any audience would be unlikely to encounter such a world outside the cinema. Often this displacement is temporal: *Metropolis* into the future; *The Golem* into the medieval past; *Die Nibelungen* into a legendary past. If not so obviously temporally displaced, they might occupy the strange half-world of *Nosferatu* or *Chronicle of the Grey House*, or the distorted grotesqueries of *Caligari* or *Genuine*. Even where the immediate setting is close to urban life, as in *The Last Laugh* or *The Street*, it is rendered alien by distortion, light, shadow, and design. Within this alienation of the films from familiar reality there is considerable varia-tion. The specific setting, for instance, is as easily rural as urban. Where it was the latter, then the excesses of expres-sionist architecture are likely; where the former, the films commonly invoked the strange landscapes of the Romantic and Gothic traditions. Social worlds vary, exhibiting little in the way of fixed patterns of sociation; there is only the individual riddled with guilt, desperation, and anxiety. The larger social world is that of the mob, the anonymous crowd.

Obviously displacement, and the visual style which encourages it, is crucial here. Style in these films reinforces the process of alienation, rendering the familiar and the intelligible beyond comprehension. It carries tremendous emotional weight, imbuing the films with feelings independent of their explicit narrative interests. Interestingly, it does not give rise to the consequences expected or desired by the expressionist theoreticians working in the other arts. The common style of the German film between 1919 and 1926 cannot be safely called expressionist. We can best see this by looking at expressionist doctrine. The concept of *abstraction* seems to be the common key. As Eisner suggests: 'The declared aim of the expressionists was to eliminate nature and attain absolute abstraction'.[7] Now 'abstraction' is a term usually applied to our processes of 'knowing' the world; by abstraction we mentally organise the chaos which surrounds us. Faced with things just as they are we would surely yield to what has been aptly called 'ontological terror'. So, by abstraction, we isolate the elements of our world, analyse them in their abstract singularity, and so render nature more intelligible. We arrive at an abstract simplification which alone enables us to see the essence of a phenomenon. We see the wood in spite of the trees. Now whatever the value of this doctrine as epistemology, the expressionists translate it into the domain of art. Expressionist art reduces its subjects to basic elements thus arriving at essences, a world of 'expressionist abstraction'.[8]

But this is still too general; there are clearly many ways in which 'expressionist abstraction' might be made manifest in film. Classic montage, for example. *Strike* and *October* are just as expressionistically abstract as the in-frame distortions of *Caligari*, *Genuine*, or *Raskolnikov*. Abstraction alone is insufficient. There is a second aim of expressionism also noted by Eisner; anti-naturalism. This is not simply a condemnation of naturalistic reproduction. It also denies validity to the naturalistic 'distortions' of impressionism. The sense can be captured in slogan-like definitions:

naturalism seeks to copy exactly; impressionism to expressively recreate: expressionism to delve beyond these mere surfaces to discover 'eternal meanings'. The combination of abstraction and anti-naturalism leads to a visual aesthetic based on freeing the object from its natural environment. This is more than a simple destruction of our normal sense of space. It involves substituting a distorted world, within which the object may be seen to be abstracted, and through which we discover truth. It is this doctrine that leads to the familiar spatial distortion, and to an acting style which tries to isolate key elements by virtue of exaggeration. Clearly enough some such beliefs find expression in the early German cinema.

Equally clearly this is only one part of the story. Though other arts may have tried to realise a pure expressionism, the cinema developed a hybrid combination with various inputs. Reinhardt's theatre, particularly his 'impressionistic' lighting and group composition, softened the jagged expressionist designs. Except for Wiene's two principal efforts, *Caligari* and *Raskolnikov*, the German style mixes expressionism and chiaroscuro together in about equal proportions, giving rise to a peculiar combination of distortion, exaggeration, abstraction, shadow, half-tone, and ambiguity. Emotionally disturbing certainly, but hardly in the philosophical sense advanced by the doctrinaire expressionists. The world created by the German style is eerie, possessing its own independent animation, darkly malevolent, and violently disturbed. Rather than revealing profound essences, these films are displaced from immediate experience and filled with desperate emotions. They are not expressionist. Indeed, the ultimate expressionist cinema would have to be entirely abstract. The early German cinema is a Romantic narrative form set in a world created by borrowed techniques.

The basic sense suggested by this stylistic pattern is mystery, and, as we shall see in the next chapter, this capacity has been widely used in the subsequent history of horror and gangster movies. This interplay of light, shadow, and design is an image of a disharmonious universe. Of such a style Kavolis says:

'. . . the image of a disharmonious universe seems likely to generate anxiety regarding man's relationship with his surroundings. The image will presumably be reflected in art styles suggestive of emotional distress experienced in relation to objects in the environment. . . . We assume the more general tendency toward deformation of visible reality to constitute the artistic expression of a sense of cosmic disharmony.'[9]

Whether distortion depends primarily on the grotesque angles and impossible perspectives of expressionist design, or the strange shadings of the chiaroscuro tradition, seems immaterial. Generally there is a mixture, and the result is largely the same. A world at odds with itself, peopled by the phantoms of both mind and spirit. Perhaps the most successful films are those that combine the styles: *Warning Shadows, Destiny, The Golem*, and *Waxworks*. Fritz Lang seems to have best mastered the mixture. In films like *Destiny, Dr Mabuse der Spieler*, and *Die Nibelungen* he combines the compositional contrasts of a modified expressionism with the skilful deployment of light for which he has since become famous. In consequence his work wears rather better than the extremities of Wiene's *Caligari*.

So, disharmony is the keynote, whatever the melody. The tortured characters of the German silent cinema are part of an alien, malevolent world, permeated by fate. They are constrained by the unknown; powerful forces wash over them; their world is dislocated within itself. They must inevitably pay Faust's price. Of course, this cluster of meanings is very generalised. By its nature artistic style deals in such generalities. It communicates an ethos, a mood, a sense of fatalism and disorder. The whole pictorial character of these visuals makes a mockery of harmony between man and environment. But within such an emotional setting some variation in theme is possible. Disharmony is an unchanging baseline which might be modified or specified in a variety of narrative structures. Kracauer, at his best in this area, singles out three such patterns. Narratives focused on the role of the tyrant; the inevitability of fate; '. . . the surge of disorderly lusts and impulses in a chaotic world'.[10] These are the principal narrative foci of the early German film.

We can interrelate them into a pattern of meanings. The many tyrants are the epitome of absolute authority. Totally unbending, unjust, and cruel, they were frequently seen as unavoidable and essential bastions against collapse into chaos. Since the whole style of the films suggests a precarious world constantly on the edge of such collapse, these authority figures occupy a crucial role. Order derives from their iron hands (Caligari, Ivan the Terrible, Haroun-al-Raschid, Mabuse, Death, etc.) and from omnipresent fate. The two are invariably intertwined, most expressively in Lang's *Destiny* where Death is both tyrant and representative of fate. Any attempt to struggle against this unholy combination can only undermine the thin fabric which holds the precarious world together; there then follows descent into chaos and an ultimate revival of authority. As Huaco concludes in his thematic analysis of *The Golem*: '. . . attempts at self-defence on the part of the oppressed can only unleash irrational, destructive forces'.[11]

So the pattern typically sees unyielding and cruel authority as a source of precarious order. The resulting world may be haunted by misery and oppression but the alternatives are not viable. Man is fated to a system revolving around an autocratic patriarch. He must repress his 'base' desires lest they bring about inevitable destruction. There are no 'heroes' in these films, though there is some pattern to the choice of protagonists. Authority figures are obviously very prominent, whether vampires or psychiatrists, arch-criminals or emperors. The seemingly more 'realistic' films are equally imbued with this familiar sense of precipitate doom, fate, and disharmony, though the protagonists here are often petty bourgeois. *Backstairs*, *The Street*, and *Shattered* threaten their characters in much the same way as do the more romantic flights of, say, Fritz Lang. Of course talents and affinities vary from director to director. Robert Wiene, over-rated because of the fame of *Caligari*, leaned most heavily on the extravagances of expressionist design. Lang, most notably in *Dr Mabuse der Spieler*, *Destiny*, and *Die*

L

Nibelungen, was rather more heavy-handed than in his later American films, repeatedly emphasising the implacability of fate and the need for stringent authority. Murnau, however was more subtle than most. *Faust* apart, his films look more closely than usual at the machinery of authority, often finding something of positive value. Nosferatu is actually defeated, and Murnau also seems least subject to the extremes of the 'German style'. While *The Last Laugh* has the definite look of a German silent film, it is more restrained than usual, both visually and morally. In documenting the collapse of authority consequent on removing its external symbols, Murnau manages to both ridicule and sympathise. Such shades of grey are unusual in the German silent cinema.

But all these are variations of emphasis which nevertheless feed off one basic corpus of themes. Particular narratives may show the disintegration and death of 'ordinary' people (*The Street, Backstairs, The Last Laugh*); a hopeless struggle against fate (*Destiny, The Golem, Die Nibelungen, The Student of Prague*); or an equally hopeless struggle against tyrannical authority (*Vanina, Waxworks, Warning Shadows*). They may adopt various attitudes. The 'revised' version of *Caligari* clearly praises the benevolent authoritarian; to oppose him is literal madness. *Destiny* is ambivalent in its attitudes to authority, other than recognising its inevitability. *Genuine* demonstrates the dire consequences of unbridled sexuality. They range from the naïve authoritarinism of the Wiene film to the differing ambiguities of Lang and Murnau. Certainly the overall thematic cluster is most easily associated with the political right; it is both illiberal and negative, imbued with a deep pessimism. But it is an unwarranted simplification – though a tempting one – to reduce the phenomenon to conservative ideology. While it is that, it is also more.

Unfortunately, such undiscriminating categorisation finds support in the traditional social structural accounts. The influence is that of a vulgar Marxism wherein the cinema is conceived as a simple ideological emanation of the class structure. Not that the case is entirely implausible. After the war the German economy collapsed, class conflict intensified, the Russian success stimulated pressure toward revolution, the SDP rose to power, the Spartacists were in full cry, and in 1919 Rosa Luxembourg and Karl Liebknecht were murdered by the Freikorps. In short, this particular capitalist society was glaringly unstable, and this instability found expression in the characteristic disharmony of the films of the early twenties. Dominated by reactionaries, the film industry sponsored films bemoaning this state of affairs, if indirectly. Where the originating artists did not hold to these views (uncommon, but clearly the case with Mayer and Janowitz, authors of *Caligari*) the industry ensured that the films were altered accordingly.[12] The cinema became a conservative weapon in the class war, and a simple epiphenomenon of the material base.

Basically there are two things wrong with this sort of account. As I have suggested, the German cinema is not so easily reduced to simple conservative ideology. It is a little more complex. Moreover, though German society was clearly in the throes of enormous convulsions, its basic contradictions are more involved than can be easily conceptualised in vulgar Marxist terms. Such theories, suspiciously implicit in Huaco, are only adequate to suitably vulgarised versions of the films themselves.[13] While it may be superficially plausible, it is only the very beginning of an account. Its errors are symmetrical to the extravagances of Kracauer and Eisner. Where they invoke idealist conceptions of soul and spirit, vulgar Marxism (or vulgar Sociologism) treats the categories of materialism similarly. The ills of capitalism were to be found in a number of societies of the period, yet only Germany produced this particular cinema. It is this particularity that is missing from the standard accounts.

The question is far from simple. It demands two sorts of answer, only one of which will be a principal focus here. This is the attempt to relate the general dynamic of that period in German society to the films. The specific detail of the link – institutions, people, events – is only possible within the more general context. So, what did produce the German cinema? As we know German society was indeed facing imminent chaos. The political extremes were in variously open conflict. The old social structure, long familiar, had fallen. An elaborate left-over of feudal domination had given way to an ill-fated attempt at democracy. Accelerated by the war, Germany was encountering the classic problems of a society undergoing rapid social change. The new forms of social relations, the pressures to democratisation, the innovations, the whole social apparatus of the society was outstripping the beliefs, attitudes, and reality-conceptions of the people. Take a simplified model. For generations a society operates on the basis of particular forms of social relations based on a rigid, hierarchical, autocratic social structure. Succeeding generations grow up to believe in the givenness of the social order, the divine rights of aristocratic rule, in the familiar social reality. Social forms are legitimated by the prevailing culture. Social relations and the beliefs of man-in-society fit each other perfectly in a vicious circle of confirmation and acceptance. Then, for many reasons, predominantly external, some part of this social edifice collapses. The old fixed structures are destroyed. Now there is a drastic disjunction between the new forms and the still well-established beliefs about what is permissible or even possible. People continue to believe in the old, though the new is increasingly common.

Not that such a phenomenon is uncommon. Some such disjunction is always present, just as some sort of social change is always present. Many of the conflicts in modern societies stem from just such incongruencies, but the German case was indeed extreme. Traditional culture was well-embedded, even in the more industrialised sectors of society. Of course even this can be overcome if those in control have the ruthlessness and perception of, for example, Lenin and Stalin in the Soviet Union. In Germany, perhaps only Rosa Luxembourg had a genuine appreciation of the situation, and she was rapidly eliminated. The culture itself is a peculiar mixture, plausibly characterised by Parsons, in a brilliant essay, as 'Prussian Conservatism'.[14] He describes it basically as combining a belief in patriarchal authoritarianism with an emphasis on the legalistically formal. The need for order and strong rule is important, and there are considerable Lutheran undercurrents.

'This world is dominated by sin, mitigated only by the restraining influence of ordained authority. Society is not and can never be a Kingdom of God on Earth, but is fundamentally a vale of tears. In its application to the role of authority, this pattern favours a certain realism, for instance with respect to the advisability of adequate military protection of one's territory but its benevolent patriarchalism readily slips over into a kind of hash authoritarianism and even into a cynical pursuit of power in defiance of the welfare of the masses of people. Government is to it a grim business. . .'[15]

All of which is reflected in the symbolic materials of social intercourse, in the emphasis on uniform as a basis for clear role definitions, in the elaborate formalism of modes of address and conversation, and in the endless strings of titles.

It is this set of beliefs which serviced the structure of pre-Wiemar Germany, and which remained as an ill-fitting left-over after the collapse of the old order. If the new system can be *made* to work, as it was in the Soviet Union, then perhaps this 'cultural lag' might be overcome. But Wiemar Germany failed demonstrably. Economic and political crises proliferated. A residual faith in the old ways was accompanied by the ever-present failures of the new. The gap grew larger instead of smaller. It is this context of acute discontinuity which finds expression in the German cinema of the period. Each individual element was derived from traditional culture; but their ultimate combination is moulded from the drastic contradictions between the culture and the social structure itself. Parsons' description of Prussian conservatism might equally apply to the thematic world of the early German cinema. Theirs was indeed a 'world dominated by sin, mitigated only by the restraining influence of ordained authority'. Benevolent patriarchalism was frequently indistinguishable from harsh authoritarianism. The films certainly expressed something of the old culture.

But as we have seen they did rather more than this. They responded to this disorganised social world, to this lack of socio-cultural harmony, with the dislocations, ambiguities and shadows of the German style. It is important to note that this is a very special impetus toward utilising expressionist techniques. In other cultural contexts expressionism developed as a *Weltanschuang* antagonistic to that of bourgeois society and definitionally opposed to the *status quo*. In collapsing the normal sense of spatial order it negated the given sense of reality. In this sense it was a revolutionary doctrine. Yet in the German cinema it came to express the opposite. Here it was adapted to convey a sense of disharmony and imminent chaos only ultimately prevented by authoritarian rule. Far from being a *Weltanschuang*, in the German cinema expressionism was incorporated into a bundle of techniques with certain specific aims. Things were wrong between the individual and his world; basic things were at odds with each other. These films combined the values of traditional German culture with an emotive evocation of contemporary disorder. Their moral conclusion was inescapable. On occasion the allegories were more specific. In an interview with Huaco, Erich Pommer (Producer of Lang's *Dr Mabuse der Spieler*) explains that the film was explicitly intended to portray the struggle between Spartacists and moderates, the arch-villain himself representing the Spartacists.[16]

It makes sense, then, to see early German cinema as an affirmation of traditional culture in the face of socio-cultural disintegration. Although they are displaced in setting, the films are 'about' the contemporary German experience in that they express a response to it. In Lang's case the parallel is deliberate. But the pattern in general need not be part of the conscious motivation of the film-makers. Movies are an articulation of the responses of their creators to their world, in this case constrained by the particular techniques available and the styles considered acceptable. For the German cinema of the early twenties the core meanings are those I have discussed. Other common factors – displacement, the dire consequences of sexuality – relate primarily to this cluster. Thus, the much remarked fascination with personal disintegration consequent upon sexual license is more than a prudish moralism.[17] It is deeply embedded in the whole pattern of culture fundamental to these German movies. The outer order derived from iron authority must be matched by an inner, psychological constraint. Powerful individual impulses, of which the sexual urge is archetypal, must be repressed in the cause of ordered survival. In this moral universe chaos is only prevented by stringent authoritarianism and widespread repression, by the promotion of the 'one-dimensional man'.[18] Ultimately this cinema is a fundamentalist response to the radical dislocations of a changing society. The old culture is erected as a bastion against social and psychological disruption, more in resignation than fervour. In its fatalistic way the German cinema simply sees no alternative.

FILM MOVEMENTS

The links between German cinema and society remain imprecise. We have seen that the films express a definite configuration of meaning. We have suggested some socio-cultural sources for these meanings, sources in social structure, in culture, and in their combination. We have seen that the German style is formed from the bits and pieces of expressionism, impressionist theatre, the cultural heritage of chiaroscuro, and the related Romantic/Gothic tradition. The resulting combination is a visual expression of the disharmonious universe created by a radically changing society. We have also seen how the thematic obsessions of the movies faithfully reflect the concerns and emphases of traditional German culture. At the level of meaning there is clearly a plausible relation between cinema and society. Part of the picture has been blocked in: but this is obviously insufficient; it can only be a rough beginning, not a culmination. It remains to discover the patterns of social process which relate the contradictions and predispositions of the larger society to the films in question. In some parts, and in some cases, these processes may be unique. An account

would begin and end with specific historical events. But
there may also be processes common to a range of comparable cases, recognisable patterns of determination. To
even begin such a formulation would require extensive
comparative materials to be endlessly sifted and re-ordered.
Film history and criticism has conducted such research with
the concept of 'film movements': a class of phenomena
which have some presumptive relation to their different social
contexts. We could do worse than to come at the problem
from this angle.

It is customary to speak of the early German cinema as a
'movement' in company with two other cases: the Soviet
cinema of the twenties and the Italian cinema of the late
forties and early fifties. The very act of labelling has served
to confirm their distinctive status. German expressionism
and Italian neo-realism are terms with wide currency, however
unsuitable they might be. And though the Soviet case has no
special name, for many critics and historians it is identified
with Soviet cinema as such. Huaco, who studies all three, terms
it 'Expressive Realism', a practice which I will follow here.
However, there has been little explicit discussion of the bases
on which these three cases are to be considered distinctive.
We can only inspect the examples themselves to discover the
implicit criteria on which such 'movements' are defined.
Inspection suggests three very obvious characteristics. First,
unlike the application of 'movement' in other arts, here the
term is limited to specific societies. In addition, the societies
in question had all experienced a drastic sociocultural
trauma immediately prior to the rise of the 'movement'.
All were involved in major wars, two meeting defeat and
the third revolution. Lastly, they all developed distinctively new approaches to cinema, at least, in their particular
time and place. They represent some form of 'aesthetic
break'.[19]

This last seems to be the more important. Limitation to a
specific society is an understandable but hardly necessary
characteristic. It reflects commercial strictures and difficulties of communication, as well as the peculiarities of
historical context. But it is surely quite reasonable to conceive

of film movements transcending national boundaries, especially in these days of what Guback terms the 'international film industry'.[20] Prior development of socio-cultural trauma is obviously an important formative influence, but surely not characteristic of a movement as such. The so-called 'British New Wave' has many of the marks of a movement but was hardly preceded by social disorder of the magnitude of the three classic cases. While it seems very likely that major disruptions will call forth an aesthetic break, they are certainly not sufficient and may not even be necessary. So, whatever the causation and context, the term 'film movement' first suggests innovation, and not simply piecemeal diffusion. The phenomenon involves a distinct grouping of films which share in the break, something Huaco describes, not without ambiguity, as 'stylistically homogenous clusters'.[21]

A movement, then, is first of all a distinct cluster of films representing a break with the films of the past. In the historic cases, Wiene's *The Cabinet of Dr Caligari*, Eisenstein's *Strike*, and Rossellini's *Open City* mark the point of disjuncture. But it is all obviously a matter of degree. Closer inspection inevitably reveals that they represent continuities as well as departures. How could it be otherwise? Even the most drastic of revolutions is forced to retain much of what has gone before. Though the German style brought much that was new, it showed little moral discontinuity. Neither the Soviet nor the Italian case can be reasonably seen as *absolute* breaks with the past. This is more than merely splitting hairs, since, if we are dealing with degree, it becomes strictly impossible to draw a line between the three historically accepted cases and any number of brief flowerings of invention scattered throughout film history. The closer one looks the more threads of continuity are seen to cross the line of fracture. There are shifts in emphasis, 'stylistically homogenous clusters', reversions, and booms, coming and going all the time. The cinema is variously dynamic and evolving. It is certainly true that the historic cases are very clear disruptions in glaringly obvious socio-cultural contexts. This is why they have received so much attention. But if they are to be truly distinct as 'movements' then some further criterion must be found. As it is they do not differ qualitatively from most other processes of changes in the cinema; they are merely massively dramatic examples.

There does seem to be a further distinguishing factor. In discussing the French *nouvelle vague* as a movement, Terry Lovell clarifies the concept:

' "Movement" is an intentional concept, implying collective action towards some conscious goal. A. F. C. Wallace's definition of "revitalisation movement" is pertinent: "a deliberate and self-conscious attempt to provide a more satisfying culture".'[22]

'Movement' is thus reserved for those aesthetic breaks consequent upon collective and self-conscious actions of the artists involved. Now there are two rough forms of change in the cinema. There are those developments which, Topsy-like, just grow: evolution, the 'normal' state of affairs. From a potent combination of commercial and social pressures, long-standing beliefs and personal inclination, commitment and whim, comes a never-ceasing process of amendment, re-emphasis, and alteration. Clearly the potential permutations are enormous, and, for this very reason as much as any, the process is hardly amenable to immediate and cryptic generalisation. Instead attention has focussed at the other extreme where common consciousness and unity of intent make analysis that much simpler. The better defined the movement, the less problematic its study. Many cases are actually mixtures of the two extremes, such as the popular genres to be discussed at length in Chapter 8. In their early days they evolved in relatively indiscriminate fashion depending, above all, on the positive feedback of commercial success. But though commerce continues to act as a sort of cybernetic governor, some degree of collective genre-consciousness also influences change. The rise of the 'psychological western', for instance, is one such mixed phase. But there does seem to be a clear gap between such mixed processes and the 'extreme' movements. The combination of radical aesthetic break and intentionality gives some sense to the distinction.

Once identified in these terms, the change is better studied. If we are able to demonstrate the structured potential of the situation (as we have roughly done for the German case) then the idea of a movement links precondition with event. Where there is no such possibility the links are that much more devious, and we are most likely to have to fall back on diffuse ideas of reflection. Hence the case-study attraction of the three historic cases. For the most part the artists involved in these movements clearly did share common goals. The Soviet post-revolutionary film-makers openly saw themselves building a new cinema in the spirit of that event. They were providing a 'more satisfying culture'. The neo-realists shared a strong political bond of anti-Nazism (many of them were Marxists), as well as a conscious recognition of their role in creating a socially responsive and responsible cinema. The French *nouvelle vague* had at its core the articulations of the *Cahiers du Cinéma* group. They were all aware of the disjunction between their desired cinema and that of the past. And though there is little in the way of evidence independent of their film-making activity, from the scattered interviews and memoriams we can infer similar characteristics on the part of the Germans. Not as clear as the others, perhaps, but sufficient to provisionally merit the 'movement' label.

Let us look once more at the German case. Seeing it as a movement allows us to borrow certain conceptualisations from elsewhere. We can, for instance, take Neil Smelser's approach to the analysis of collective behaviour, recognising that its utility is only as a simple basis of organisation.[23] He classifies the essential determinants of collective behaviour under a set of headings: structural conduciveness, structural strain; generalised belief; precipitating factors, mobilisation; social controls. All of them play some part in determining the consequent episode of collective behaviour, in our case, the movement. First, the structured context itself must permit such a possibility. This given, there must be some socio-cultural root for the development, conceptualised by

Smelser in the unsatisfactory term 'strain'. There must be a general belief which spreads through the group pinpointing their common antipathies and aims. There must be some final precipitating event and some basis and pattern of mobilisation for action. Finally, we must include the potential restraining influences of the larger social context; their means of controlling the episode, if means they have.[24] All of which is hardly a theory, more a pattern into which we might organise our ideas on the range of crucial factors influencing the German movement. They can be usefully taken in two groups, with the addition of the rather separate 'social control' category.

Conduciveness and Strain. These two headings encompass most of the contextual factors involved in precipitating a film movement. Some derive from the larger socio-cultural world; others from the more immediate context of film making. The former has already been discussed at some length. In that discussion we saw how the concerns of traditional German culture were reflected in the thematic obsessions of the films. How 'strain' in German society, specifically the disjunction between established culture and new social forms, found expression in the dominant style of the period. How they combined in the movies to proffer an authoritarian resolution of the prevalent contradictions of Wiemar Germany. The socio-cultural situation was surely conducive to some form of aesthetic break; its specific content dictated a good deal of the form of that break.

There were also a number of developments, largely within the institution of the cinema, which facilitated subsequent events. Almost all began in the war years and came to fruition in the early twenties. This is not just temporal coincidence. Apart from its obviously far-reaching effects in the society at large, the war itself had a good deal of material influence on the cinema. It generally stimulated production. Cut off from what was rapidly becoming the standard source of movies – America – the German film industry was forced to plough its own furrow. One indirect consequence, later to prove very important, was that the

German cinema survived rather longer in the face of the American than did its European contemporaries, though whether the consequences were as extensive as Rositi suggests is a moot point.[25] But it is certainly true that the war years saw a great deal of basic development in the German industry. Production facilities expanded, film-makers, performers, and writers gained experience, and, stimulated by the propaganda need, the industry increased the number of domestic outlets for its product. In stimulating these developments, the war ensured that the basic materials for an aesthetic break were actually available. The magnificent technical apparatus, later to prove so effective, was cajoled into growth by war and blockade. Not unnaturally this was paralleled by an increasing elaboration of the commercial structure, progressively approaching monopoly.[26] The early twenties saw a rapid assimilation of the many small production companies into the cartel-like UFA. Decla-Bioscop, a crucial moving force in the movement, was thus assimilated in 1921. Such a structure is clearly conducive to considerable centralised control, and did apparently result in widespread ideological homogeneity. So, along with the material preconditions for extensive output came the organisational preconditions for its control.

By 1919, however, the commercial need was to maintain the war induced industry against the revived challenge of American movies, a need which gave rise to the basic internal 'stains" of Wiemar cinema. Erich Pommer in his interview with Huaco:

'Germany was defeated; how could she make films that would compete with the others? It would have been impossible to try and imitate Hollywood or the French. So we tried something new: the expressionist or stylised films. This was possible because Germany had an overflow of good artists and writers, a strong literary tradition, and a great tradition of theater. This provided a basis of good trained actors. World War I finished the French industry; the problem for Germany was to try to compete with Hollywood.'[27]

In this way a commercially conscious industry is subject to competitive pressures toward something new, toward an aesthetic break. We have seen some of the factors which go to determine the precise form of the break; those contextual elements touched on briefly here and extensively discussed earlier in the chapter. Pommer adds some more, and one might also point to the educational, social, and political backgrounds of the film-makers themselves.[28] The social, cultural, and commercial situations were thus conducive to some development. The technical facilities were there, as were the technicians to operate them. The 'strains', social and cinematic, were clearly established. The scene was set.

Belief, Precipitation, and Mobilisation. It is unfortunate that there is not the same independent evidence of collective belief among the German film-makers as there is for the other historic cases. We can only assume that in the closed world of UFA domination there was a good deal of interaction. There is surely no doubt that these men shared many latent beliefs; they had studied in similar contexts, worked within the orbit of Reinhardt's theatre, came from similar classes, and so on. But they have left no *Cahiers du Cinéma*, no film school, and no body of theoretical writings. We can only recognise that certain topics were current in German intellectual life of that period and that there is no reason to exempt the German film-makers from these concerns. Expressionism in art, concern with the state of German society, and what Lang once described as 'pessimism for its own sake'[29] were some of the issues of the period. It seems reasonable to hypothesise that the film-makers did come to believe in the potential value of their newly developed style (Pommer, who dominated production, certainly believed in its commercial potential) and in their common 'authoritarian' response to the situation. Present data permits us no more.

The precipitating factor is rather easier to recognise. As one would expect it has a strong commercial component. Because of Pommer's perseverence and public relations skills, *The Cabinet of Dr Caligari*, a failure in 1919, became a startling success in 1920.[30] As we have seen the preconditions were all present. They needed only a trigger, and that was provided by this sudden proof that the new style had commercial potential. The safes were unlocked, as aesthetic, moral, political, and commercial interests joined hands over the grotesque somnambulist's coffin. The German style began its mobilisation, and continued in full flood to the middle of the decade. Its expansion was paralleled by that of the industry itself, and Pommer rode his support of *Caligari* to control of UFA. His company Decla produced *Caligari*. The following year Bioscop remade *The Golem*, directed by Paul Wegener, and carrying many of the marks of the fledgling movement. Decla and Bioscop then merged, films like *Genuine* (the only commercial failure of the group), and *Destiny* established the pattern, and Pommer drew together the threads with UFA. After two years the movement was in full swing.

Social Control. Apart from the ever present commercial restraints – persistent financial failures have a way of disappearing – there seem to have been two major sources of control. One stems from the domination of the industry by men of particular attitudes. The occasional and dramatic 'conspiracy theory' accusations were not without basis. Kracauer mentions the Phoebus scandal, when it was discovered that this film company had been extensively financed by secret Reichswehr funds, and he notes that the Prussian conservative, Hugenberg, took control of UFA after Pommer's departure.[31] It seem likely that control by the right of the political spectrum ensured certain limits on what was and was not permitted. The second source of control is more indirect, and was sufficiently 'positive' to bring about the effective end of the movement. It began in the notorious inflation of 1923, an economic disaster which had not initially had drastic effects on the film industry. The measures introduced to deal with the crisis, however, were far from beneficial to the movement.

In 1924 came the Dawes Plan, an attempt to solve the worst of the German economic problem. In the cinema it brought in a great deal of American investment while

drastically cutting the export market. Most historians seem
to agree that the American film industry enthusiastically
grasped this opportunity to infiltrate and undermine. The
Parafumet agreement of 1926 is a major example, its terms
permitting MGM and Paramount to plant both feet solidly
in the doorway. Not only did their investment guarantee
them 50 per cent exhibition in Germany, it also, quite
fatally for the movement, precipitated the wholesale departure of German film-makers to American shores. Of the
major figures Lang held out the longest. Berger, Dupont,
Leni, Lubitsch, Murnau, and Pick were soon gone, accompanied by Jannings, the major acting figure, and lesser
performers like Pola Negri and Conrad Viedt. By the end
of the decade many more had followed them. In this way the
American industry exercised fatal control, ensuring the
decline of the movement by removing its major members.
In 1927 Pommer found himself unable to refuse an American
offer. With Lang he had just produced *Metropolis*: perhaps
this event and this film were the symbolic ends of the whole
episode.

Of course many of the predisposing factors were still there.
German society was far from stable and would not be so
until the Third Reich. Indeed, many of the events and
inclinations which we have seen to be central to the 'expressionist' movement may also have played their part in
subsequent German developments. Kracauer sees a continuous chain running from *Caligari* to Hitler, a thesis which is,
at the least, plausible. But in removing the artists, the
American industry had eliminated one of a whole set of
essential factors, leaving the impetus, of which this cinema
had been an expression, to find other channels of development. What had been a crucial cultural configuration, as
someone once said, died a quiet death.

It is not easy to conclude a discussion such as this. By
taking the German movement in some detail I have tried to
illustrate some of the ways in which society affects the
cinema. It is clear that the most traditional postures in the
sociology of art – different forms of materialism – are not
completely wrong, but certainly inadequate. The closer one

looks, the less simply deterministic is the picture, the more rich the interrelations between culture, social structure, institution, and society. It seems likely that this is even more true for cases other than the historic movements. In a 'movement' we are dealing with a distinct sub-culture, its members conscious of their position and their goals, artificially compressed in time, and representing more or less radical breaks with the past. Such singularity has some advantages for the sociologist which he would not find in more 'normal' circumstances. There, the social processes, of which these are crystallised examples, are more blurred and indirect. But they do belong to the same world, to the same sorts of associations between institution and society. They are some part of understanding the cinema. To understand them further we must move on to the 'popular genres'.

References

[1] See Karl Marx, *The Eighteenth Brumaire of Louis Bonaparte*, Moscow Pub. Hse, Moscow, 1967, and *The Class Struggle in France, 1848–50*, Moscow, 1968.

[2] G. V. Plekhanov, *Art and Social Life*, Lawrence & Wishart, London, 1953; Ernst Fischer, *The Necessity of Art*, Penguin, Harmondsworth, 1963; Georg Lukacs, *The Historical Novel*, Merlin, London, 1962; Lucien Goldmann, *The Hidden God*, Routledge, London, 1964; Louis Althusser, *For Marx*, Penguin, 1969.

[3] Claude Lévi-Strauss, *Structural Anthropology*, Penguin, Harmondsworth, 1968, pp. 207–8.

[4] S. Kracauer, *From Caligari to Hitler*; L. Eisner (see Selected Bibliography.) For a discussion of these two studies, partly utilised in the present chapter, see A. Tudor, 'Elective Affinities' (Selected Bibliography).

[5] L. Eisner, *op. cit.*, p. 51.

[6] S. Kracauer, *op. cit.*, pp. 60, 107, 217.

[7] L. Eisner, *op. cit.*, p. 151.

[8] See Wilhelm Worringer, *Abstraction and Empathy*, Routledge, London, 1953.

M

[9] Vytautas Kavolis, *Artistic Expression – a Sociological Analysis*, Cornell Univ. Press, Ithaca, New York, 1968, pp. 117–18. Kavolis goes on to quote evidence in support of this assertion.

[10] S. Kracauer, *op. cit.*, p. 96.

[11] G. Huaco, *The Sociology of Film Art*, p. 41 (Selected Bibliography).

[12] For an account of the *Caligari* case see S. Kracauer, *op. cit.*, Chapter 5. Basically Pommer and Wiene placed the original story in a framing plot which ensures that the doctor was ultimately seen as benevolent and the story itself the nightmare of a lunatic.

[13] See G. Huaco, *op. cit.*, 'Introduction', and especially pp. 18–22. This is hardly the place to enter into an extended discussion of Huaco's sociological framework, though it is difficult to resist commenting on his rather odd combination of Marx and Smelser. For a lengthy review, see A. Tudor, 'Sociology and the Cinema', *Views*, **11**, 1966, pp. 62–4.

[14] Talcott Parsons, 'Democracy and Social Structure in Pre-Nazi Germany', in his *Essays in Sociological Theory*, Free Press, Glencoe (Ill.), 1964.

[15] T. Parsons, *ibid.*, pp. 109–10.

[16] G. Huaco, *op. cit.*, pp. 45–6.

[17] Huaco finds it extremely common; Kracauer embeds it in one of his three major categories, i.e. 'instinct films'.

[18] Cf. Marcuse's discussion of repressive society: H. Marcuse, *Eros and Civilisation*, Routledge, London, 1969, and *One Dimensional Man*, Routledge, London, 1968.

[19] There may be some analogues to Kuhn's well-known account of 'paradigm change' in science. See Thomas Kuhn, *The Structure of Scientific Revolutions*, Chicago Univ. Press, Chicago, 1962. However, as T. Lovell suggests, caution is to be recommended in making such parallels. See her discussion of the question in T. Lovell, 'Sociology of Aesthetic Structures and Contextualism', especially pp. 337–8 (Selected Bibliography). Cf. also the concept of the 'epistemological break' in L. Althusser, *op. cit.*

[20] T. Guback (Selected Bibliography).

[21] See G. Huaco, *op. cit.*, 'Introduction'.

[22] T. Lovell, 'Sociology and the Cinema" *Screen*, **12**, 1, 1971. On revitalisation movements see A. F. C. Wallace, 'Revitalisation Movements', *American Anthropologist*, **58**, 1956.

[23] See T. Lovell, 'Sociology and the Cinema', *op. cit.*, and the rather differently organised discussion in 'Sociology of Aesthetic Structures and Contextualism', *op. cit.* The latter reflects her dissatisfaction with the Smelserian analysis as a 'mere organisation' (personal correspondence).

[24] Niel J. Smelser, *Theory of Collective Behaviour*, Routledge, London, 1962,

pp. 13–20. This, of course, is just one crude element from Smelser's extensive and elaborate theory.

[25] G. Galli and F. Rositi (Selected Bibliography).

[26] Of the standard histories only H. H. Wollenberg, *Fifty Years of German Film*, London, 1948, seems to have any dispute about the monopoly claim.

[27] G. Huaco, *op. cit.*, pp. 35–6.

[28] For a brief breakdown see *ibid.*, pp. 85–8.

[29] From Fritz Lang, 'Happily Ever After', *Penguin Film Review*, No. 5, London, 1948. Quoted in Paul M. Jenson, *The Cinema of Fritz Lang*, New York, London, 1969, p. 13.

[30] For Pommer's own account see G. Huaco, *op. cit.*, p. 34.

[31] See S. Kracauer, *op. cit.*, pp. 133–4.

Chapter 8

Cinema and Society: Popular Genres

Unlike film 'movements', the 'popular' cinema has usually been thought of in terms of its consequences for society; its genres conceived to be meeting some need for catharisis, for acting out, for diversion, and for the affirmation of widely held values. This is intelligible partly in terms of cultural prejudice. Genres, as part of popular cinema, belong to mass culture. Their sociological significance is assumed to lie in their role as determinants of the actions of the 'masses'. But 'movements' are respected as art: the articulation of important themes by intellectuals. They come within the domain of the sociology of art and knowledge.[1] Ironically enough, that context has made it seem more sensible to see movies as determined by society.

However, there are better reasons than this for the distinction, sketchy though it may be. Popularity, for instance. Hollywood genres are among the world's most widespread cultural forms. It thus seems almost perverse not to ask what consequences such a popular form may have for the societies in which it appears. 'Film movements' do not have such popularity; their appeal is more limited. There are also distinctions of substance. Genre movies are only rarely disturbing, innovative, or openly 'deviant'. There are obvious commercial reasons why this should be so. The very existence of a set of conventionalised genre parameters constrains movies toward a norm. A genre is a relatively fixed culture pattern. It defines a moral and social world, as well as a physical and historical environment. By its nature, its very familiarity, it inclines toward reassurance. Certainly, outstanding film-makers may use a genre in unusual ways; the existence of established rules makes a film which breaks them that much more striking. In recent years Sam Peckinpah's westerns have employed such techniques, most notably *The Wild Bunch* and *Ride the High Country*. 'Movements', although they also become established cultural patterns, exist by virtue of their deviation. They are something new. Seen contemporaneously they are often thought of as radical, some sort of new cinematic experience. However, this should not disguise that fact that their social dynamics are similar to those of the genres. They develop a particular cultural pattern and an audience educated in their special characteristics. Both constitute cinematic subcultures.

There is a similar social process here. The cinema (comprising audience, communicators, and medium) throws up many potential sub-institutions. Like religious sects these innovations either survive briefly as a distinct pattern (e.g. Italian neo-realism), or become established as a regular part of the cinematic scene (e.g. the western). Either way they are part of a complete circle of causation; they act on society and society acts on them. What starts life as a movement may end as an established genre, though the three genres I shall explore (the western, the gangster movie, the horror movie) did not start in this way. These three all evolved fairly slowly and from relatively clear roots. The gangster movie showed the most dramatic growth but this is easily understood in terms of 'cashing in' on current affairs, and not as a sudden and radical break. These genres represent a kind of evolution – a 'survival of the popular'. Bit by bit communicators produce new variations, audiences accept or reject them, they are continued or discarded, and so the genre slowly evolves. Stage by stage it shifts from 'sect' to 'denomination'.

This rather slower development of the genres is intimately involved with the open commercial motivations of their beginnings. In the enormous expansion of operations of the First World War, mass production brought with it the concomitant of all economies of scale: standardisation. According to Jacobs, by 1918 every studio planned some part of its production in terms of 'formula pictures': action pictures, westerns, 'shockers', comedies, and the like.[2]

Producers experimented to find popular subjects, categorised them, and used these categories to define their future efforts, finally giving rise to the elaborate classifications of Hollywood audience research.[3] Inevitably this 'what works once, works again' principle led to a cyclical tendency in the popular genres. The pattern repeats itself at intervals considered commercially judicious. In this way the popular genres grew up with the cinema itself. They had no unique identifiable beginnings, and it made more sense to look at their consequences than their genesis. Of course there have been attempts to explain their rise and popularity. A number of French analysts of the western have argued that its popularity and development had much to do with a need to have American national identity affirmed. They suggest that the early silent westerns, independent of language as they were, met some such need among American immigrant populations. Alan Lovell makes a pertinent comment on this thesis:

'. . .it seems reasonable to suggest that the cinema acted as a focus for national consciousness in America at the beginning of the century except that when one looks at the films (*The Great Train Robbery*, the Bronco Billy series, Tom Mix films) they seem to have very little in them that could possibly feed national consciousness.'[4]

To talk about consequences, however, it is necessary to talk about meanings. There are a number of traditional ways of dealing with such issues. Generally they see popular culture as a means of satisfying frustrated needs and as a way of confirming widely accepted attitudes. There is obviously some truth here, but such arguments are not improved by their tendency toward mass psychoanalysis. Barker, for example, sees the western as a special sort of fantasy in which the audience identifies with the hero. This is unexceptionable. However, he fills the thesis out with some wilder psychoanalytic claims:

'The cowboy's faithful horse – the object of such solicitude, pride, and respect – probably represents the hero's narcisstically overvalued phallus and also the father as totem animal.'[5]

It is difficult to see how one could hope to evaluate such a claim! Emery, also on the western, is no less problematic, though a little less extravagant. He sees the appeal as primarily Oedipal; the conflict between superego and id is manifested in good-versus-bad.[6] On the horror movie Clarens waxes more poetic:

'. . . we are to consider the Horror Film as the Cinema of Obsession, the rendering unto film of the immanent fears of mankind: damnation, demonic possession, old age, death, in brief, the night side of life. In Jungian fashion, I feel more compelled to single out and explore the visionary than the psychological.'[7]

These approaches – though in practice this is much less true of Clarens' useful historical discussion – rest their analysis on some view of the 'collective unconscious'. In translating the movie into psychoanalytic language they borrow spurious legitimacy from the widespread belief that we can thus dig below the surface. Without prior acceptance of the vast apparatus of psychoanalytic theory this faith is misplaced.

Because of such characteristic extravagance there seems some case for a more prosaic analysis. The question at issue is the potential meanings of a popular genre to its audience. From such simple groundwork it might be possible to get some idea of the emphases and functions of popular culture. So, this chapter will be given over to analysing the patterns of meaning to be found in three major surviving genres. All three of them are well established, the western and the gangster movie quite exceptionally so. These two are widely permeated through television as well as the movies. Horror movies are rather less widespread and more openly sub-cultural in their appeal. As we have already seen they command 'special show' status. But all three of them have passed through similar developments and have fairly clear histories. I shall treat each one in roughly the same fashion. Starting with a survey of their development, I shall make only some mention of the social factors influencing that development before analysing the main patterns of meaning which characterise the genre. My guideline for this 'content analysis' is the paradigm developed in Chapter 5. In the first and most famous case, the western, this will be preceded by a brief discussion of one particular critical perspective on the genre, the reasons for which should become clear. Once given this base-line description of the three genres it is reasonable to discuss the potential social role of such patterns of meaning without making totally illegitimate assumptions. In other words this discussion is strictly exploratory; it makes no claims to be a full and detailed sociological account.

THE WESTERN

If there is a single keynote to contemporary discussion of the western it lies with Henry Nash Smith.[8] He sees two broad symbolic clusters hanging over the treatment of the West in American culture: the 'Garden of the World' and the 'Great American Desert'. Although the symbol of the Garden has predominated, that of the Desert has been a potent force. The imagery is truly dual. Now Nash Smith is not concerned with cinema, and it is fair to say that most applications of these ideas to film have retained their spirit rather than their detail. The imagery of Garden and Desert has been invoked as a critical cue to trigger off whole series of more specific contrasts. Kitses suggests eighteen such pairings arranged in three sub-groups of six: the sub-distinctions are those between individual and community, nature and culture, west and east, while the whole set fall under the master distinction between Wilderness and Civilisation.[9] This more complex analysis points up the simplifications inherent in taking the straight Garden–Desert contrast, or, for that matter, the familiar moral-heroic image of the westerner so well expressed by Robert Warshow.[10] The western deals in more complex distinctions than this, though its very familarity may delude us into underestimation. The Wilderness may be a context for an agrarian dream (as in *Wagon Master* or *Drums Along the Mohawk*), or an intrinsically antagonistic desert (as in *Fort Apache*). Civilisation may be both the community spirit of the pioneering township (the 'Sunday morning' sequence of *My Darling Clementine*), or unwanted 'control' from back East (the military high-ups unseen but felt in *Rio Grande* or *Fort Apache*). The simple distinction between Wilderness and Civilisation is a key; it is not also the whole melody. The western is richer than that.

One thing, though, is immediately notable: all the examples just quoted are films made by John Ford. It is a remarkable characteristic of the western that one director has figured so prominently in it. From his first feature, *Straight Shooting*, in 1917, through to *Cheyenne Autumn* in 1964, he has charted most reaches of the genre. And where he has led the rest have followed, many of the characteristic images and interests of the western deriving from Ford's particular articulation of American history. To trace the changing shape of his westerns is to follow the contours of the genre from its beginnings in romantic dream to the progressive souring of the sixties and seventies. So, inevitably, Ford provides the standard example for the Garden–Desert conception. *The Man Who Shot Liberty Valance* straddles the two images; its twin heroes encompass the contrast. Doniphon (John Wayne), the pragmatic, individual, man of the west, loses the girl and his dream of a ranch, finally dying a pauper. His fate is sealed by his unselfish actions: he shoots Liberty Valance in such a situation that Stoddart (James Stewart) is credited with the success. On this basis Stoddart wins both girl and a successful political career; he is the eastern-trained lawyer and through him Civilization is brought west, but only at the expense of Doniphon and the individualistic integrity for which he stands. One recurrent image binds the elements together, uniting in itself components of both Garden and Desert: the cactus-rose, its final sad resting place on Doniphon's coffin. They grew liberally around his projected ranch, and this was his dream, to keep the best of Garden and Desert, Wilderness and Civilisation. The film's poignancy lies in the demonstrable impossibility of preserving the western spirit in the face of

lisation. In *The Man Who Shot Liberty Valance* and *The
__hers* Wayne finally sees out the earlier aspirations of
Ford's Henry Fonda in *Drums Along the Mohawk* and *My
Darling Clementine*.

In this context it is easy to see why Nash Smith's conception has proved so attractive. It is a general formulation
which makes sense out of a number of facets of the western.
In one straightforward conception it is possible to capture
the typical environments, social structures, and themes which
inform the genre, The frontier spirit, the creation of 'civilisation', law enforcement, subjugation of the 'natural savage',
and the wagon train, are all quite sensibly linked within the
master conception. Even so, to *start* by abstracting Garden
and Desert invites a highly selective view. And although
selectivity is unavoidable it must be possible to start with
more open parameters than this. The risk in reducing the
genre to this 'master theme' is that we by-pass inflections
which are thereby rendered insignificant. Revenge, for
example, is one of the most common narrative patterns of
the western. As such it has no particular affinity with the
Garden–Desert conception. Yet it has been central to many
westerns; the code of honour that it represents is an integral
part of the western landscape. It would be a very limited
account which failed to include such an important element.
So, although the Nash Smith imagery has surely been
established as an important part of any analysis of the
western, it is not all. It is a useful backdrop against which we
can consider the history and content of the genre.

There was a good deal already to hand when the movies
latched onto the western. Some of the popular conventions
had already found expression in the dime novel and other
fiction of the period.[11] The familiar image of the cowboy
was already established. Besides, action was predictably
proving a great attraction in the new medium; what else in
moving pictures? And what better context than the largely
imaginary world of the silent movie frontier? The very
first influential story film, Edwin S. Porter's *The Great Train
Robbery*, was a primitive combination of a roughly western
setting with a good deal of action interest. That was in 1903.

But what Jacobs refers to as 'a flood of western pictures' came round 1907 when some film companies moved west. As in the other movies of the time the primitive story line was all-important. It was sufficient to make exciting narrative sense. But year by year the movies became more sophisticated. By the time the westerns shift out of the two-reelers and into features we are in the era of Bronco Billy, William S. Hart, Tom Mix and Hoot Gibson.[12] It was in this situation that the historic cowboys overlapped with those in the movies – Ford talks of meeting Wyatt Earp and a number of friends from Tombstone.[13] And it is in this formative period that the pattern of the genre was first outlined. Here the morally scrupulous cowboy hero comes to the fore. The western is born.

So far the success of the western seems largely immanent to the genre. The proven capacity of the medium for exploiting action, plus this idealised historic and geographic context, seem just as important as any thesis invoking 'national identity'. Following Alan Lovell's excellent discussion we can see that it is later, in the early twenties, that more generally significant developments come. In Cruze's *The Covered Wagon* and Ford's *The Iron Horse* begins the shift from a handily located action picture to a celebration of the historic move west. The crudely developed cowboy hero now had the beginning of a fitting context. With these films the genre was opened to '. . . the full force of Western history; inside it played all the themes, legends, and heroes associated with that history'.[14] A romanticised history could now go hand in hand with a romanticised hero. The classical period had begun; its climacteric, Lovell argues, lay in *My Darling Clementine*, a western integrating all the basic elements. Which is not to say that the two intervening decades showed no changes in the genre. One thing evident as early as *The Covered Wagon* was a certain 'documentary' inclination, a detailed and realistic surface to the film. This injection of realism – 'naturalism' is a better word for it – has stayed with the western for most of its development. The 'French thesis' on the western tends to see increasing realism in the thirties as a response to the concerns of the depression,[15] and it is obviously true that some films of the period, not just westerns, betray a concern with 'realistic social issues'. But a large part of the naturalism of the western must surely have derived from a combination of growing technical accomplishment applied to the historical and physical context of the movies. The events and settings of the western demanded naturalistic treatment; for years they were almost the only films shot anywhere but on tawdry sets. Western naturalism must owe its development as much as to the internal requirements of the genre as to outside social and political factors.

However they stand on the classical period, most writers seem to agree on the major post-classical innovation, though their terms may differ somewhat. At that time the westerns of the fifties were labelled 'psychological'. *Shane, 3.10 to Yuma, The Left-handed Gun,* and others, pushed psychological interplay to the fore. André Bazin saw the development as more wide-ranging than a simple injection of psychological interest. What he called the 'sur-western' was '. . . a western that is ashamed to be just itself, and seeks to justify its existence by some sort of supplementary interest, whether aesthetic, sociological, moral, psychological, or erotic'.[16] In 1955 he saw *High Noon* and *Shane* as paradigm examples of the 'sur-western', the former dealing in moral allegory, the latter coming full circle and justifying itself in terms of the western myth. But for Bazin any sort of elaboration beyond the simplicity of *Stagecoach* is such a shift; even *My Darling Clementine* is described as baroque! Nevertheless the general observation is plausible enough. As in so many cultural areas the fifties and sixties have seen an increasing psychological sophistication in the western, with some extreme manifestations such as *The Left-handed Gun* or *Warlock*. This period also saw a more critical exploration of the traditional themes, a much more elaborate style, and, especially in the sixties, more open attention to the mechanics of violence. In the fifties these alterations in emphasis might be personnified in Anthony Mann's *Man of the West*; in the sixties the equivalent must be Sam Peckinpah's *The Wild Bunch*. They both forced paths in which others have followed.[17]

This rise of the 'sur-western' is perhaps the only crucial

innovation in the genre since the twenties. As Bazin suggests it has been a quite sweeping change, and fifteen years after its first diagnosis there seems even more force to the argument. Westerns have become increasingly self-conscious about their genre status. *Shane* may well incestuously feed off the western myth; certainly Stevens goes out of his way to invoke the traditional trappings and primitive colour symbolism: but compared to Peckinpah's *The Ballad of Cable Hogue*, a movie openly and affectionately mocking the western stereotypes, *Shane* seems restrained. Nor is it just for the more 'intellectual' directors like Peckinpah or Penn (in *Little Big Man*) to push this self-awareness to its limits. The sixties saw a flurry of parodies (*Cat Ballou, Support your Local Sheriff, The Good Guys and the Bad Guys*), of self-consciously 'mythical' Italian westerns (*A Fistful of Dollars, Once Upon a Time in the West, The Good, the Bad, and the Ugly*), and of 'evening westerns' set in the decline of the mythical western era (*Lawman, Butch Cassidy and the Sundance Kid, The Hunting Party*). A final component of reflexive consciousness has been explicitly introduced into the genre. These films say 'Look at us; we are drawing on the western genre'. It is hard to imagine where they can go from here.

For this to be possible there must obviously be an enormous stable background against which individual movies are played out. The genre is dead; long live the genre! The world of the western retains many of its traditional characteristics, fixed points around which differing emphases revolve. This is most obvious in the basic physical trappings. Their simple surface appearance signals the genre of the film. Pistols, holsters, horses, saloons, stagecoaches, townships, and the others, 'place' the movie for an audience. Basically we are shown them naturalistically. The distortions and stylisations common to gangster and horror movies are the exception in the western. Of course particular directors have imported such techniques into the genre. Fritz Lang, whose stylisation of light and shade is so effective in gangster movies like *The Big Heat*, injects something of that surface mystery into *The Return of Frank James*. But these rare exceptions apart, romantic naturalism is very much the order of the day. The image of the lone figure in the western landscape, the open spaces of mountain, desert, and prairie, the magic of rivers, wagon trains, and columns of cavalry. These are typical of the western. Of course the imagery *is* stylised, but rather differently to the gloomy half-worlds we shall shortly encounter. Here the style serves almost to accentuate the reality, to dress up the epic push west in the finest clothes available. So, in line with the general Garden–Desert thesis, the predominant images are those of the wild and beautiful western vista. Aridity and dinginess are found in only a minority of the films: William Wellman's *The Ox-Bow Incident* is a classic example, and Andre de Toth's *Day of the Outlaw* a superb baroque variation.

There is a whole complex of moral, emotional, and historic interaction here. Since the early days the loner has figured prominently. The individualistic ethos is deeply embedded in the genre, but it is an individualism of a special kind. Unlike the ruthless achievers of the gangster movie the westerner is 'inner-directed'; Reisman's term for contemporary puritanism fits well here.[18] He is, as Warshow suggested, a man with a code, and it is that code which leads him on. The extremes of this inner constraint inform every one of the major thematic structures of the western; as we shall see they each use the lone figure as a crucial element. The western world is structured around him. As the repetitive B-pictures confirm, he is the final essential *reductio* of the genre. He is the minimum requirement of the cheapest, most ill-conceived, rehash. Even in the beautifully integrated world of classic John Ford, individual autonomy and integrity of character are crucial factors.

In the classic period the loner was frequently interstitial; he mediated between the various sub-groups of the movie, fleetingly essential to all, but ultimately passing on 'into the sunset' (in *The Gunfighter* even after he is dead!). Wyatt Earp, in *My Darling Clementine*, is a richly developed example of this centrality. He mediates between violence and savagery, peace and civilisation. In his way he belongs to both. Early in the film his attempt to civilise himself by getting a shave is interrupted by a drunken Indian letting loose with a revolver. The respectable citizens of Tombstone cannot deal with the situation. They cluster in the darkened street while the Indian fires his gun in the brightly lit saloon. Only Earp can bridge the gap between them and deal with the situation. But like all the professional gunmen of the genre his role is ephemeral. He must join civilisation or move on. At the end of *My Darling Clementine* he preserves both possibilities by riding off in the hope of some day returning to Clementine.

The loner may be a central figure, but he generally exists in a social environment. A few movies have an absolute minimum of social structuring – Mann's impressive *The Naked Spur* involves only five characters (plus attacking Indians) interacting in an entirely non-social wilderness – but most westerns rely in some part on the familiar social structures. Inevitably the most basic pattern is the family. One stage more complex than the lone man against the wilderness, the family provides a close-knit unit for dealing with the antagonisms of both nature and man. Conflict within the family is usually resolved in the course of the film. Families exist on both sides of the moral fence: Earps and Clantons in the many remakes of the familiar story, or the villainous Cleggs in *Wagon Master*. They may be informally adoptive as is the relation between Dunson and Garth in *Red River*. They may be all-male quasi-families like the group in *Rio Bravo*. They may become the whole rationale as in TV series like *The High Chapparal*. They may even be quite grotesque like the Hammonds in *Ride the High Country*. They are usually patriarchal and intensely loyal, but in all these manifestations they provide a vital focus for involvement. If the emotional centre of the western is the solitary hero, he is not infrequently drawn into some surrogate family relationship. And the further one steps away from this small group context, the less the involvement. The community, of course, retains some demand on individual loyalty, as does the familiar symbol of Old Glory fluttering in the breeze. Like a series of Chinese boxes these successive social levels contain the individual hero. How strongly they are developed varies from film to film.

Everyday events in this world are moulded by an elaborate set of rituals, each suited to a different level of social organisation. The ritual actions of the loner are the rock-bottom of the genre. Drinking, gambling, and the other minutiae of western leisure follow well-established patterns. The face-off and the quick draw are the rites the hero must pass through for the preservation of his vaunted integrity. The man of the west lives typically by these codes, though he may be drawn into successively enveloping social worlds, and his style of life thus partly transformed. The family unit, especially in its collective rituals of eating and working together, is an obvious locus. *Shane* plays on it at great length, Shane himself becoming a special part of the family. Indeed, mealtimes, be they in town dining-rooms or around camp-fires, are standard devices for incorporating the loner. Further up the scale of social generality we find other rituals. Like the savages against whom it is contrasted, the Community has its own ways of affirming solidarity. John Ford is a prime mover here. His methods have been much imitated: open-air church ceremonials filled with the emotionalism of 'We Will Gather at the River' or 'Rock of Ages'; the dances, community or cavalry; Old Glory hoisted in celebration of national or communal identity. It is not easy to suppress emotion at the dances of *My Darling Clementine* and *Fort Apache*, or the fluttering flag of *Drums Along the Mohawk*.

Most of the standard western narratives grow out of this well-defined and ritually elaborate world. Even the most 'revisionist' movies of the modern era draw on the same basic elements, pushing them to the limit and even rendering them grotesque. There are many permutations, for the western is the richest of all genres in the variations it allows. None the less, it is possible to single out a basic group of narrative patterns which may be present, singly or collectively, in individual films. Three of them derive primarily from the 'loner' element, though in their richest incarnations they are usually embedded in a more complex context. The commonest include the paradigm western figure: the solitary gunman, freelance or employed, marshal or bounty hunter.

In Guillot's sample this hero was the victor in over 90 per cent of the films, and, in contrast to most Hollywood heroes, he was aged between forty and fifty in more than half the films.[19] Out of this role come the many narratives based on the enforcement of law and order in the variously primitive western communities. Such 'social' conflict Guillot finds to be the commonest form in the western. Often tied to it comes that most characteristic of western constituents, the revenge story. Like the law-and-order narrative this is frequently a main involvement of the lone figure, though sometimes it may involve a whole family. The third narrative focusing on the individual is that involving the 'economic conflict' of cattlemen-versus-settlers, the plot dynamic flowing from the fight of small against large. This obviously merges into a rather more community-oriented narrative; the small farmers may also constitute a defensive community.

This community, in one form or another, is the basis for the other three major narrative patterns. First there is that whole cluster revolving round primitive communal endeavours. Pioneering, wagon training, railroad building, and the general accoutrements of the push west, often celebrate the community as much as the individual. Likewise with that other much exploited cluster involving defence against the Indian. Although we may still retain a B-picture stereotype of Indian wars settled by individual combat between solitary hero and chief's son, much of the force of these movies is actually vested in the community struggle against the rampaging Indian. This applies whether the community is a wagon train, a group of isolated homesteads, a town, or the much rarer early settlers of *Drums Along the Mohawk*. It may also take on varied complications, as it does in the individual–community tensions of *The Magnificent Seven*, where bandits take the place of Indians. Lastly there is the narrative which frequently rests on the community–Indian conflict but in a special set of terms: the Cavalry films. From *She Wore a Yellow Ribbon* to Raoul Walsh's underrated *A Distant Trumpet* they promote a fascinating if uneasy combination of collective military values and individual inner-directed heroics.

N

In a sense the cavalry narrative most clearly states the basic dramatic tensions of this genre-world. The individual hero looks within for his motivation and justification, but his final obligation is to the military community, its rituals and its values; the cavalry crystallises collective restraint on western individualism. There is a justly famous moment in *Fort Apache*. As the troop rides out to battle, with all the pomp and splendour Ford usually gives to such occasions, one of the watching women describes their disappearance into the distance: 'I can't see them any more – all I can see is the flags.' This merging of the individual into the community is one of the principal dimensions of the genre-world. It makes for a certain ambivalence. Though the emotional weight of many westerns leans toward the individual hero, the moral implications of most of the narratives value the communities. Ultimately the solitary hero is either drawn into the community finding a new identity within it, or he simply 'rides on'. In the more bitter westerns of the fifties and sixties the individualist may find himself simply excluded from both familial and community setting. Ethan Edwards in *The Searchers* is ultimately shut off from human contact.

Which returns us to where we began: the contrast between wilderness and civilisation. These two polarities, individual and community, wilderness and civilisation, provide the basic tensions of the western's moral universe. Of course they are hardly independent. The western individual has clear affinities with the wilderness, the community ethos with civilisation. Individual and civilisation, community and wilderness exist in a state of uneasy tension. The world of the one is forever yielding to the world of the other, though strange alliances may be struck along the way. This landscape is nicely consummated in the good-humoured parodies of Peckinpah's *Ballad of Cable Hogue*. Cable is established as the Individual, the man of the desert and the snakes, the man who cannot tolerate the community. In the final surreal sequence of the movie he succumbs with no sign of injury. He has been run down by a motor car in the middle of his beloved desert. To make things worse the car engine is not even running; it rolls down a slope and he tries unsuccessfully to halt its progress. Knocked down by civilisation, surrounded by mourning representatives of the community which has depended on his enterprise (banker and priest), he dies in the midst of his wilderness, having completed his revenge and gained the love of his lady. His successor, to whom he has shown the true westerner's mercy, is about to change his entrepreneurial water-hole into an even more entrepreneurial gas-station. On a brass bedstead the middle of the desert, and accompanied by a peroration, all tensions are resolved. Civilisation overtakes wilderness, community overtakes the individual. The western comes to an end.

But of course it does not, the genre remaining a rich mine of meanings. This lengthy description is designed to suggest the basic parameters of this particular pattern of popular culture. It should also suggest the impossibility of sensibly locating single, distinct causal factors to explain the development of such a genre. Its evolutionary development demands an equally complex explanatory account. Simple equations between social and political events and claimed emphases in the genre are far from satisfactory. Indeed, it is arguable that the genre was not 'caused' in this strong sense at all. What does seem more significant, however, is the status of the western as a very widely diffused pattern of culture. For many hours of their lives audiences participate, in cinemas and in television, in this genre world. They involve themselves in its evaluations, in its emotions, in its very fabric. For a while the reality of film and audience is one. What sense can we make of the importance of this cultural pattern? How do people use these meanings? What part do they play in our societies? These questions will be revisited in the perspective afforded by analysing our other two genres.

GANGSTER MOVIES

Unlike the western, gangster movies were not extensively predated by American history. Of course they did grow out of public consciousness of historic events, but the construction of the genre was almost contemporaneous with the construction of the events themselves. Perhaps the obviousness of this link had slackened interest in the gangster movie: there are very few systematic attempts at analysis. Apart from the usual elaborately imperceptive filmographies, there is only one English language study which tries to dig below the surface of the genre.[20] Other than as a focus for plastic nostalgia, the gangster movie remains remarkably undiscussed. And there is certainly no equivalent to the Garden–Desert thesis, and no body of writings similar to the impressive French materials on the western.

But there is the history, the familiar pattern of innovation, acceptance, decline, and repetition, a history which begins with *Little Caesar* in 1930. Not that there were no silent movies about crime and racketeering. Jacobs mentions a string of twenties films, featuring Lon Chaney as master criminal, including *The Penalty, Partners of the Night*, and *One Million in Jewels*.[21] Chaney moved successfully between these primitive gangster movies and the closely related horror movies of the time, a link which is not without significance. As we shall see the two genres are variously related. Better remembered now, however, are Josef Von Sternberg's underworld films made in rapid succession between 1927 and 1929: *Underworld, The Dragnet, Docks of New York*, and *Thunderbolt*. Although even then fascinated by the pictorial, the Sternberg movies also display that feel for desolate urban environs so much admired in *The Salvation Hunters*. This sordid and conventionalised realism was to be one major characteristic of the first full flowering of the gangster movie. It was stimulated by the late twenties boom in publicity for gangster activities. The fame of Capone and the notorious St Valentine's Day massacre of 1929 created a storm of publicity. Quick to see the possibilities, the studios reacted, and on the crest of this wave came Mervyn Le Roy's *Little Caesar*. And although it has dated a good deal it is still not difficult to see why this bleak story of Rico's rise and fall was so successful. Although these were the early indulgent days of sound the dialogue remains fairly terse;

action is all. Rico claws his way to the top and is precipitately eliminated.

The decade which followed *Little Caesar* saw the classic development of the genre. The rise-and-fall pattern became very common. *The Public Enemy* and *Scarface*, made in the two years following, differed from *Little Caeser* mainly in the intensity of their violence, though the Hawks film is much the most interesting. *The Public Enemy*, of course, came up with that bastion of the genre James Cagney, as well as the new, brassy, female co-star epitomised by Jean Harlow. The genre stuck by this pattern for as long as it remained commercially viable. Unlike the western, these classic gangster movies are rarely great achievements; none of them exhibit the depth and artistry of, for example, their German equivalent, Fritz Lang's *M*. The genre was much more limiting than the western of the same period, and the minor additions of the thirties hardly expanded its potentialities. *G-Men* and *Bullets or Ballots* shifted the mid-decade emphasis to the law-enforcer as hero, though he was generally only the gangster character shifted sides. Ironically enough, in Kieghley's two movies he was played by Cagney and Robinson. And even this was only a logical extension of the sinister, tough, and heavily stylised policeman of *Little Caesar*. Similarly with the other lauded innovation of the period, the 'discovery' of the social causes of crime. Though principally developed in the Dead End Kids movies of the late thirties, especially Michael Curtis's *Angels with Dirty Faces*, it was there from the beginning in *The Public Enemy*. The laboured childhood sequences of that film were clearly designed to give some sense of the social development of the criminal. It has been suggested that this reflects the influence of the Chicago School.[22] If so it is a greatly vulgarised influence.

The forties see the first decline of the classic gangster movie. As in the western, the end of this decade was to see a shift toward a more sophisticated and baroque form. The war years interregnum was filled with B-picture repeats and that peculiar sub-genre the 'private eye' movie. Bogart, established as out-and-out villain in the thirties gangster movies, became the best known hero here. The sub-genre's brief development was largely a combination of the sophisticated detective thrillers of the previous decade (e.g. *The Thin Man*) with the seedy physical world of the gangster movies: and, of course, Raymond Chandler. But whatever their retrospective popularity, the private eye movies were only a ripple on the pond. The gangster movie re-emerged at the end of the forties, and with it a new fascination with the psychological peculiarities of the gangster. This was the beginning of the disturbed and psychopathic 'hero'. In 1947 *Kiss of Death* saw one of the most famous: Richard Widmark's first appearance as a sadistic gunman with a maniacal laugh. Two years later Raoul Walsh capped a varied career with *White Heat*, Cagney's psychotic headaches and his peculiar relationship with his mother providing the basic motivational rationale of the movie.

This psychological focus is the last major input to the genre. The decades following show some change in emphasis but nothing radically new. Thus the cycle of fifties movies in 'dramatised documentary' style emphasises one element of the classic pattern. Similarly with the quality B-pictures of that decade made by directors like Don Siegel, Phil Karlson, and Roger Corman. Even the private eye movie had its resurgence in the sixties with star vehicles like *Marlowe* and *Tony Rome*. They stuck pretty much to the classic pattern, adding colour, more esoteric violence, and more perverse sexuality. So, paralleling development in the western, 'psychological' gangster movies become prominent. Interestingly, the late sixties and early seventies have seen a further similarity: the development of increasing genre self-consciousness. Don Siegel, especially, has made a series of successful movies which, like Peckinpah's 'evening westerns', make some open obeisance to their genre origins. Films like *Dirty Harry*, *Madigan*, and John Boorman's *Point Blank*, are highly sophisticated developments of the genre. They reflect an increasingly widespread characteristic of modern cinema: open awareness of the traditional genre conventions.

In the gangster movie these conventions are fairly simple.

There are not the riches of the western here, nor the same capacity for evoking deeply held convictions. The world of the gangster is frighteningly desolate. If the western is a kind of agrarian dream, then the gangster movie is surely an urban nightmare. Its most prominent characteristic is its urban context. As Warshow has argued, the gangster is above all a man of the city.[23] This scene was depressingly set in the classic period. Central characters came from the streets and were returned to them to die. *Angels with Dirty Faces* typically saw Cagney rise from the slums. Rico, in *Little Caesar*, dies, disbelievingly, in a back-alley, beneath a poster advertising the dancing talents of his former partner. In *The Public Enemy* the beginning of the end comes for Cagney when he staggers, seriously wounded, into an overflowing gutter. And *The Roaring Twenties* provides him with that famous and much parodied 'death run', down a block and across the snow-covered steps of a church.

The films are honeycombed with half-lit alleys and seedy bars; prohibition joints and smoky rooms; waterfronts and warehouses; the ever present neon signs; and that mobile arm of the city, the motor car. Before one can even consider the trappings of gangsterdom, the guns, the clothing, the brutalities of everyday interaction, it is essential to comprehend this urban milieu. '. . . that dangerous and sad city of the imagination', Warshow calls it. And it is given this sense primarily through photography. It is often a world of deep shadows, of an ill-lit city at night. The extreme contrasts of light and shade are vital to it. And where it becomes possible to see more than this blurred outline, the city is garish, sordid, and seedy. So strongly is this image established that it is difficult to see even the most luxurious settings (such as the high-class night-clubs which occasionally appear) in anything but the same way. Significantly, many of the lighting and camera effects are the same as those of the horror movie. They share much the same origins in the German silent tradition. Indeed, if horror movies take place in a world dominated by the supernatural, gangster movies are located in a sub-natural counterpart. A true underworld. Where the one is bestial – Dracula, Frankenstein, monster,

Werewolf, and Mummy – the other is brutalised. The gangster is barely human.

This selective imagery accounts for much of the emotional force the gangster movies share. It creates an eerie world, at its best one which exudes a perpetual aura of malevolence. Coleridge's 'frightful fiend' lurks as much here as in the horror movie, a comparison reinforced by the demoniac intensity of the central gangster characters. Cagney is a perfect example. His screen persona, forever bound up with the genre, is a bundle of inexplicable nervous energy. The puzzle is the source of this ultimately self-destructive single-mindedness; so often the gangsters seem like puppets manipulated by their world. And the environment itself suggests dimly understood and inexplicable forces constraining and destroying its characters, just as it does in the horror movie and in the German silent cinema from whence it came. Many of the films have produced implausible and thumbnail explanations. In the silent period for instance:

'*The Penalty* displayed Lon Chaney as "the legless wonder" who has sworn revenge on society because both of his legs were amputated by a careless doctor after an accident. Bitter and violent, he becomes ruler of the underworld. The removal of a blood clot from his brain by a surgical operation finally restores him to decency. Ridiculous though such a solution appears to us today [1939], in the light of more recent realism regarding crime, it was accepted as plausible then.'[24]

Ironically enough Jacobs's 'more recent realism' does not now look as plausible as he thought. The late thirties gangster movies attempt to demonstrate some sort of link between criminality and social background seems supplementary to the main thrust of the genre. It was just as mystificatory as the blood clot and the psychiatric determinism of later years, partly because that sort of straightforward causal explanation was antipathetic to the emotional tone of the movies. Emotional and 'factual' meanings conflict, and mystery inevitably turns out to be more efficaceous than maladjustment. It is interesting to speculate that, had it not been for the influence of the 'German style', the gangster movie might have led to something like Italian neo-realism. It did not because its basic impetus remained mystificatory rather than socially realistic.

The brutal universe so created is mechanistic. It has little in the way of social and emotional riches. In fact its social world is simply a network of crude exploitation. Man climbs upon man to survive at the top of the heap. Where there is a family context – as in *The Public Enemy* – it is ineffectual.[25] There are 'big shots', there are loners (a characteristic of heroes whether police or gangster), and there are endless streams of subservients. Loyalty, other than the occasional emotional attachment formed in early days, is absent. Violence, murder, and sudden death are the basic order of things. Moral compunction is rare and generally short-lived; indeed issues of morality are barely invoked. In this world most characters are not in positions where they can make choices, and without choice, morals can have little meaning. Unlike the western there is no code governing the violence, no set of rules for the regulation of this war of all against all. It is a heartless, fatalistic, obsessive, and amoral environment. There is not much leeway here.

This is reflected in the limited variation of narrative structure. The simplest and most repeated pattern is that of the first three crucial genre-defining movies: *Little Caesar*, *The Public Enemy*, and *Scarface*. Rise-and-fall. Many a film has revolved around this straightforward device. Obviously such a narrative is easily incorporated into the mechanistic world of the gangster movie. These characters set out to 'make it' at any cost, a price invariably underlined by their callous treatment of former associates, women, and even close friends. The all-powerful individual is glorified in his achievements; there is usually much more rise than fall. This is very different to the celebration of individualism in the western where there is some suggestion of larger limitations and obligations, where community and family are felt to have some meaning. For the gangster there is no such context. His self-interested individualism is totally unfettered.

His is not the challenge of individual integrity to a hostile world; it is material ambition. Even where the central character is on the side of law and order he exhibits the same characteristics; he bucks against the rules and the given authority they represent. The much employed under-cover agent is constrained to imitate the gangster by virtue of his situation. Not simply because he must convince those he seeks to betray, but because in any case he does not have a structured world of his own. He is occupationally a loner, obliged by his position to deny individual integrity, forced to betray his apparent associates, and to claim a world peopled with fictitious wife, mother, family, and friends. He is symmetrical with the gangster. *White Heat* presents this at the limit. The agent is completely emotionless, an extension of the electronic gadgetry that he handles so well, an asocial isolated robot. Cagney's gangster, by contrast, is 'over-involved' to the point of insanity; he wants the top of the world. But both are manifestations of the same amoral individualistic theme.

Whatever the sub-variations of the genre there is some development of this individualism. It is there in the private eye thrillers and in the traditional rise-and-fall. It is there in the 'revenge' movies like *The Big Heat* and *Underworld USA*, and it is still there in the modern idiom of *Point Blank* and *Dirty Harry*. It is there even where it is explicitly invoked in popular Freudian terms, as in *White Heat* and *Baby Face Nelson*. It is the cowboy's world but without his integrity and without his richness of character. In a way it is the American Dream seen through a glass darkly. Rampant individualism overcomes all; society is reduced to a fierce and frightening 'state of nature'.[26] The gangster kicks out at an incompre-hensible world. He is constrained by it, and it is a world that the very style of the movies betrays as antagonistic and unknowable. Whatever the crude explanation – be it blood clot, slum, or Oedipus complex – the gangster movie is fascinated by the consequences; by the machinery of an almost instinctive, self-centred, and anti-social response to unasked for and unavoidable constraints. The westerner fights for some half-understood principle. The gangster fights partly for himself and partly for the hell of it. He does indeed occupy an underworld.

HORROR MOVIES

The horror movie is one of the few cinematic genres which is largely non-American in its origins. This is in two senses: it developed first in Europe, specifically in Germany; on take-over by the American industry it still retained a mythical, central European setting. Its classic development, in the Universal studios of the thirties, remained fairly faithful to the Transylvanian mythos, only occasionally shifting to a native American context. So, unlike the two preceding cases, the horror movie has little or nothing of American history and culture at its root. It has no obvious intrinsic American attachments. This lack of specificity has made the genre much more geographically mobile; the centre of gravity of horror production has not been fixed in any one country. While only the French have approximated to gangster movies, and the Italians to westerns, all and sundry have made some contribution to horror: from Germany in the silent era, through Italian pictorialism and Japanese sadism, and finally to the methodical exploitation of Britain's Hammer Films.

This variation in source is counterbalanced by the basic simplicity of the genre. The crystallised rules of horror are very straightforward. In this respect it is indeed the American input of the thirties which is so important; the boom years of Universal Studios do most to define the genre. Obviously the German silent era provided much of the materials, in terms of technique if not of narrative and characterisation. Murnau even made an odd version of the Dracula story, *Nosferatu*, in 1921, though it is some way from the more full-blooded studio versions of later years. But most of the German 'horror' movies are Gothic novels of high Romanticism. It is their wrongly named 'expressionist' style which provides grist for the later Horror mills, their ability to suggest a strange half-seen world of light, shade, and mist. Films like *The Chronicle of the Grey House* or *The Student of Prague* demonstrate this romantic chiaroscuro tradition.[27] Its visual style was to contribute a great deal to the development of both gangster movies and horror movies in the years to come.

The American silent period also saw its own developments of the genre, by the last year of the silent film already under the influence of the 'German style'. But Clarens reports that *Frankenstein* appeared in the 1910 Edison catalogue, though we know no print of it today.[28] Certainly the early history of the American cinema saw a formula picture category of 'shockers'. By 1920 the commercial machinery was well aware of the potentialities. *Dr Jekyll and Mr Hyde* had been variously adapted, and the literature was scoured for other likely sources. Successful plays were also used as raw materials. And, as we have already noted, Lon Chaney became a major success of the twenties shuttling between early gangster and horror movies. He marks the real beginning of that phenomenal skill at grotesque make-up later used to such advantage. His vampire in the 1927 *London after Midnight* remains one of the nastiest of images.

All came to fruition in the early thirties. The stylistic influences from Germany, the borrowings from Gothic, Romantic, and Horrific literature, the long-developed commercial tradition of the 'shockers', and the line in brilliant individual grotesquery pioneered by Chaney, all combined in the Universal melting pot. The only thing finally missing was Chaney himself who had sadly died at his prime in 1930. But even he was soon to be replaced by the twin pillars of the genre: Bela Lugosi and Boris Karloff. Karloff, surely, was his equal. But it was Lugosi who made the first major sally in Tod Browning's 1931 version of *Dracula*. The film became the studio's major source of income for that year and the floodgates were finally opened. It was followed later in the year by James Whale's *Frankenstein*. For this film the make-up artist Jack Pierce and the immortal Karloff created an outstanding monster. This figure, arguably borrowed from Goya,[29] has become one of the most instantly recognisable in twentieth-century popular culture. And because of Karloff the film is still reasonably watchable today, which is more than can be said for many of its contemporaries. It was also heavily influenced by the German silent cinema; the opening graveyard scene, with its tilted crosses and leafless trees, setting this stylistic mood immediately.

Dracula and *Frankenstein* are the defining movies of the classic horror film. Like so many such adaptations they twist and simplify their literary sources. Though Bram Stoker might have recognised some kinship to his rather turgid novel, Mary Shelley would surely have been much dismayed. Karloff's performance alone battles seriously for the spirit of the novel: horror movies seem inevitably to be great simplifiers. From these forthright beginnings there were three main immediate developments. First there were the inevitable sequels and sequels to sequels. Plots were wildly distorted to ensure the survival of key characters. *Dracula's Daughter, The Bride of Frankenstein, Mark of the Vampire*, began a long cycle which climaxed in the inane combination movies of the forties: *Frankenstein meets the Wolf-man, House of Frankenstein, House of Dracula*. These last two combined all the beasts in the horror stable with the exception of the Mummy. One can only assume that the addition of a remnant of ancient Egypt was beyond the ingenuity of even these film-makers. Seldom has a genre been wrung so dry. The second development was the initial creation of this pantheon of characters. The most telling was probably Karl Freund's *The Mummy*, again embellished with a fine performance from Karloff, but the werewolf was no doubt nearer to the melodramatic epicentre of the genre. He survived a number of movies principally memorable for their remarkably weak plot lines. The third development returned to the literature. *The Invisible Man, Murders in the Rue Morgue, Burn Witch Burn*, and the like, provided a further source of raw materials. The tills continued to fill.

These were the staples of the classic period. Of course there were other horror movies on the fringes, some of them very impressive – Browning's long banned *Freaks* for instance. And there were separate inputs which also had their beginnings in the German and American silent film, and beyond them in Méliès. Lang had used models extensively in his

German films: the city in *Metropolis* as well as the animated
dragon in *Siegfried*. An American, Willis O'Brien, carried
the technique further than everyone else, thus beginning a
series of films whose *raison d'être* lay in their animated and
generally prehistoric monsters. After a number of shorts he
graduated to *The Lost World* in 1925, adapted from Conan
Doyle. Its most famous thirties off-spring was *King Kong*
(though its 1949 grandchild *Mighty Joe Young* leaves the rest
standing for sheer hilarity; John Ford is credited as producer
on this one and Ben Johnson plays cowboy to the friendly
ape), and the tradition has remained alive through endless
remakes of *One Million BC*, through the science-fiction
monsters of the fifties and the Godzillas and Mothras of the
Japanese industry. All this was a parallel and occasionally
interlinked growth distinct from the mainstream of the
horror movie. Similar considerations apply to the science-
fiction boom of the fifties, though all three share the same
narrative strategy if not the same visual style. The science-
fiction bug-eyed monster movies were predominantly
naturalistic in their handling of their unnatural materials.
They signalled an interregnum following the last, but
stylish, gasp of the classic horror movie in the war-time films
produced by Val Lewton.[30]

The genre has been thoroughly revived in the late fifties,
and throughout the sixties, by the activities of one company:
Hammer Films. Of course others were and are in the
business, and there have always been some movies on the
market. But with *The Curse of Frankenstein*, and a very good
Dracula in 1958, they restarted the whole cycle. Mummys,
werewolves, sequels, literary adaptations, and some original
and impressive material; the mixture as before. This period
also saw, with apologies to Bazin, the rise of the 'sur-horror-
movie'. Movies which draw on the genre materials very
much as a means to an end rather than as an end in itself.
Jack Arnold (in *The Incredible Shrinking Man* and *The Creature
from the Black Lagoon*) made such attempts. Roger Corman in
his Poe adaptations (especially *The Tomb of Ligeia* and *The
Masque of the Red Death*) has not been averse to imposing his
mark. And the perfect example – combining elements of

gangster movie, horror movie, and science-fiction – Don Siegel's *Invasion of the Body Snatchers*. But it does seem that the genre has not proved as stimulating in this respect as have our other two cases.

Hammer dominance continues, repeating many of the thirties cycles. But there has been some leaning toward psychologisation. The pioneering psychoanalytic element in *Peeping Tom* has found some reflection in later Hammer products. The new generation of Hammer directors, especially, seem to have been encouraged in their search for new twists. The Dracula story has been openly sexualised, something only occasionally and covertly suggested in the past. Loosely based on Le Fanu, *The Vampire Lovers* has exploited Ingrid Pitt's considerable talents in its combination of Lesbianism and Vampirism, though not with the subtlety of Vadim's *Blood and Roses*. Ingrid Pitt also features in *Countess Dracula*, an unsuccessful but interesting attempt to return to the historic bases of the Dracula myth. And *Hands of the Ripper* takes the classic techniques and welds them into a peculiarly fascinating psychoanalytic maze. Interestingly, in comparison to the other cases, the horror movie has not become so self-conscious. Perhaps its intrinsic limitations make such a development unlikely, apart from the occasional parody.

It is a very limited genre, and the limitations are first set in the world of the classic horror movie. In this world, clearly borrowed in part from the Gothic novel, we find Lord and peasant, castle and village, forest and mountain. In short, Transylvania. This is the sense given to the horror world whatever its detailed geography. Nineteenth-century town, twentieth-century London, ancient and modern Egypt, whatever the setting it is immanent supernaturalism which stands out. This is why the 'German style' was so important. Its mystery of light and shade was highly effective. Though the Gothic landscape helps, the style itself is capable of infecting almost any subject matter with its eerie tone. *Invasion of the Body Snatchers* does so in an American small town setting; *Night of the Demon* in modern, rural, home counties England; a number of movies in Victorian London. The sense of mystery, of lurkers in the shadows, is the constant factor. The mechanism is very difficult to the western, where the environment makes so much of the genre; here the style of the genre makes the environment.

Our emotional responses in this world derive very much from shock and the expectation of it. Depth of characterisation, also a source of involvement, is rare, much rarer than in the western or gangster film. The principal performers in the horror movie – Lon Chaney, Bela Lugosi, Boris Karloff, Christopher Lee, Peter Cushing, Vincent Price – are rarely stars in the traditional identification-projection pattern. They are not charismatic figures of the stature of John Wayne, Henry Fonda, James Cagney, or James Stewart. Emotional involvement is primarily located in the *situations* of the horror movie, with a corresponding stress on narrative pattern. The visual tone of the genre provides a sort of base-line of mystery: the narrative builds its pattern of shock on top of this. In principle, such a method will work in any environment, urban or rural, ancient or modern. In practice, the horror movie has been most successful in a semi-rural and unspecified 'period' setting.

It would be easy to be misled into thinking that horror movies invoke a very specific social world. But this would be to overstress the classic period. Transylvania certainly did have a clear and simple social structure: that of Lord and peasant. The malevolent and decadent aristocracy contrasted with the friendly, if frightened and stupid, peasantry. But the further through the genre we move the less prominent this becomes. It is reduced to 'local colour': a source of victims and bawdy inn scenes. By and large horror movies have little in the way of fixed patterns of sociation. Certainly their image of the world is one of exploitation, the evil bringing death and misery to the rest. It is in the monster's nature to be thus; it is in the order of things for the rest to be victims. But as a social world the horror movie is remarkably empty of distinctive characteristics. Its events are located in whatever social context they can be made to make sense.

One begins to see why the genre is so limited. It does not have those potential resonances which inform other genres.

Apart from its obvious fatalism, the horror world has little which is really its own, other than a fairly narrow range of themes and narratives. Its conventions are unidimensional and straightforward. It is even possible to distinguish a single basic horror narrative to which all conform, something we might label the 'seek-it-out-and-destroy-it' pattern. The expression is borrowed from Dr Van Helsing of the Universal studios' Dracula series. The movies always included the long-awaited moment when his analysis of the situation led to the inescapable conclusion: 'We must seek it out and destroy it.' The language itself reflects the predelictions of the genre. Evil ones are sought not searched out, destroyed not killed; and, of course, they are *its*. But this narrative structure spreads far beyond the limits of Count Dracula's Transylvanian castle. The whole genre revolves around the creation or discovery of an *it*, *its* recognition, seeking, and destruction. Allowing for a slightly more open end (for sequels), this plot line goes from *Dracula* and *Frankenstein* to *Witchfinder General* and *Hands of the Ripper*, from *The Werewolf of London* and *The Invisible Ray* to *The Blob* and *The Beast from 20,000 Fathoms*. The ultimate pruning in title and plot came with movies like *It* and *Them*.

Within this narrative pattern the strategy is a simple one of cumulative shock. Tension is built, dissipated through shock, and rebuilt. Hands on foreground banisters, figures emerging from shadows, ravening vampires in sudden close-up; all the clichés find their place here. These simple narrative patterns, combined with a predominantly visual evocation of atmosphere through lighting, photography and set design, form the style of the classic horror movie. Within it we find a limited set of themes. They have been developed at different stages of the genre, and they can also be named from the movies themselves. The earliest comes in large part from the initial literary inspiration; it might fittingly be called the Dracula theme. Basically it presents the aristocrat as decadent, unfeeling, and exploitative. His destruction is invariably achieved through the services of some intelligent bourgeois from some metropolitan and educational centre. Count Dracula and Dr Van Helsing are the paradigms here.

o

The bourgeois comes to the aid of the people against the aristocracy.

As I have suggested this theme is progressively played down; indeed, its successor was already combined with it in *Frankenstein*, and this film can give it its name. Here the real villain is the creator of the *it*: the mad scientist. Madness here is a synonym for irresponsible and inhuman, and antagonism shifts from the decadent aristocrat to the scientist. Many of the fifties bug-eyed monster movies were founded on some such premise, often linking it in with the development of nuclear weaponry. The bomb released enough beasts from caves, ice, or the bottom of the sea, to populate a galactic zoo. And though the monster provides the traditional horror focus, the scientist must also be humanised or, more often, destroyed. The favourite denouement sees the monster somehow turn on his creator/liberator. But this antagonism is only one side of the horror movie's attitude to the scientist. The fifties also brought a new theme and a peculiar respect for the individual scientist who stood out against the bureacratic indecisiveness which placed the world in peril. The fact that he may have caused the peril in the first place is now presented as a justifiable risk for advancing knowledge. Although the distant prototype may well be Van Helsing, the name best associated with this theme is surely that of Quatermass. The Donleavy character in *The Quatermass Experiment* and *Quatermass II* (and, in a rather different way, in *Quatermass and the Pit*) is a hard-hitting, incorruptible, terse, anti-bureaucratic superman. Red tape falls apart before him, and his seeming lack of sentiment and human feeling is celebrated as an individual struggle against impersonal bureaucracy. In some of the more traditional combinations it is his scientific scepticism that is singled out, while the rest is ignored; the black magic movies play on such a contrast. Will he be convinced in time?

All these themes have retained some force since their inception, while the sixties have seen unlikely thematic combinations where once characters were merely shoved together in times of flagging inspiration. Heresies have even advanced as far as humanitarian doctors trying to cure disturbed vampires! If such psychologisation gains any force, then one can imagine the effects. The simple fatalism of the genre would be undermined and relativised by such a development. As the German silent cinema recognised, in this world the more that is left unexplained and inexplicit the better it is. Horror movies begin and end with something which is definitionally unknowable. It may be fought, held at bay, even defeated. It may be wrapped in the mythology of science, magic, or space; disguised as a blob of jelly, a stegasaurus, or an invisible ray. But it somehow transcends us mere mortals; and when it has been finally defeated there still remains, to borrow a Lovecraft title, a lurker at the threshold. The horror movie *must* believe in the absolute status of that threshold. That is both its limitation and its virtue.

PATTERNS OF MEANING

It is commonplace to see popular culture as basically integrative, as conserving and supporting the given institutions of society. Most 'mass culture' views in some way approximate this image. But often they do not specify the detail of the mechanisms involved; they claim simply that mass culture is 'escapist' or that it is fundamentally 'conservative'. The absence of detail in such argument is disturbing. It suggests, as always, that knowledge has been replaced by assumption. It may be that popular culture is widely used as a means of 'escape'; it may indeed be that almost all culture is thus employed. But without specifying this 'escapism' in terms of the meaning popular culture has to its consumers, we are far from understanding the processes involved. Of course some such attempts have been made. In their well-known study Wolfenstein and Leites look at movies '. . . to see what are the recurrent day-dreams which enter into the consciousness of millions of movie-goers'.[31] They rightly recognise that these 'day-dreams' play a part in the complex interaction between beliefs and action, between society and culture. They are both escape from the unsatisfactory and articulation of the valued. To understand their workings Wolfenstein and Leites invoke the familiar categories of psychoanalysis, though, to their credit, not in the sort of extravagant terms we have had occasion to mention.

The 'catharsis' argument need not even go this far in analysing the social importance of movies. The simple concept of 'acting out' has provided plenty to be going on with. Take the themes of the horror movie. All of them – Dracula, Frankenstein, and Quatermass – are easily seen as providing contexts in which felt tensions may be acted through to acceptable catharctic conclusions. The first in relation to social distinctions of class and exploitation. The second in relation to the scientist and science as a source of disturbance and strain. The third in relation to bureaucracy and authority as a source of frustration. Each movie context is then easily conceptualised as a world for 'acting out', a world of fantasy in which fear and antagonism may be vented. Such arguments – provided they are extensively supported by analysis – are plausible if superficial. They underlie many discussions of the 'conservative' functions of popular culture.

In a sense, however, they are negative discussions. Men-in-society face certain sources of disturbance; popular culture is a 'drug' for dealing with this 'pathology'. Attempts to look at the more active consequences of popular movies are rarer than these 'aspirin' analyses. This stems partly from the prejudices of the 'mass culture' thesis, and partly from the difficulty that stronger discussions require stronger assumptions. Such an approach would need to explore the typical patterns of meaning in the movies and demonstrate their potential consequences for social process. Galli and Rositi make an interesting comparative attempt.[32] They argue that, from 1928 onwards, Germany was unique in resisting the spread of American cinema. In the rest of Europe this particular pattern of culture was to become variously institutionalised. The meanings it incarnated were distinct from those found in the German cinema of the period, and in many respects the two cinemas were diametrically opposed. Rather as Weber saw the Protestant ethic as the unique factor in the rise of capitalism, so Galli and Rositi's thesis leads to the view that German popular culture is a crucial element in the rise of Naziism. Of course they only sketch in a potential account, but they do at least enter into more sociological detail than one finds in the 'classic' discussion of the question: Kracauer's *From Caligari to Hitler*.[33]

This is an 'active' conception in that it conceives the movies as playing a part other than simple catharsis. The patterns of meaning repeated in the films are interpreted as constitutive of the social world. They are more than just aspirin. Galli and Rositi treat movies as patterns of culture as well as escapist day-dreams. This hardly exhausts their potential cultural significance, but it does provide a beginning analysis of the relations between such patterns of culture and the societies in which they are manifested. We can follow a similar speculative route in relation to the meanings of our three popular genres. Of course this does not focus on specifics; I am not here concerned with a particular historic development, but two of these genres at least are extraordinarily widespread. As patterns of popular culture they are the commonest currency of all. For this reason their analysis in itself is significant; they are a very important and widely diffused part of social process.

Of the most prominent elements in the three genres only one is completely shared: the use of violence as the ultimate necessary solution to crucial problems. It is easy to underestimate this element precisely because it is so familiar; it is present in so many of our popular genres. Occasionally, in the western, this violence may be unwillingly applied, somehow forced by circumstance. But whatever compunction there may be in motivation, the desired solution still follows. Violence works like magic. Other emphases are associated with this stress. The ethic of revenge, for instance, is very much a part of these genre-worlds. Or the fascination with the trappings of violence, mechanised or not. Dramatic resolution so often derives from their presentation: the gunfire of the face-off, the blazing sub-machine gun, the werewolf's silver bullet, or the staking of the vampire. They provide both a dramatic and narrative consummation of the genre movies. In terms of plot, in terms of emotion, and in terms of morality, violence resolves all problems and tensions. It closes the book.

This context of meaning has remained largely constant through the history of the various genres. The substance of the violence has varied according to fashion and censorship, recent years seeing a proliferation of blood and detail. The indignation that this development has occasioned seems misplaced, based, as it is, on an unlikely premise. The argument broadly suggests that in the old days violence was acceptable because it was 'clean' and distanced. When people were shot they simply fell over. Now that we see blood, wounds, and pain, the violence is no longer respectable. It is too 'real'. Which argument is a red herring. However clean or dirty, the meaning of the violence has remained much the same; it provides the only practicable solution to the fictional situation. It might be argued that increasing realism of presentation demonstrates how high the price is in pain and loss, but surely not that this is somehow 'worse' violence than that which has always permeated the genre.[34]

Which is not to say that violence in popular culture has nothing to do with violence in the social world. The traditional genre acceptance of the violent solution is an entrenched part of our western cultures. The movies (and the other media) form one part of socialisation, adult and adolescent, *one* source of attitudes and beliefs. Their stress on the violent solution is hardly unique. They are repeating a pattern of culture, in dramatic terms, which an adolescent, say, will also find elsewhere: in his family, amongst his peers, in the history texts he reads at school, and in many of the institutions of his society. Civilised societies are officially conducting much publicised wars and supporting widely advertised institutions specialising in violence. Blaming popular culture for the violence of modern societies is pernicious scape-goating; there is much more wrong here than just the movies. The genres play only one part in the circle of cause and confirmation. One can blame them for violence about as convincingly as one can blame a hydrogen atom for a nuclear explosion.

The controversial potential of the violence issue has drawn attention away from a rather more disturbing element in the popular genres. Besides being given to the 'violent solution', coercion – resting on the threat of violence – is a common basis of interaction. Violent actions themselves are only the logical extension of this basically coercive image of human relations. In the gangster movie and the horror movie this is reinforced by other characteristics to which we shall shortly return, but even in the western, which differs from the others in a number of respects, non-coercive ways of getting things done are demonstrably less successful. This pattern is rather more diffuse than the actual recourse to violence, and possibly more socially acceptable. While modern societies do accept a considerable range of open violence there are also certain customary restraints on its intensity. Movie violence is more extreme than that which we might expect to encounter in everyday life. But the various forms of coercive relationship – threats of violence, of deprivation, of emotional injury – are much less restricted and so more widespread and damaging. The fact that such patterns of interaction are widely tolerated reflects the degree to which they find legitimation in our cultures. The importance of the 'violent solution' and the emphasis on coercion in our popular genres is one link in this legitimating process.

This theme of coercion runs like a thread through the popular genres. It is also present in their attitude to women and their evident belief in male dominance. With rare exceptions women take a secondary and exploited place to men. Even the exceptions – Calamity Jane for example – are ultimately assimilated. Her myth has her taking on the more acceptable characteristics of feminity under the influence of 'true love'. In fact this 'romantic love syndrome' is the major area of the genres in which the female role is developed. All three of my cases pay it variable attention. In the horror movie it is usually limited to a sub-plot; the traditional commercial 'love-interest' formula. Gangster movies are served similarly, though the romantic paring may be a contrast to the inhumanity of the central gangster. Where women figure more prominently in the gangster movies they do so as objects of lust and disdain rather than love and respect. The exception to this rule is the peculiar role of the mother in gangster movies and westerns. They are invariably figures of diffuse attachment and often matriarchs. At their extremes (Ma Barker in *Bloody Mama*, Cagney's mother in *White Heat*) they are the main source of (evil) power, though more often their committment is to the family in a less powerful but more conventional form. This matriarchal sub-pattern is standard, usually where the male father figure has disappeared. It is not inconsistent with the popular genres' general attitude to women.

Predictably, sexuality varies with the emphasis on romantic love. Where male dominance and romantic love combine in the presentation of inter-sex relations, as in the western, open sexuality is minimal. In gangster and horror movies, where romantic love is largely sub-plotted, the main narrative may well exhibit a more open sexual dimension. The 'molls' of the classic gangster movies – from Jean Harlow through to Gloria Grahame – exude a brassy confidence; relations have open sexual connotations. By contrast the romantic sub-plots remain quite asexual. Similarly with the horror movie. Where inter-sex relations are emphasised they tend toward perversity. Vampire and female victim have been long recognised in these terms, a recognition which recent genre developments have brought to the fore. But sexuality is absent from the romantic preoccupations of those in pursuit of the *it*; it is almost as if such 'impurity' would damage their ability to seek and destroy. Where it is encountered in the western, sexuality is similarly isolated. It is the domain of the implicitly labelled prostitutes of saloon and hotel. In short, sexuality is associated with the world of masculine domination, coercion, and violence; romantic love with a world still dominated by the male, but characterised by the more insidious and socially acceptable coercions of everday interaction. One might add that the latter is generally pretty lifeless and unreal; it is clear where the emotional interests of the movies rest.

These patterns intermesh with a further cluster, present in all three genres, but varying in emphasis from case to case. It revolves around the degree to which individuals are constrained by their world or free to influence it in some way; the relation between people and the larger social context; and the degree to which actions are governed by clearly defined obligations of ritual. The western differs most from the other two. In many respects it celebrates man's ability to impinge on his environment. The push west, the pioneering spirit, the growth of the Garden from the Desert, all reflect this optimism. Not that there is no tension. As we have seen the strain between Wilderness and Civilisation, Individual and Community, informs the basics of the genre. It is the conflict between self and community which makes the western so fascinating. The family, the town, the cavalry troop, all make for some restraint on the individualism of the pioneering spirit. This complex of mutuality and conflict, of uneasy symbiosis between individual and community, is the rationale of so many westerns. In the classic formulation these difficulties are largely resolved by the integrity of the hero. His code of honour ensures that his individualistic talents are harnessed to the needs of the community. In terms of the famous cliché: 'A man must do what a man must do'. Not because he has no choice, but because his principles dictate his choice. Once the choice is made, the ensuing actions, inevitably violent, are governed by distinct sets of rituals and expectations. There is some balance between determination and freedom.

In contrast gangster and horror movies suggest a much more fatalistic universe. Its state is given; an individual can only struggle to survive. He does so by ruthless egocentricism or magical inspiration. He is not a creator. He either destroys for his own advancement (gangsters and *its*), or he defends himself by seeking and destroying (*it*-catchers and agents). Either way the mood is a deep pessimism to contrast with the qualified optimism of the western. Compare the rituals of the western to those of the horror movie. In the former their function is to affirm an ideal of community spirit or individual good. In the latter they are simply manipulative means to a defensive end. The true central characters of gangster and horror movies are the gangsters and monsters themselves. The world may be finally and implausibly rescued from their threat, but the fascination lies with them and not with their defeat.

These are the main generalised meanings of our three popular genres. They dramatise, repeat, and underline an interpretative account of acceptable social order. It is not entirely consistent from genre to genre and it shows variation from movie to movie, but there is some pattern to the sort of world which these popular genres create. They stress the need for violent solutions, coercive interaction, brutality, and revenge. They show us a world in which male domination is taken for granted, in which love and sexuality are divorced, in which a whitewashed romantic love is an expectation. For the most part they promulgate a strong individualism, sometimes tempered by ethical restraint, often simply indulgent. One might argue that in so doing they are reflecting common characteristics of the societies in which they are so popular, and it is certainly true that our societies are coercive, male-dominated, exploitative and self-interested. But reflection is too simple a concept. In dramatising these traits the movies participate in a continual and complex social process. They articulate for us the bases of our social lives; they give the underlying regularities of our societies' concrete form. They are both reflection and cause; a link in a closed circle. We act, we create, we form, and even change our societies. Our popular culture expresses the irreducibles of these operations. Through it succeeding generations imbibe the standards and expectations which service our social structure. The circle closes. But no one of these elements is a prime cause or even essential to the process. Culture – our body of ideas, artefacts, and beliefs separated from any of us as individuals – is the shelter beneath which society operates. It mystifies, justifies, and reifies the actions and structures which make up our social system. Like popular religion before it, our popular cultures find ways to justify the unjustifiable. They underwrite exploitation, self-interest, and hypocrisy. Their sin is not original. We can only be grateful that, again like religion, they have also produced some great experiences, genuine works of art. Popular culture is not to blame for the ills of our society: we are.

References

[1] It is significant that the main sociological study of 'movements' refers to 'film art' and not just to film. See G. Huaco, *The Sociology of Film Art* (see Selected Bibliography).

[2] L. Jacobs, pp. 163–4 (Selected Bibliography).

[3] For a good summary see L. Handel, *Hollywood Looks at its Audience* (Selected Bibliography).

[4] Alan Lovell, 'The Western', Paper given to the BFI Educ. Dept. Seminar, March 1967. He discusses a number of the French writers including J. L. Rieupeyrout, *La Grande Adventure du Western*, Paris, 1963 and A. Bazin, 'l'Évolution du Western' (Selected Bibliography).

[5] W. J. Barker, p. 275 (Selected Bibliography).

[6] F. E. Emery (Selected Bibliography).

[7] C. Clarens, p. 13 (Selected Bibliography).

[8] Henry Nash Smith, *Virgin Land*, Random Hse, New York, 1957, especially Book 3. The application of Smith's ideas to the western is given some general consideration in Colin McArthur, 'The Roots of the Western', *Cinema*, 4, 1969.

[9] J. Kitses, p. 11 (Selected Bibliography).

[10] R. Warshow, 'The Westerner' (Selected Bibliography).

[11] See H. Nash Smith, *op. cit.* for the literary antecedents to the 'myth'.

[12] For an affectionate account see George N. Fenin and William K. Everson, *The Western*, New York, 1962.

[13] See Peter Bogdanovich, *John Ford*, Studio Vista, London, 1968, pp. 84–5.

[14] A. Lovell, *op. cit.*, p. 5.

[15] See J. L. Rieupeyrout, *op. cit.*, and J. Wagner, *op. cit.*

[16] A. Bazin, *op. cit.*, quoted from the BFI Educ. Dept. translation.

[17] J. Kitses, *op. cit.*, discusses Mann and Peckinpah at some length, as well as Budd Boetticher.

[18] See David Reisman, with Nathan Glazer and Reuel Denney, *The Lonely Crowd*, Yale Univ. Press, New Haven, London, 1961. In this context, also see P. Homans (Selected Bibliography), and R. Warshow, *op. cit.*

[19] Alain Guillot, 'Aspects Politique du Cinéma Americain', *L'Année Sociologique*, **11**, 1960, p. 131.

[20] C. McArthur (Selected Bibliography).

[21] L. Jacobs, *op. cit.*, pp. 408–9. Since I have not been able to see these movies I have to rely on Jacobs' account.

[22] C. McArthur, p. 63 (Selected Bibliography).

[23] R. Warshow, 'The Gangster as Tragic Hero', in his *The Immediate Experience, op. cit.*

[24] L. Jacobs, *op. cit.*, pp. 408–9.

[25] There are two main areas of rather odd exceptions. The one encompasses those movies which deal with the quasi-family of the Mafia; *The Godfather* takes this to high class 'Peyton Place' limits. It has little to do with the gangster movie at this extreme of its development. The other either deals with the genuine family of *Bloody Mama* or the part related familial group of *Bonnie and Clyde*. All these share the notion of the family as the criminal unit.

[26] V. F. Perkins likens the world of Fuller's *Underworld USA* to that presented by Thomas Hobbes. See David Will and Peter Wollen (Eds), *Samuel Fuller*, Cinema Pubs. of Edinburgh Festival, Edinburgh, 1969, p. 72.

[27] See L. Eisner (Selected Bibliography). See also Chapter 7 of this book.

[28] C. Clarens, *op. cit.*, pp. 54–5.

[29] See the illustration in Raymond Durgnat, 'Truth is Stranger than Fiction', *Films and Filming*, January, 1965, p. 45.

[30] For an account see Joel E. Siegel, *Val Lewton: The Reality of Terror*, Secker & Warburg, London, 1973.

[31] M. Wolfenstein and N. Leites, *Movies*, p. 13 (Selected Bibliography).

[32] G. Galli and F. Rositi (Selected Bibliography).

[33] S. Kracauer, *From Caligari to Hitler* (Selected Bibliography).

[34] The previously invoked *Straw Dogs/Clockwork Orange* affair is revealing in this context. See C. Barr, 'Straw Dogs, A Clockwork Orange and the Critics'. See also Andrew Tudor, 'Screen Violence', *New Society*, 19 July 1973.

Chapter 9

Patterns of Change

The two preceding chapters have been largely empirical, concentrating exclusively on the character and development of certain cultural patterns. Of course, these patterns may not be untypical. Some aspects of the German 'movement' are echoed in post-war Italy, though the substance of the movies is very different. And the attitudes and beliefs expressed in the genre-worlds of westerns, gangster movies, and horror movies are not unique to these three; they are surely much more widespread. Genre concerns are implicit in much popular culture. Indeed, even where substance differs, the popular genres may still serve as socially legitimating devices, used by different people for varying but 'conservative' ends. Now, plausible though they might be, none of these generalisations follow directly from my empirical analyses. If they did, the pursuit of knowledge would be grotesquely simple, the leap from particular to general quite empty of hazard. But it is not, and I have not intended that it should appear so. These empirical materials are basically exploratory, and, as such, they can stand by themselves as one part of studying the cinema. Not that they are complete. There are other events and factors important to the German case, and, however detailed it may seem, my portrait of the three genres is little more than a sketch. Nor are they conceptually elaborate. In fact, I have tried to avoid building conceptual castles at this stage, feeling that the basic information itself is presently a paramount need.

I have already suggested why this should be so. Because the mass society imagery has been so influential, and because that model does not encourage detailed and sympathetic exploration of mass culture, we have very little genuine sociology of the cinema. Not many sociologists have attempted a disciplined study of film's role within society. The label 'mass' predisposes its users to see only mass characteristics; who needs to research into what is already defined as obvious? And there are more simplifications than this. In Chapter 6 I argued that many traditional perspectives on the media were *unable* to conceptualise the full range of interrelations between cinema and society. That demonstration was roundabout and laborious, I would be the first to admit, but it does serve some purpose. Viewing the various approaches in terms of a simple classification helps us appreciate their inherent limitations and emphases. This is no place for reiteration, especially since Chapter 6 was primarily intended as a conceptual precursor to the empirical analyses which follow it. But invoking it here serves as a reminder that, while we do have need for method, for abstraction, and for a conceptual language, their provision is quite pointless if they are so general as to far exceed our store of empirical materials. Since the mass society distortion has ensured that our basic information remains thus limited, I have preferred to concentrate on relatively 'low-level' empirical analysis as a strategy for further advancing the macro-sociology of film.

All that given, it must also be said that there is a considerable strain toward generality in sociology just as there is in any other scientific activity. But in aiming for generality we must sacrifice detail, and in demanding detail we must sacrifice generality. Whatever balance we strike depends on present situations and purposes, on what we know and what we do not know, and on why we want to know it in the first place. So even with the limited materials assembled here there is some temptation to make more general statements. I intend to yield to that temptation, but only briefly, and only because the attempt to generalise and synthesise has its pay-off for further empirical analysis. This chapter's sketchy discussion, however, is not *justified* by the materials I have previously invoked, though it does grow out of them. Nor does this chapter formulate an encompassing theory, though theory is its interest, and it sets many of the problems with which any theory would have to contend. Any author is tempted to 'draw conclusions', even from richly varied subject-matter and undisciplined analysis. I hope the reader will tolerate mine even though they are more conceptual conjectures than conclusions. If not, then at least there is some comfort in their brevity.

A MODEL OF CHANGE

In discussing the pattern of development in the popular genres I used the term 'evolution'. One must be careful with such analogies. Though suggestive, they can be misleading, especially when they encourage us to view a changing entity as undergoing a completely autonomous process of development. Obviously this cannot be the case with cinema. Any such cultural pattern is inevitably embedded in a world of more or less complex social actions. Culture does not evolve as such; it is not realistically autonomous as is a distinct animal species. To speak in general of cultural evolution—even without any overtones of 'progress'—is to run all sorts of risks of misunderstanding.[1] But the term is defensible. The term 'evolution' is a good description of the apparent pattern of genre development, implying that the observed character of the change is, at least, consistent with a postulated evolutionary process. Explaining this pattern, however, is a problem of a different order, requiring us to consider factors other than the cultural development itself. Let us see where these questions will take us.

The popular genre's developmental pattern is evolutionary in a fairly straightforward sense. The conventions, images, and typical narratives of a genre are built up by addition, selective emphasis, and re-emphasis on a roughly trial-and-error basis. This much is clear from Chapter 8. In the horror movie, for instance, Universal Studio's simple formula was sufficient for most of the thirties: simple seek-and-destroy narratives featuring Dracula, Frankenstein, Werewolf, or a Mummy. But sooner or later familiarity breeds contempt, a harsh judgement rapidly reflected in box-office returns. Film-makers are subjected to pressures (largely commercial but with important aesthetic components) demanding the introduction of something new, the subsequent innovation is tested over a period, and it is either assimilated into the genre or it disappears. Sometimes, as in the horror movie, the genre goes through a period of mock-innovation before it actually begins to incorporate new elements. This usually involves endless permutations and combinations of the basic materials giving rise to the familiar cyclical patterns of popularity. The forties produced all those unintentionally hilarious and short-lived movies which tried to cram the whole pantheon of horror characters into one improbable plot: *House of Dracula* is as good an example as any. But the more important changes are those involving new characters and, less often, new themes and styles. Thus the fifties saw the rise of a Quatermass-type character far beyond the confines of *The Quatermass Experiment* and *Quatermass II*. This stereotypical scientific superman survived the subsequent vicissitudes of the genre characteristically well.

Character innovations, however, are only a minor part of genre development, even if they do provide convenient labels for more far-reaching changes. The horror movie's thematic progression through 'Dracula', 'Frankenstein', and 'Quatermass' themes has been a much more substantial process, though more diffuse stylistic changes have been quite rare in this genre. There is no developmental disjunction as significant as the much noted shift from western to 'sur-western'. Indeed, the most blatant attempts to introduce new and commercially viable styles in the horror movie have usually been laughably crude failures, verging into self-parody and gimmickry, and rejected in short order by critical audiences. The luminous plastic skeleton which rattled across the auditorium during screenings of *The House on Haunted Hill* and the 3-D thrills of *House of Wax* are typically vulgarised failures. Perhaps more than any other genre, the horror movie established very simple parameters in its classic period, amending them very little in the years that follow.

If this makes horror movie evolution seem very crude then it must be stressed that the horror movie is the simplest of genres. But not all can be tarred with the same brush, and much genre development is quite subtle. In the western, for example, it is not easy to pin down the points at which this or that inflection entered the genre, for, by their very nature, such changes are spread over a period. Perhaps just one movie, then another, or even a whole group, adopt a particular innovation. If the audience accepts it as part of the genre sub-culture, then it is a viable addition, joining the body of materials which other genre-movies may utilise. Of course any given movie need not and does not utilise everything the genre has to offer, for a genre is a 'reservoir' of culture which can be mobilised in all sorts of ways. If you prefer the biological analogy, the genre is rather like a species. It changes its shape, it evolves, sometimes evolving new sub-species within it. The overall process is one of slow, cumulative change, as the genre progressively differentiates.[2] The simpler cases differentiate very little: Universal's stock of materials, styles, and characters underwent only minor changes. The western, by comparison, is highly differentiated. Where horror movie narratives stick very much to the one pattern, the western has developed half-a-dozen specialised narrative structures. Where the horror movie retains a limited and thinly drawn band of characters, the western has shown an increasing capacity for deeper characterisation. And where the horror movie has limited itself to one major cluster of techniques, the western has proved able to adapt to all sorts of variations. These are some of the reasons for the riches of the modern western; it is one of our most differentiated and elaborate genres.

So far, then, evolutionary change in the popular genres appears to have three main characteristics. First, in that innovations are added to an existent corpus rather than replacing redundant elements, it is cumulative. Second, in that these innovations must be basically consistent with what is already present, it is 'conservative'. Third, in that

P

these processes lead to the crystallisation of specialist sub-genres, it involves differentiation. Though this generalisation derives from detailed analysis of only three genres, it seems sufficiently plausible to deserve persistence. It might even be useful to see much popular cinema history as some sort of evolutionary 'branching tree'. Growing from a few primitive roots in the early days of the fiction-film, the tree branches out into the various 'formula pictures' of the nineteen-tens and nineteen-twenties, and then into the classic flowering of the major genres of the nineteen-thirties. Inevitably, some branches lead to evolutionary dead-ends, now forgotten; others branch and branch again. The strongest survive as part of modern popular culture, perhaps primarily on television. Others cling to a tenuous niche in the cinema (the Hollywood musical), while others are remembered only as the subjects of a cultural nostalgia. Films like *Casablanca*, or the swashbuckling epics of *Robin Hood* or *The Mark of Zorro*, invariably occasion the 'they don't make movies like that any more' cliché, neither living parts of modern popular cinema nor extinct and forgotten species. But they might always be revived, just as *Whats up Doc?* revives the great tradition of *Bringing Up Baby* and *Monkey Business*.

So the evolutionary analogy may be useful in describing a typical pattern of change in the popular genres. It is certainly true that genre differentiation is cumulative, conservative, and slow. But terms like 'evolution' and 'differentiation' are not merely descriptive; they also carry explanatory connotations. They are associated with characteristic ways of explaining change. At their simplest they rest on the slogan of classic adaptive evolution: 'survival of the fittest'. Vulgarly expressed, whatever survives does so because it successfully adapts to the demands of the environment in which it exists. Obviously that cannot be literally true of a cultural pattern. Culture survives because there are people who ensure that it does, either because it is useful to them, or because they think it useful to society at large. Of course they may be quite wrong about the consequences of a particular pattern, just as they undoubtedly have a very diffuse concept of utility. In fact cultural artefacts often survive only because powerful élites like to see themselves as the guardians of aesthetic and moral value, or, more cynically, because 'culture' helps them maintain their élite position. For such reasons the precise dynamics of culture survival vary considerably and are not amenable to simple generalisation; there are many different ways in which something can be 'useful'. Often relations of power and authority are crucial formative factors, though, in the popular genres, sheer weight of audience opinion is the primary determinant. But even this is not a direct effect, since audience influence is mediated primarily through the images communicators hold, and only finally through financial veto at the box office. We must therefore expect some amendments to a simple 'survival of the commercially fittest'.

It is here that the argument must become complex, perhaps too much so for the present context. Once more we can see the problem in relation to the classic analogy. The nineteenth-century development of the theory of biological evolution did two different things. It provided a viable description of the evolutionary relation between various known species, and it made general sense out of this observed pattern in terms of 'natural selection'. But the gap between the empirical pattern and the general theory of natural selection remained wide, for, although the theory makes broad sense, the detailed links were almost all missing. A number of questions were still to be answered. What are the actual mechanisms of natural selection? How does an adaptation develop and become established over the generations? How can we avoid 'hidden hand' arguments, or teleological concepts of progress? Biology had to await complex developments in genetics before it could begin to understand the natural selection mechanisms. Sociological use of an evolutionary model faces exactly analogous problems. The pattern of development of the popular genres does seem aptly described as 'evolutionary'. 'Commercial selection' does seem something like the beginnings of a plausible account. But to advance any further by connecting the two we have to understand the particular social processes whereby commercially viable innovations are selected, established, and assimilated.

This seems to me to be one of the most important problem areas in the development of a sociological history of the popular cinema. Considerable care is needed, for, once given 'commercial selection', it is too easy to slip into unacceptable 'free market' explanations of cultural change. This would obviously be unsound. Although some part of the process is amenable to analysis in market terms, the approximation is very rough. The various socio-cultural constraints on market 'freedom', and the organisational structures which act as mediators in the selection process, all demand further research. Their understanding is the linking aim of the microscopic communication model and these more macroscopic interests. We would thus have to explore particular instances of genre development, discovering how audiences develop 'sub-cultures of taste', how communicators develop audience images, and how the all-important feedback relation between audience and genre actually operates. It is clear that change in the popular cinema has been something of a hit-and-miss affair. Adaptive evolution, in this context, has meant seeking around for the right formula in a situation of limited and ambiguous information. Unpredictability is further compounded by the cultural heterogeneity of audience and communicator, and the peculiarly distorting information channels which connect the two groups. Gans has rightly drawn attention to the importance of these processes in his various discussions of taste sub-cultures and audience-images.[3] Though this, too, seems a reasonable beginning, there is little else that we can say in the absence of further and more rigorously directed research. We are not lacking in research in this field, but the research is lacking in some idea of where it should be looking.

Allowing for many limitations, I hope to have established that the evolutionary analogy could be usefully applied to change in the popular genres. Crude though it is, it certainly seems less crude than the traditional macro-sociological models of cultural change. Those perspectives devote most of their energies to isolating determining factors exogenous to the institution in question, for instance by relating particular cultural changes to changes in the larger social structure. Though this is not totally uninteresting, it does have strict limitations, and it faces just the same problems in isolating intervening mechanisms. For the popular cinema the link is inevitably seen in audience terms, and we find such propositions as those which relate the rise of the western to the need for national identity among immigrant Americans. The moment one tries to fill in the gaps in such an account one arrives at similar problems to those I have already mentioned: the dynamics of genre sub-cultures. So, although the adaptive problem may be set exogenously by the larger socio-cultural environment, the link between this problem and the evolutionary 'response' it calls forth is heavily constrained by factors specific to the institutional context. This is one of the reasons why it is so difficult to discover simple relations between society and cinematic development, the initial social impetus undergoing all sorts of transformations within the institution. Where we have to develop models of this process of interlocking imputs and feedback, evolutionary imagery seems to offer us a little more leverage.

Of course there are some circumstances where the simpler links do make sense, and where the straightforward evolutionary imagery is less suitable. This is most prominently the case in situations of major cultural innovation. Minor innovations, found typically in processes of genre development, are almost totally bound up in their institutional context. Major innovations, though they cannot be totally independent, do tend to 'overcome' the normal institutional constraints. Instead of the sub-cultural context moulding the innovation, the innovation carries the sub-culture with it. In these 'aesthetic break' situations the more direct approach is helpful, as it was in my analysis of a film movement. Generally speaking, film movements have a brief 'life', they reflect speedy and even precipitate cultural change, they are neither cumulative nor conservative in relation to previously established cultural patterns (though they may be politically or socially reactionary), and, in sum, they are 'revolutionary' rather than 'evolutionary'. Historically they are more brief fashions than established developments, though they may partly survive through adoption into established genres. As we have seen, this was the case with the German style first developed in the German film movement of the early twenties.

Indeed, the German case seems not untypical. Though commercial pressures were obviously important (Pommer, for one, emphasises them), they did not feature in the usual cumulative evolutionary role. The whole process of change seems to be compressed, and, once given *Caligari's* initial breakthrough, the socio-cultural context which led the communicators into the aesthetic break seems also to have guaranteed a commercially viable audience who accepted that break. Film history exhibits few such extreme changes, for the film movement is a relatively uncommon phenomenon. Under normal circumstances audience and communicator negotiate small changes within sub-cultures. In these atypical situations it is as if these negotiations were carried on independent of the specific institutional context and at a more general societal level. The extremes of the socio-cultural situation come to dominate both the institution's production pattern and the audience's desires and expectations. In this way the movement is able to by-pass all the normal processes through which we create a cultural context for communication, this short circuiting process being a precondition for a major innovation. This is why movements only occur in the wake of severe socio-cultural trauma. Wars, economic disasters, and revolutions produce atypical situations within which such short-cuts are possible; dislocation of established order opens the way for major cultural change. Precisely what change depends on the sort of detailed factors that I have discussed in relation to the German case.

So the actual course of such an innovation depends on particular empirical circumstances; it is not amenable to immediate generalisation. A film movement is an unusual phenomenon, largely isolated from the normal context of cinematic development. It is directly drawn into major socio-cultural change, and, unlike the popular genres, it is not insulated from the outside world in a specialised sub-cultural cocoon. Of course social developments always influence the cinema as they do nearly every other institution. But such influences are usually piecemeal, mediated through all sorts of controls, and generally lagging behind outside developments. The outside influences on the popular cinema, then, are very indirect, while the film movement is free from much of this buffering. It crystallises a unique situation into an 'aesthetic break', a major change which finds brief acceptance with communicator and audience alike. However, the fact of this difference, important though it is, cannot disguise the common characteristics of the two forms of change. The one is very much a compressed version of the other. 'Evolution' and 'revolution', in this context at least, are far from being diametrical opposites. The one fuses the typical processes of the other into a highly specialised and very uncommon process of change.

UNDERLYING IMAGES

As I have already suggested, this view of change in the cinema arises from the empirical analyses of the previous two chapters. But it also rests on an implicit image of the sorts of relations which typically hold between cinema and society, on a particular idea of the cinema's social role. Some sense of this imagery is given by my emphasis on audience 'needs' and the development of genre sub-cultures which satisfy them. This is basic to the evolutionary argument. Through a series of selection mechanisms the popular genres are conceived to evolve forms adapted to their environment, and that environment basically consists in the movie audience and its needs. The main communication channel for articulating audience wants is commercial: audiences 'use' the cinema and they pay for that use. So, unless the movies can keep up with any change in audience requirements, unless they can adapt, any sub-species will go into decline. One must stress that this process is unlikely to operate in its pure form. For one thing simple commercial sanctions do not allow much leeway in the expression of audience response, and for another the whole process can be highly distorted by power relations and varying attitudes and beliefs. Thus, an audience may be deprived of 'what it wants', for example, by an élitist communicator with a crusading spirit. So, because we are dealing with a *human* process the pure 'mechanical' model has to be open to modification according to the demands of specific empirical situations.

All of which makes it difficult to be very specific about the social role of the movies, though the perspective one brings to such analysis does reflect certain general sensitising images. For instance, at the end of Chapter 8 I suggested that the patterns of meaning implicit in the popular genres might well play a part in both causing and legitimating social actions. It sounds plausible, and this style of assertion is quite common. Looked at a little more closely it is found to rest on the same sort of audience/sub-culture imagery that underlies my analysis of cultural change in the cinema. In effect, popular culture is conceived to be *simultaneously* the cause, justification, and consequence of various patterns of social behaviour. Too many studies have tried to break down this complex interaction prematurely, thus favouring one or another of these roles to the exclusion of the rest. Once again the exact role of a particular institution within society has to be discovered in detailed analysis. But such work must be conducted within some sort of perspective which, at least, seems consistent with what evidence we already have. This is what is embedded in my underlying images, and it is this that I must try to get at here.

I have already mentioned one interesting example of such a general perspective, namely Berger's 'sacred canopy' analysis. This work, and his co-authored study with Luckmann, offers us a general picture of the role of culture in society.[4] It is especially relevant here because Berger is much concerned to avoid isolating the different 'moments' of the complex interactive process. While he insists that, however indirectly, we are responsible for creating our own cultures ('we', here, must include past generations), he also recognises that these cultural products become reified. We come to experience cultural phenomena (beliefs, knowledge, ideas, etc.) as independent of our volition, as something autonomous and 'out there'. What men once produced becomes an apparently independent given pattern of culture which, precisely because of its independence, offers us a shelter of meaning and order against a potentially chaotic world. In the case of religious culture, a sacred canopy. Language is surely the most general of such cultural defences for it can be used in such a wide variety of contexts. But other cultural institutions, significantly the media, can and do play a part in this process of cultural encapsulation.

None of this involves conceiving the media as direct causes of behavioural patterns and social developments. As we have already seen the evidence is overwhelmingly in favour of more indirect relations. Nor do people automatically respond to culture in the prescribed manner in stimulus–response fashion; the process is creative in that people *use* culture more or less consciously and in a variety of ways. There seem to be two main levels to this process, one making rather stronger claims than the other. The former is the process in which the movies, as part of our culture, provide us with a cultural 'map' through which we can interpret the world. The latter is the more general process whereby the movies are used to justify or legitimate beliefs, actions, and ideas, rather than as specified sources of cultural order. The 'map-giving' function is obviously a socialisation process, and its importance might thus be expected to decline with age. But for children and adolescents it figures prominently in learning basic techniques for dealing with our world. We learn from our environment: from family, from peer-group, from school, and, in this century, from film, TV, and the other media. We have already seen that there is some common pattern to three of the popular genres, a pattern which seems likely to be rather more widespread. This given, then the combination of this pattern (consistently expressed in the popular cinema and on TV) with other socialisation sources might be a significant factor in many children's socialisation experiences. Of course, it is true that these patterns are common because they are in part determined by other aspects of our societies and cultures. We do live in unjust, hypocritical, and violent environments. But it is when such values are repeated over a wide range of socialisation experiences that they become constituent elements in the 'maps' we carry around in our heads. The media play one part, albeit an important part, in this process of collective articulation, though they frequently receive the blame for all of it.

In this way, then, socialisation gives us the basic materials which we use in comprehending and handling our environment. It does so only in general terms, forming predispositions and capacities; later we fill in the detail out of our own unique histories. Naturally enough, this detail can change in later life, though the overall pattern is normally retained. As we also know, people do not like to be faced with experiences which contradict the general outlines of their attitudes and beliefs. Minor discrepancies are easily ignored, and more important ones selectively re-interpreted so rendering them consistent with the basic pattern. Once socialisation provides them with a 'world-view' most people are unwilling to let it go without a fight, and it is here that the second level processes come into operation. By providing what is almost an extended peer-group the popular genres can reinforce this strain toward retention; in the fiction-film, peopled with living characters, this is almost literally the case. By continually demonstrating that one's beliefs and attitudes are not mere personal eccentricities, the movies, like other expressions of culture, can act as legitimators.

Once more this is a very general suggestion, even apparently suggesting mass homogeneity. However, while there are some meanings almost universally present in the movies, what they serve to legitimate may vary a good deal. The popular genres cover a wide cultural range. They provide a store of meanings, so to speak, on which different audiences with different needs may draw. Any particular audience might accept one emphasis while successfully ignoring another, or even entirely changing its meaning by re-interpretation. It is not clear quite how far audiences can use the movies entirely for their own legitimating purposes; I am inclined to think that a film (and, indeed, a genre) offers some fixed structure which sets limits on selective interpretation. But the process depends so much on specific characteristics of both individuals and films that it is difficult to make any hard and fast rules. No doubt analysis of genre-languages will help to specify the range of meaning inherent to a genre and so allow us to explore the ways in which these meanings are used by particular audiences. Cinema audiences comprise different sub-cultures of taste, and, though they may all use the movies as legitimators, the substantive values that the films legitimate may vary from sub-culture to sub-culture. Meaning is far from being a simple constant.

So the image which underlies a large part of my discussion presents the cinema as socialiser and legitimator, though only one such institution within society. There is a chain of reasoning, arguably still incomplete, which goes from here to the pattern of genre development I analysed as 'evolutionary'. Audiences use the movies as one way of dealing with the demands and pressures society puts upon them. If we are careful to use the terms in the most general of senses, audiences use the movies to gratify their needs. To commercially survive the cinema must supply the goods by adapting to changing requirements of its audience/environment. In response to this come the genres, the primary means by which the movies can be built into a stable sub-culture. Communicators and audiences negotiate the genre with one another, and out of the minutiae of this negotiation comes the macro-pattern of genre evolution. Filling in the murky detail of these processes remains the major task of the macro-sociology of the cinema. In the movies we have a lot of history to play with, more than any other modern medium. If we can begin to understand the interplay between movies and society then we might be better off in trying to understand what is happening to us now with television. If we could do that we would have filled in one link in a fascinatingly tangled chain.

So what? It *is* a good question. I have asked it of myself, especially where I have been concerned with such speculative generalisations as these. Of course, there is no short answer. I believe that sociology has to find ways of uniting discrete bodies of data into workable and general models. Inevitably that involves crude approximations, analogies of limited use, and all sorts of cavalier attitudes to empirical detail. But I cannot justify that belief here, nor, indeed, could I ever totally justify it. For it is finally an act of faith, a commitment to the idea that this way of going about things is the only way that will finally allow us to understand the workings of our social world. What we need in this area is detailed empirical work, I have no doubt of that; but it would be of little use without some self-consciousness about the sorts of images we are using and the sorts of models we should be trying to build. In this chapter I have been playing with such ideas, ambivalently and imprecisely, rather more than in the rest of the book. A permissible indulgence, I hope. If not, then you must find what you can.

References

[1] Some of the wilder products of evolutionary thinking in modern sociology fall into all sorts of such traps. On cultural issues see, for example, R. N. Bellah, 'Religious Evolution', *American Sociological Review*, **29**, 3, 1964. For an illuminating discussion of neo-evolutionism see Robert A. Nisbet, *Social Change and History*, O.U.P., London, New York, 1969, especially Part 3. His strictures on metaphor are not irrelevent here.

[2] The analysis of differentiation has been a precursor to evolutionary analogies in sociology, generally in functionalist theories and under the

guise of 'structural differentiation'. Here I am using the term to refer to a process whereby specialised sub-units develop from what was originally a homogeneous phenomenon.

[3] See H. Gans, 'The Creator – Audience Relationship – the Mass Media', and 'Popular Culture in America' (see Selected Bibliography).

[4] See Peter L. Berger, *The Sacred Canopy*, Shocken Bks, New York, 1967 (the English ed. under the title *The Social Reality of Religion*), and Peter L. Berger and Thomas Luckmann, *The Social Construction of Reality*, Penguin, Harmondsworth, 1967.

Selected Bibliography

This select bibliography is largely limited to materials directly relevant to the sociology and psychology of the cinema. More general references on the media, on sociology, and on film criticism are limited to a very few. Bibliographies on such subjects are quite common; bibliographies on the sociology of film are not. Many references are to texts in languages other than English, a characteristic which reflects a general pattern in the literature. Much that is important is not available in English. I have not been able to consult every reference here, especially those in more 'distant' languages such as Polish. I include them for the consideration of those who are able to do so.

ABRAMS, MARK, 'The British Cinema Audience, 1949', *Quarterly of Film, Radio and Television*, **4**, Spring 1950, pp. 251–5.

ADAIR, JOHN, and WORTH, SOL, 'The Navajo as Film-Maker: a Brief Report of Research on the Cross-Cultural Aspects of Film Communication', *American Anthropologist*, **69**, 1, 1967, pp. 76–8.

ADLER, KENNETH P., 'Art Films and Eggheads', *Studies in Public Communication*, **2**, Summer 1959, pp. 7–15.

ADLER, MORTIMORE J., *Art and Prudence: a Study in Practical Philosophy*, Longman, Green, New York, 1937.

ALBERT, P. S., 'The Role of the Mass Media and the Effect of Aggressive Film Content upon Children's Aggressive Responses and Identification Choices', *Genetic Psychology Monographs*, **55**, 1957, pp. 221–85.

ALBRECHT, GERDE, 'Sozialpsychologische Faktoren im Wandel der DEFA-Filme', *Kölner Zeitschrift für Soziologie und Sozial Psychologie*, **17**, 2, 1965, pp. 245–53.

ANAST, PHILIP, 'Differential Movie Appeals as Correlates of Attendance', *Journalism Quarterly*, **44**, 1, 1967, pp. 86–90.

Annals, The, The Motion Picture Industry, **254**, American Academy of Political and Social Science, Philadelphia, 1947.

ARNSTINE, DONALD G., 'Value-Models and Education: Content in the Popular Arts', *Journal of Educational Sociology*, **35**, 1, 1961, pp. 41–8.

AUSTER, DONALD, 'A Content Analysis of Business and Labour Sponsored Films', *Social Problems*, **9**, 4, 1962, pp. 323–36.

BABITSKY, PAUL, and RIMBERG, JOHN, *The Soviet Film Industry*, Praeger, New York, 1955.

BARKER, W. J., 'The Stereotyped Western Story', *Psychoanalytical Quarterly*, **24**, 1955, pp. 270–80.

BARR, CHARLES, 'CinemaScope: Before and After', *Film Quarterly*, **16**, 4, 1963, reprinted (abridged) in MacCann, Richard Dyer (Ed.), *Film: a*

Montage of Theories, New York, 1966; '*Straw Dogs, A Clockwork Orange,* and the Critics', *Screen*, **13**, 2, 1972, pp. 17–31.

BASTIDE, ROGER, 'L'Amerique Latine Vue à Travers le Miroir de son Cinéma', *Revue de Psychologie des Peuples*, **15**, 4, 1960, pp. 366–79.

BATICLE, YOELINE, 'Les Enseignantes Face à la Culture Cinématographique: les Ciné-Clubs dans le Second Degré', *Communications*, **5**, 1965, pp. 88–93.

BATZ, JEAN-CLAUDE, *À Propos de la Crise de l'Industrie du Cinéma*, Université Libre de Bruxelles Institut de Sociologie, 1963.

BAZIN, ANDRÉ, 'L'évolution du Western', *Cahiers du Cinéma*, December, 1955; *Qu'est-ce que le Cinéma?*, Vol. I, *Ontologie et Langage*, Éditions du Cerf, Paris, 1958; *Qu'est-ce que le Cinéma?*, Vol. II, *Le Cinéma et les Autres Arts*, Éditions du Cerf, Paris, 1959; *Qu'est-ce que le Cinéma?*, Vol. III, *Cinéma et Sociologie*, Editions du Cerf, Paris, 1961; *Qu'est-ce que le Cinéma?*, Vol. IV, *Une Esthetique de la Réalité: le néo-réalisme*, Éditions du Cerf, Paris, 1962, *What is Cinema?*, Univ. California Press, Berkeley and Los Angeles, 1967, *What is Cinema?*, Vol. II, Univ. California Press, Berkeley and Los Angeles, 1972.

BELSON, WILLIAM A., 'The Effect of Television on Cinema Going', *Audio-Visual Communication Review*, **6**, 2, 1958, pp. 131–9.

BENHAM, ALBERT, 'War or Peace in the Movies', *Public Opinion Quarterly*, **1**, 4, 1947, pp. 109–13.

BERKOWITZ, LEONARD, 'Aggressive Cues in Aggressive Behaviour and Hostility Catharsis', *Psychological Review*, **71**, 1964, pp. 104–22; 'Some Aspects of Observed Aggression', *Journal of Personality and Social Psychology*, **2**, 3, 1965, pp. 359–69.

BERKOWITZ, LEONARD, CORWIN, R. and HEIRONIMUS, M., 'Film Violence and Subsequent Aggressive Tendencies', *Public Opinion Quarterly*, **27**, 2, 1963, pp. 217–29.

BERKOWITZ, LEONARD and GEEN, RUSSELL G., 'Film Violence and the Cue Properties of Available Targets', *Journal of Personality and Social Psychology*, **3**, 5, 1966, pp. 525–30.

BERKOWITZ, LEONARD and RAWLINGS, EDNA, 'Effects of Film Violence on Inhibitions Against Subsequent Aggression', *Journal of Abnormal and Social Psychology*, **66**, 5, 1963, pp. 405–12.

BLUMER, HERBERT, *Movies and Conduct*, Macmillan, New York, 1935; 'The Moulding of Mass Behavior through the Motion Picture', *Publications of the American Sociological Society*, **XXIX**, 1936.

BLUMER, HERBERT, and HAUSER, P. M., *Movies, Delinquency, and Crime*, Macmillan, New York, 1933.

BOLLE DE BAL, FRANCOISE, 'Possibilité Actuelles de la Recherché en Belgique sur le Cinéma et son Publique', *Études et Recherches-Techniques de Diffusion Collectif*, **5**, 1961.

BOSE, A. B., 'Mass Communication: The Cinema in India', *Indian Journal of Social Research*, **4**, 1963, pp. 80–2.

BREMOND, CLAUDE, 'Education Cinématographique et Culture de Masse', *Communications*, **2**, 1963, pp. 154–8; 'Le Public Français et le

Film Japonais', *Communications*, **6**, 1965, pp. 103–42; 'Ethique du Film et Morale du Censeur', *Communications*, **9**, 1967, pp. 28–53.

BROWNING, H., and SORRELL, A., 'Cinemas and Cinema Going in Great Britain', *Journal of the Royal Statistical Society*, **117**, 2, Series A (General), 1954, pp. 133–65.

BRUEL, OLAF, 'Psychic Trauma through the Cinema – an Illustrative Case', *International Journal of Sexology*, **7**, 2, 1953, pp. 61–8.

BRUNER, JEROME, and FOWLER, GEORGE, 'The Strategy of Terror: Audience Response to *Blitzkrieg im Westen*', *Journal of Abnormal and Social Psychology*, **36**, 1941, pp. 561–74.

BRUYN, G. DE, 'Filmpropaganda voor Paraatheid', *Mens en Maatschappij*, **31**, 5, 1956.

CATRICE, PAUL, 'Le Cinéma peut-il Contribuer à l'Amitie entre les Peuples', *Revue de Psychologie des Peuples*, **16**, 4, 1961, pp. 417–25; 'Problèmes Juifs à Travers le Cinéma', *Revue de Psychologie des Peuples*, **16**, 4, 1961, pp. 391–416; 'Le Cinéma en Amerique Latine', *Revue de Psychologie des Peuples*, **18**, 4, 1963, pp. 424–7.

CAWELTI, J. G., 'Prolegomena to the Western', *Studies in Public Communication*, **4**, 1962, pp. 57–70.

CENTRE NATIONAL DE LA CINÉMATOGRAPHIE, 'Cinéma Français, Perspectives 1970', *Bulletin d'Information*, Series 92, 1965, pp. 1–104.

CHARTERS, W. W., *Motion Pictures and Youth*, Macmillan, New York, 1935.

CLARENS, CARLOS, *Horror Movies*, Secker & Warburg, London, 1968.

COOPER, EUNICE, and DINERMAN, H., 'Analysis of the Film "Don't be a Sucker": a Study in Communication', *Public Opinion Quarterly*, **15**, 2, 1951, pp. 243–64.

COOPER, EUNICE, and JAHODA, MARIE, 'The Evasion of Propaganda: How Prejudiced People Respond to Anti-Prejudiced Propaganda', *Journal of Psychology*, **26**, 1948.

CRESSEY, PAUL G., 'The Motion Picture as Informal Education', *Journal of Educational Sociology*, **8**, 1, 1934; 'The Influence of Moving Pictures on Students in India', *American Journal of Sociology*, **41**, 3, 1935, pp. 341–50; ' The Motion Picture Experience as Modified by Social Background and Personality', *American Sociological Review*, **3**, 4, 1938, pp. 516–25.

CRIPPS, THOMAS R., 'The Death of Rastus: Negroes in American Film since 1945', *Phylon*, **28**, 3, 1967, pp. 267–75.

CRISTANTI, P., *Arte e cinema nella loro funzione sociale*, AUIEA, Rome, 1954.

DACRUZ, EFREN BORAJO, 'Esquema General de los Effectos Sociologicos del Cine', *Revista International de Sociologica*, **17**, 66, 1959, pp. 225–30.

DADEK, WALTER, 'Der Gegen Wärtige Stand der Filmsoziologie', *Kölner Zeitschrift für Soziologie und Sozial Psychologie*, **12**, 3, 1960, pp. 516–33.

DALE, EDGAR, *Children's Attendance at Motion Pictures*, Macmillan, New York, 1933; *The Content of Motion Pictures*, Macmillan, New York, 1933b; 'Motion Picture Industry and Public Relations', *Public Opinion Quarterly*, **3**, 2, 1939, pp. 251–62.

DELL'ORBO, R., 'Tematica Sociale nello Suiluppo del Neorealismo Cinematografico', *Civitas*, **9**, 3, 1952, pp. 71–80.

DIEZ DEL CORRAL, L., 'Les Supuestos Histórico Sociológicos del Cine Italiano', *Revista de Estudiōs Politicos*, **80**, 1955, pp. 83–99.

DUMĀZEDIER, JOFFRE, 'Loisir Cinématographique et Culture Populaire', *Revue de l' Institute de Sociologie Solvay*, **3**, 1959, pp. 349–70.

EISNER, LOTTE H., *The Haunted Screen*, Thames & Hudson, London, 1969.

ELKIN, FREDERICK, 'The Psychological Appeal of the Hollywood Western', *Journal of Educational Sociology*, **24**, 1950, pp. 72–85; 'The Value Implications of Popular Films', *Sociology and Social Research*, **38**, 5, 1954, pp. 320–2.

EMERY, F. E., 'Psychological Effects of the Western Film: A Study in Television Viewing' (two parts), *Human Relations*, **12**, 3, 1959, pp. 195–213, 215–32.

ESAER, ERIC, 'Analyse du film "Persona" de I. Bergman', *Revue de l'Institute de Sociologie*, **1**, 1971, pp. 97–134.

EVES, VICKI, 'The Structure of the British Film Industry', *Screen*, **11**, 1, 1970, pp. 41–54.

EZRATTY, SACHRA, 'Films and Society', *Impact of Science on Society*, **13**, 2, 1963, pp. 147–69.

FALEWICZ, JAN, 'Effects of Criticism on Urban Film Tastes', *Polish Sociological Bulletin*, **1**, (9), 1964, pp. 90–5.

FEABREGAT CUNEO, ROBERTO, 'El Proceso del Cine en el Mundo y en la Cultura y la Deformacion de los Temas Culturales al Traves del Cine', *Revista Mexicana de Sociologia*, **19**, 2, 1957, pp. 387–404.

FEARING, F., 'Influence of the Movies on Attitudes and Behaviour', *Annals of the American Academy of Political and Social Science*, **254**, 1947, pp. 70–80, reprinted in McQuail, Denis (Ed.), *Sociology of Mass Communications*, Penguin Books, Harmondsworth, 1972, pp. 119–34; 'A Word of Caution for the Intelligent Consumer of Motion Pictures', *Quarterly of Film, Radio, and Television*, **6**, 1951, pp. 129–42.

FEDERATION OF BRITISH FILM-MAKERS, *Cinema Going in Greater London*, London, 1963.

FERRAROTTI, FRANCO, 'Cinema e Societa: Un Rapporto Ambiguo, da Approfondire', *La Critica Sociologica*, **1**, 3, 1967, pp. 88–99.

FIELDING, R., 'Mirror of Discontent: "The March of Time" and its Politically Controversial Film Issues', *Western Political Quarterly*, **12**, 1, 1959, pp. 145–52.

FILMER, PAUL, 'Three Frankenheimer Films: A Sociological Approach', *Screen*, **10**, 4, 1969, pp. 160–73.

FREIDSON, ELIOT, 'Communication Research and the Concept of the Mass', *American Sociological Review*, **18**, 3, 1953, pp. 313–17.

FRENCH, PHILIP, 'Violence in the Cinema', in Larsen, Otto N. (Ed.), *Violence and the Mass Media*, Harper & Row, New York; Evanston, London, 1968.

Q

FYOCK, JAMES A., 'Content Analysis of Films: New Slant on an Old Technique', *Journalism Quarterly*, **45**, 4, 1968, pp. 687–91.

GALLI, G., and ROSITI, F., 'The Cinema and Political Collective Trends in the American and German Crises of 1930–32', *Ikon*, **19**, 1966, pp. 125–66.

GANS, HERBERT J., 'The Creator-Audience Relationship in the Mass Media: An Analysis of Movie Making", in Rosenberg, Bernard, and White, David Manning (Eds), *Mass Culture: the Popular Arts in America*, Free Press, Glencoe (Ill.), 1957; 'Hollywood Films on British Screens: An Analysis of the Functions of American Popular Culture Abroad', *Social Problems*, **9**, 4, 1961, pp. 324–8; 'The Rise of the Problem Film: An Analysis of Changes in Hollywood Films and the American Audience', *Social Problems*, **11**, 4, 1964, pp. 327–35; 'Popular Culture in America: Social Problem in a Mass Society or Social Asset in a Pluralist Society', in Becker, Howard S. (Ed.), *Social Problems: A Modern Approach*, Wiley, New York, London, Sydney, 1966.

GEDULD, Harry M., *Film Makers on Film Making*, Penguin Books, Harmondsworth, 1967.

GEERTS, CLAUDE, 'Les Telespectateurs et le Cinéma', *Études de Radio-Television*, **15**, 1969, pp. 70–81.

GJERDE, W., *A Study to Determine the Effectiveness of a Planned Film Programme in Selected Counties in Iowa*, University Microfilms, Ann Arbor, 1955.

GLUCKSMANN, ANDRÉ, 'Rapport sur les Recherches Concernants les Effects sur la Jeunesse des Scenes de Violence au Cinéma et à la Television', *Communications*, **7**, 1966, pp. 74–119; *Violence on the Screen*, British Film Institute Education Department, London, 1971 (English language version of the above).

GOLDMANN, ANNE, and LEENHARDT, JACQUES, 'Essai de Sociologie du Cinéma: Morgan ou l'Impossible Révolution; Blow Up: Essai d'Analyse', *L'Homme et la Société*, **6**, 1967, pp. 171–9.

GOULD, KENNETH M., 'Cinepatriotism', *Social Forces*, **7**, 1, 1928, pp. 120–9.

GOVAERTS, FRANCE, and MANDL, P. E., 'Présentations des Informations et Dialectique du Temps dans le Langage Filmique', *Études de Radio-Television*, **5**, 1964, pp. 25–42.

GREGARIO, DOMINICA DE, 'Cinema and TV Audiences in Italy', *Gazette*, **11**, 1, 1965, pp. 68–81.

GRIERSON, JOHN, *Grierson on Documentary*, Forsyth Hardy (Ed.), Faber & Faber, London, 1966.

GRITTI, JULES, 'La Télévision en Regard du Cinéma: Vrai ou Faux Problème?', *Communications*, **7**, 1966, pp. 27–39.

GUBACK, THOMAS H., *The International Film Industry*, Indiana Univ. Press, Bloomington, London, 1969.

GUILLOT, ALAIN, 'Aspects Politiques du Cinéma Américain', *L'Année Sociologique*, **11**, 1960, pp. 109–62.

HALEY, JAY, 'The Appeal of the Moving Picture', *Quarterly of Film, Radio and Television*, 4, 1952, pp. 361–74.

HALL, STUART, and WHANNELL, PADDY, *The Popular Arts*, Hutchinson, London, 1964.

HANDEL, LEO, *Hollywood Looks at its Audience*, Univ. Illinois Press, Urbana, 1950; 'La Bourse des Vedettes', *Communications*, 2, 1963, pp. 86–104.

HARRIS, THOMAS, 'The Building of Popular Images: Grace Kelly and Marilyn Monroe', *Studies in Public Communication*, 1, 1957, pp. 45–8.

HMSO, *Report on the Tendencies to Monopoly in the Cinematographic Film Industry*, London, 1944; *Films: A Report on the Supply of Films for Exhibition in Cinemas*, London, 1966.

HIRSCH, PAUL M., 'Processing Fads and Fashions: An Organization-Set Analysis of Cultural Industry Systems', *American Journal of Sociology*, 77, 4, 1972, pp. 639–59.

HOLLAND, NORMAN N., 'The Puzzling Movies: Three Analyses and a Guess at their Appeal', *Journal of Social Issues*, 20, 1, 1964, pp. 71–96.

HOMANS, PETER, 'Puritanism Revisited: An Analysis of the Contemporary Screen-Image Western', *Studies in Public Communication*, 3, 1961, pp. 73–84.

HONIGMANN, J., *Information for Pakistan: Report of Research on Inter-Cultural Communication through Films*, Univ. North Carolina Press, Chapel Hill, 1953.

HONIGMANN, J., and DOORSLAYER, M. VAN, 'Some Themes in Indian Film Reviews', *The Eastern Anthropologist*, 10, 2, 1956–7, pp. 87–96.

HOUSEMAN, J., 'How – and What – does a Movie Communicate?', *Quarterly of Film, Radio, and Television*, 10, 3, 1956, pp. 227–38.

HOVLAND, CARL, LUMSDAINE, ARTHUR, and SHEFFIELD, FRED D., *Experiments in Mass Communications*, Wiley, New York, 1949.

HUACO, GEORGE A., 'Toward a Sociology of Film Art', *Berkeley Journal of Sociology*, 7, 1, 1962, pp. 63–84; *The Sociology of Film Art*, Basic Books, New York, London, 1965.

HUGHES, ROBERT (Ed.), *Film: Book 1, The Audience and the Filmmaker*, Grove Press, New York, 1959; *Film: Book 2, Films of Peace and War*, Grove Press New York, 1962.

HULETT, J. E., 'Estimating the Net Effect of a Commercial Motion Picture upon the Trend of Local Public Opinion', *American Sociological Review*, 14, 2, 1949, pp. 263–75.

HULL, DAVID STEWART, *Film in the Third Reich*, Univ. California Press, Berkeley & Los Angeles, 1969.

HURLEY, Neil, P., 'The Cinema of Tomorrow', *Social Order*, 7, 5, 1957, pp. 207–14.

IMAMURA, TAIHEI, 'The Japanese Spirit as it Appears in Movies', in Kato, Hudetoshi (Ed.), *Japanese Popular Culture*, Charles E. Tuttle, Rutland (Vt.), 1959.

Q*

INGARDEN, ROMAN, 'Leopold Blaustein – Teoretyk Radia i Filmu', *Zeszty Prasojznawcze*, **4**, 3, 1963, pp. 86–93.

INSTITUT DE SOCIOLOGIE SOLVAY, *Le Cinéma, Fait Social*, Brussels, 1960.

JACOBS, LEWIS, *The Rise of the American Film*, Teachers College Press, New York, 1968.

JARVIE, I. C., 'Film and the Communication of Values', *European Journal of Sociology*, **10**, 2, 1969, pp. 205–219; *Toward a Sociology of the Cinema*, Routledge, London, 1970.

JINDAL, AKALAUKA, 'Sociological Research on Films', *Sociological Bulletin*, **9**, 2, 1960, pp. 56–72.

JONES, DOROTHY B., 'Quantitative Analysis of Motion Picture Content', *Public Opinion Quarterly*, **6**, 3, 1942, pp. 411–28; 'Quantitative Analysis of Motion Picture Content', *Public Opinion Quarterly*, **14**, 3, 1950, pp. 554–8.

KAHN, G., *Hollywood on Trial*, Boni & Goer, New York, 1948.

KATZ, ELIHU, and LAZARSFELD, PAUL F., *Personal Influence*, Free Press, Glencoe (Ill.), 1955.

KELLY, TERENCE, *The Competitive Cinema*, Institute of Economic Affairs, London, 1965.

KENDALL, P., and WOLFE, K., 'The Analysis of Deviant Cases in Communication Research', in Lazarsfeld, Paul F., and Stanton, Frank (Eds), *Communications Research 1948–9*, Harper & Row, New York, 1949.

KITSES, JIM, *Horizons West*, Thames & Hudson, London, 1969.

KLEIN, ROBERT J., 'Film Censorship: The American and British Experience', *Villanova Law Review*, **12**, 3, 1967, pp. 419–56.

KOENIGIL, MARK, *Movies in Society*, Speller & Sons, New York, 1962.

KOLAJA, JIRI, and FOSTER, ARNOLD W., ' "Berlin, the Symphony of a City" as a Theme of Visual Rhythm', *Journal of Aesthetics and Art Criticism*, 1965, pp. 353–357.

KOLODZIEJCZYK, WLADZIMIERZ, 'Stereotypy: Modele 'Swiata Kina' a Aspicacje Zyciowe Wybranej Kategorii Mlodziezy', *Pizeglad Socjologiczny*, **17**, 1, 1963, pp. 115–18.

KRACAUER, SIEGFRIED, 'The Conquest of Europe on the Screen and the Nazi Newsreel, 1939–40', *Social Research*, **10**, 3, 1943, pp. 337–57; 'Hollywood's Terror Films: Do They Reflect an American State of Mind', *Commentary*, **2**, 1946, pp. 132–6; *From Caligari to Hitler*, Princeton Univ. Press, Princeton, 1947; 'National Types as Hollywood Presents Them', *Public Opinion Quarterly*, **13**, 1949, pp. 53–72; *Theory of Film*, Oxford Univ. Press, New York, 1965.

LANDAU, J. M., 'The Arab Cinema', *Middle East Affairs*, **11**, 4, 1953, pp. 349–58.

LAZARSFELD, PAUL F., 'Audience Research in the Movie Field', *Annals of the American Academy of Political and Social Science*, **254**, 1947, pp. 160–8.

LEISER, E., 'Den Tyska Filmens Politisering', *Tiden*, **49**, 4, 1957.

LEYDA, JAY, *Kino*, Allen & Unwin, London, 1960.

LOVELL, ALAN, *Don Siegel – American Cinema*, British Film Institute Education Department, London, 1969.

LOVELL, ALAN, and HILLIER, JIM, *Studies in Documentary*, Secker & Warburg, London, 1972.

LOVELL, TERRY, 'An Approach to the Sociology of Film', in Wollen, Peter (Ed.), *Working Papers on the Cinema: Sociology and Semilogy*, British Film Institute Education Department, London, 1969; 'Sociology and the Cinema', *Screen*, **12**, 1, 1971, pp. 15–26; 'Sociology of Aesthetic Structures and Contextualism', in McQuail, Denis, (Ed.) *Sociology of Mass Communications*, Penguin Books, Harmondsworth, 1972.

McARTHUR, COLIN, *Underworld USA*, Secker & Warburg, London, 1972.

McCANN, R. D. (Ed.), *Film and Society*, Scribner, New York, 1964.

McCLINTOCK, M., 'Une Force Vitale du Système Pedagogique Américain: le Cinéma', *Synthèses*, **71**, 7, 1952, pp. 204–11.

MACCOBY, ELEANOR E., LEVIN, HARRY, and SELYA, BRUCE M., 'The Effects of Emotional Arousal on the Retention of Aggressive and Non-Aggressive Movie Content', *American Psychologist*, **10**, 1955, pp. 359–67; 'The Effects of Emotional Arousal on the Retention of Film Content: A Failure to Replicate', *Journal of Abnormal and Social Psychology*, **53**, 3, 1956, pp. 373–4.

MACCOBY, ELEANOR E., and WILSON, WILLIAM C., 'Identification and Observational Learning from Films', *Journal of Abnormal and Social Psychology*, **55**, 1, 1957, pp. 76–87.

MACCOBY, ELEANOR E., and WILSON, WILLIAM C., and BURTON, ROGER V., 'Differential Movie-Viewing Behaviour of Male and Female Viewers', *Journal of Personality*, **26**, 1958, pp. 259–67.

McCOY, E. P., 'Influence of Color on Audiences Rated Perception of Reality in Film', *AV Communication Review*, **10**, 1, 1962, pp. 70–3.

MAGGOWAN, K., 'The Screen's "New Look" – Wider and Deeper', *Quarterly of Film, Radio, and Television*, **11**, 2, 1956, pp. 109–30.

MATHUR, AJIT K., 'Movies and the Students', *Journal of Social Research*, **1**, 1, 1960, pp. 29–37.

MAY, MARK A., and SHUTTLEWORTH, FRANK K, *The Social Conduct and Attitudes of Movie Fans*, Macmillan, New York, 1933.

MAYER, ARTHUR L., 'Fact into Film', *Public Opinion Quarterly*, **8**, 2, 1944, pp. 206–225.

MAYER, J. P., *Sociology of Film*, Faber & Faber, London, 1946; *British Cinemas and their Audiences*, Dobson, London, 1948.

METZ, CHRISTIAN, 'Le Cinéma: Langue ou Langage', *Communications*, **4**, 1964, pp. 52–90; 'La Grande Syntagmatique du Film Narratif', *Communications*, **8**, 1966, pp. 120–4; 'Le Dire et le Dit au Cinéma: vers le Déclin d'un Vraisemblable?', *Communications*, **11**, 1968, pp. 22–33; *Essais sur la Signification au Cinéma*, Vols. 1 & 2, Klincksieck, Paris, 1968 & 1972; 'Propositions Méthodologiques pour l'Analyse du Film', *Social Science Information*, **7**, 4, 1968, pp. 107–19, translated as 'Methodological

246   *Image and Influence*

Propositions for the Analysis of Film' *Screen*, **14**, 1/2, 1973, pp. 89–101; *Langage et Cinéma*, Larousse, Paris, 1971.

MIALARET, G., *The Psychology of the Use of Audio-Visual Aids in Primary Education*, Harrap, London, 1966.

MICHALEK, BOLESLAW, 'Wokol Polskiego Filmu o Wspolizesnosci', *Kultura i Spoleczenstwo*, **6**, 2, 1962, pp. 245–54.

MILLARD, W. J., *A Study in the Sociology of Communications: Determinants and Consequences of Exposure to American Motion Picture Film in the Near and Middle East*, Univ. Microfilms, Ann Arbor, 1955.

MINAMI, HIROSHI, 'A Survey of Post-War Japanese Movies', in Kato, Hudetoshi (Ed.), *Japanese Popular Culture*, Charles E. Tuttle, Rutland (Vt.), 1959.

MORIN, EDGAR, 'Préliminaires à une Sociologie du Cinéma', *Cahiers Internationaux de Sociologie*, **17**, 1954, pp. 101–11; *The Stars*, Grove Press, New York, 1960; 'Conditions d'Apparation de la Nouvelle Vague', *Communications*, **1**, 1961, pp. 139–41.

MORIN, EDGAR, and BREMOND, CLAUDE, 'An International Survey on the Film Hero', *International Social Science Journal*, **15**, 1, 1963, pp. 113–19.

MORIN, VIOLETTE, 'James Bond Connery: le Mobile', *Communications*, **6**, 1965, pp. 88–102.

NELSON, DONALD M., 'The Independent Producer', *Annals of the American Acadamy of Political and Social Science*, **254**, 1947, pp. 49–57.

NUSSBAUM, MARTIN, 'Sociological Symbolism of the "Adult Western" ', *Social Forces*, **39**, 1, 1960, pp. 25–8.

OLSEN, MARVIN E., 'Motion Picture Attendence and Social Isolation', *Sociological Quarterly*, **1**, 2, 1960, pp. 107–16.

OSGOOD, CHARLES E., 'The Cross-Cultural Generality of Visual-Verbal Synesthetic Tendencies', *Behavioural Science*, April 1960, pp. 146–9.

PEP, *The British Film Industry*, London, 1952.

PERKINS, V. F., *Film as Film*, Penguin Books, Harmondsworth, 1972.

PETERS, J. M., 'Die Struktur der Filmsprache', *Publizistik*, **7**, 4, 1962, pp. 195–205.

POFFENBERGER, THOMAS M., 'A Technique for Evaluating Family Life and Mental Health Films', *Marriage and Family Living*, **18**, 3, 1956, pp. 219–23.

POLLIET, J., 'Petite Sociologie du Cinéma', *Chronique Sociale de France*, **62**, 4–5, 1954.

POWDERMAKER, HORTENSE, 'An Anthropologist looks at the Movies', *Annals of the American Academy of Political and Social Science*, **254**, 1947, pp. 80–7; *Hollywood: the Dream Factory*, Little Brown, Boston, 1950.

PRYLUCK, CALVIN, 'Structural Analysis of Motion Pictures as a Symbol System', *AV Communication Review*, **16**, 4, 1968, pp. 372–402.

PRYLUCK, CALVIN, and SNOW, R. E., 'Toward a Psycholinguistics of Cinema', *AV Communication Review*, **15**, 1, 1967, pp. 54–75.

RAO, T. N., 'Is the Cinema a Social Educator?', *Educational Review*, **60**, 2, 1954, pp. 2–26.

RATHS, LOUIS E., and TRAGER, FRANK N., 'Public Opinion and *Crossfire*', *Journal of Educational Sociology*, **21**, 1948, pp. 345–68.

REISMAN, DAVID, 'The Oral Tradition, the Written Word, and the Screen Image', *Film Culture*, **2**, 3, 1956.

RIEGEL, O. W., 'Nationalism in Press, Radio, and Cinema', *American Sociological Review*, **3**, 4, 1938, pp. 510–15.

RIMBERG, JOHN, 'Social Problems as Depicted in the Soviet Film – A Research Note', *Social Problems*, **7**, 4, 1960, pp. 351–5.

ROSENTHAL, SOLOMON P., 'Change of Socio-Economic Attitudes under Radical Motion Picture Propaganda', *Archives of Psychology*, **25**, 1934.

ROSITI, FRANCO, 'Cineclubs in Italy', *Ikon*, **19**, 1966, pp. 229–31.

ROSS, LILLIAN, *Picture*, Penguin Books, Harmondsworth, 1962.

ROSS, MURRAY, *Stars and Strikes: Unionization of Hollywood*, New York, 1941; 'Labor Relations in Hollywood', *Annals of the American Academy of Political and Social Science*, **254**, 1947, pp. 58–64.

ROSTEN, LEO C., 'A "Middletown" Study of Hollywood', *Public Opinion Quarterly*, **3**, 2, 1939, pp. 314–20; *Hollywood: The Movie Colony, The Movie Makers*, Harcourt Brace, New York, 1941.

ROUCEK, JOSEPH S., 'The Mythical Aspects of the "Wild West" in American Mass Media of Communication', *Indian Journal of Social Research*, **7**, 2, 1966, pp. 137–44; 'Las Tendencias de la Television Northamericana y sus Relaciones con Hollywood', *Revista Espanola de la Opinion Publica*, **10**, 1967, pp. 127–50.

ROWSON, S., 'A Statistical Survey of the Cinema Industry in Great Britain in 1934', *Journal of the Royal Statistical Society*, Series A, **99**, 1936, pp. 67–119.

SAFILIOS-ROTHSCHILD, CONSTANTINA, ' "Good" and "Bad" Girls in Modern Greek Movies', *Journal of Marriage and the Family*, **30**, 3, 1968, pp. 527–31.

SAKSENA, R. N., 'Films et Heros de Films en Inde', *Communications*, **1**, 1961, pp. 60–9.

SCHWARTZ, JACK, 'The Portrayal of Educators in Motion Pictures, 1950–8', *Journal of Educational Sociology*, **34**, 2, 1960, pp. 82–90; 'The Morality Seekers: A Study of Organised Film Criticism in the United States', in Larsen, Otto N., *Violence and the Mass Media*, Harper & Row, New York, Evanston, London, 1968.

SIEGAL, ALBERTA E., 'Film-mediated Fantasy Aggression and Strength of Aggressive Drive', *Child Development*, **29**, 1, 1958.

SINHA, D., 'Sociological Aspects of Film', *Science and Culture*, **20**, 6, 1954, pp. 281–3.

SMYTHE, DALLAS W., GREGORY, JOHN R., OSTRIN, ALVIN, CALVIN, OLIVER P., and MORONEY, WILLIAM, 'Portrait of a First-Run Audience', *Quarterly of Film, Radio, and Television*, **9**, 3, 1955, pp. 390–409.

SMYTHE, DALLAS W., LUSK, PARKER B., and LEWIS, CHARLES A., 'Portrait

of an Art-Theater Audience', *Quarterly of Film, Radio, and Television*, **8**, 1, 1953, pp. 28–50.
SODERBERGH, PETER A., 'Hollywood and the South, 1930–60', *Mississippi Quarterly*, **19**, 1, 1965–6; 'On War and the Movies: A Reappraisal', *Centennial Review*, **11**, 3, 1967.
SPANISH INSTITUTE OF PUBLIC OPINION, 'Productores Cinematograficos', *Revista Espanola de la Opinion Publica*, **6**, 1966, pp. 295–380; 'Estudio Sobre Cine', *Revista Espanola de la Opinion Publica*, **11**, 1968, pp. 189–320.
SPRAOS, JOHN, *The Decline of the Cinema*, Allen & Unwin, London, 1962.
STEPUN, F., 'Das Wesen des films – Ein sociologischer Versuch', *Soziologische Forschung in unserer Zeit*, Köln und Opladen Westdeutscher Verlag, 1952, pp. 241–7.
SUMNER, R. L., *Hollywood Cesspool: A Startling Survey of Movieland Lives and Morals, Pictures, and Results*, Sword of the Lord Press, Wheaton (Ill.), 1955.

TEIXEIRA DE SALLES, F., 'Aspectos Politicos-Socais do "Western" ', *Revista Brasileira de Estudes Politicos*, **14**, 1962, pp. 129–54.
THORP, MARGARET FARRAND, *America at the Movies*, Yale Univ. Press, New Haven, 1939.
THURSTONE, L. I., and PETERSON, R. C., *Motion Pictures and the Social Attitudes of Children*, Macmillan, New York, 1933.
TINACCI-MANNELLI, GILBERTO, 'Cinema e Sociologia. In Marque a un Convegno', *Rassegna Italiana di Sociologica*, **4**, 2, 1962, pp. 313–20; 'Influenza dell'Apparatenza Socio-Culturale Deglie Spettatori sull Accettazione e Interpretzione di un Film Africano', *Rassegna Italiana di Sociologia,*' **4**, 1, 1963, pp. 91–126; 'Reazioni di Tre Gruppi Sociali Diversi a un Film-Inquiesta Sulla Gioventu', *Rassegna Italiana di Sociologia*, **5**, 1, 1964, pp. 133–49.
TOEPLITZ, JERZY, 'Polska Kronika Filmowa – Dorabek XX-Lecia', *Zeszyc Prasoznawcze*, **5**, 3, 1964, pp. 92–105.
TRACHTENBERG, STANLEY, 'Undercutting with Sincerity: the Strategy of the Serious Film', *Midwest Quarterly*, **7**, 3, 1966, pp. 281–95.
TUDOR, ANDREW, 'Film and the Measurement of its Effects', *Screen*, **10**, 4/5, 1969, pp. 148–59; 'Sociological Perspectives on Film Aesthetics', in Wollen, Peter (Ed.), *Working Papers on the Cinema: Sociology and Semiology*, British Film Institute Education Department, London, 1969; 'Film, Communication and Content', in Tunstall, Jeremy (Ed.), *Media Sociology*, Constable, London, 1970; 'Genre: Theory and Mispractice in Film Criticism', *Screen*, **11**, 6, 1970, pp. 33–43; 'Elective Affinities: the Myth of German Expressionism', *Screen*, **12**, 3, 1971, pp. 143–50; *Theories of Film*, Secker & Warburg, London, 1973.
TWOMEY, JOHN E., 'Some Considerations in the Rise of the Art-Film Theater', *Quarterly of Film, Radio, and Television*, **10**, 3, 1956.

UENO, I., 'Motion Picture Industry', *Contemporary Japan*, **23**, 1–3, 1954, pp. 57–74.

UNESCO, *Film and Cinema Statistics*, Department of Social Sciences, Paris, 1955; 'The Influence of the Cinema on Children and Adolescents – an Annotated International Bibliography', *Reports and Papers on Mass Communications*, No. 31, 1961; 'An International Survey on the Film Hero', *International Social Science Journal*, **15**, 1, 1963.

URBANO, SALUSTIANO DEL CAMPO, 'El Publico Cinematografico', *Revista Espanola de la Opinion Publica*, **8**, 1967, pp. 209–78.

URUNO, FUIJO, 'Audience of Motion Pictures – an Analysis', *Japanese Journalism Review*, **9**, 1959, pp. 108–34.

WALL, W. D., and SIMSON, W. A., 'The Effects of Cinema Attendance on the Behaviour of Adolescents as seen by their Contemporaries', *British Journal of Educational Psychology*, **19**, 1, 1949, pp. 53–61; 'The Responses of Adolescent Groups to Certain Films', Parts I & II, *British Journal of Educational Psychology*, **20**, 1950, pp. 153–63, and **21**, 1951, pp. 81–8.

WALL, W. D., and SMITH, E. M., 'The Film Choice of Adolescents', *British Journal of Educational Psychology*, **19**, 2, 1949, pp. 121–36.

WALTERS, R. H., THOMAS, E. L., and ACKER, C. W., 'Enhancement of Punitive Behaviour by Audio-Visual Display', *Science*, **136**, 1962, pp. 872–3.

WANGER, WALTER, 'The Role of Movies in Morale', *American Journal of Sociology*, **47**, 3, 1941, pp. 378–83; 'OWI and Motion Pictures', *Public Opinion Quarterly*, **7**, 1, 1943, pp. 100–10; 'Donald Duck and Diplomacy', *Public Opinion Quarterly*, **14**, 3, 1950, pp. 443–52.

WARSHOW, ROBERT, *The Immediate Experience*, Doubleday, New York, 1962.

WEST, FRANK, 'Semiology and the Cinema', in Wollen, Peter (Ed.), *Working Papers on the Cinema: Sociology and Semiology*, British Film Institute Education Department, London, 1969.

WIESE, MILDRED J., and COLE, STEWART G., 'A Study of Children's Attitudes and the Influence of a Commercial Motion Picture', *Journal of Psychology*, **21**, 1946, pp. 151–71.

WOLFENSTEIN, MARTHA, and LEITES, NATHAN, 'An Analysis of Themes and Plots in Motion Pictures', *Annals of the American Academy of Political and Social Science*, **254**, 1947, pp. 41–8; *Movies: a Psychological Study*, Free Press, Glencoe (Ill.), 1950; 'Trends in French Films', *Journal of Social Issues*, **11**, 2, 1955, pp. 42–51.

WOLLEN, PETER, 'Cinema and Semiology: Some Points of Contact', in Wollen, Peter (Ed.), *Working Papers on the Cinema: Sociology and Semiology*. British Film Institute Education Department, London, 1969; *Signs and Meaning in the Cinema*, Secker & Warburg, London, 1969, 2nd ed., 1973.

WORTH, SOL, 'Cognitive Aspects of Sequence in Visual Communication', WORTH, SOL, 'Film as a Non-art: An Approach to the Study of Film', *The American Scholar*, **35**, 2, 1966, pp. 322–34; 'Cognitive Aspects of

Sequence in Visual Communication', *AV Communication Review*, **16**, 2, 1968, pp. 121–45.

WORTH, SOL, and ADAIR, JOHN, 'Navajo Filmmakers', *American Anthropologist*, **72**, 1, 1970, pp. 9–34.

ZYGULSKI, KAZIMIERZ, 'Film i Kultura Masowa', *Kultura i Spoleczenstwo*, **3**, 3, 1959, pp. 81–102.

Index